ON ANGER

COGNITIVE APPROACHES TO LITERATURE AND CULTURE SERIES
EDITED BY FREDERICK LUIS ALDAMA, ARTURO J. ALDAMA,
AND PATRICK COLM HOGAN

Cognitive Approaches to Literature and Culture includes monographs and edited volumes that incorporate cutting-edge research in cognitive science, neuroscience, psychology, linguistics, narrative theory, and related fields, exploring how this research bears on and illuminates cultural phenomena such as, but not limited to, literature, film, drama, music, dance, visual art, digital media, and comics. The volumes published in this series represent both specialized scholarship and interdisciplinary investigations that are deeply sensitive to cultural specifics and grounded in a cross-cultural understanding of shared emotive and cognitive principles.

ON ANGER

Race, Cognition, Narrative

BY SUE J. KIM

UNIVERSITY OF TEXAS PRESS ◆ *Austin*

Requests for permission to reproduce material from this work should be
sent to:
   Permissions
   University of Texas Press
   P.O. Box 7819
   Austin, TX 78713-7819
   http://utpress.utexas.edu/index.php/rp-form

♾ The paper used in this book meets the minimum requirements of ANSI/NISO
Z39.48-1992 (R1997) (Permanence of Paper).

LIBRARY OF CONGRESS CATALOGING-IN-PUBLICATION DATA

Kim, Sue J.
   On anger : race, cognition, narrative / by Sue J. Kim.
      pages   cm. — (Cognitive approaches to literature and culture series)
   Includes bibliographical references and index.
   ISBN 978-0-292-74841-5 (cloth : alk. paper)
   1. Anger in literature.   2. Mass media—Social aspects.   3. Anger—Social
aspects.   I. Title.
   PN56.A6K57   2013
   809'.93353—dc23

                                                                    2012046594

doi:10.7560/748415

TO THE JUSTLY ANGRY

CONTENTS

Acknowledgments   ix

INTRODUCTION   I

CHAPTER I. Anger as Cognition   13

CHAPTER 2. Anger as Culture   43

CHAPTER 3. Liberal Anger: Technologies of Anger in *Crash*   70

CHAPTER 4. Temporality and the Politics of Reading Kingston's
The Woman Warrior   84

CHAPTER 5. Anger and Space in Dangarembga's *Nervous Conditions*
and *The Book of Not*   IOI

CHAPTER 6. Estranging Rage: Ngugi's *Devil on the Cross* and
Wizard of the Crow   129

CHAPTER 7. "This Game Is Rigged": *The Wire* and
Agency Attribution   152

CONCLUSION. Anger and Outrage   175

Notes   179

Works Cited   195

Index   209

ACKNOWLEDGMENTS

I HAVE MANY PEOPLE AND ORGANIZATIONS to thank for help with *On Anger*. Of course, all errors and flaws are my own.

First, multitudinous thanks go to Frederick Luis Aldama, without whose constant support this book would not have been possible. I also thank his University of Texas Press Cognitive Approaches to Literature and Culture Series co-editors, Arturo Aldama and Patrick Colm Hogan; my editor at UT Press, Jim Burr; the reviewers of my manuscript; and Mary Silverstein.

At the University of Alabama at Birmingham, I thank English Department Chair Peter Bellis; Linda Frost (now at EKU); Jill Pruett; Daniel Siegel; Gale Temple; and graduate research assistants Sarah Harrell, Kimberly Nesmith, and Anamaria Santiago. Mervyn H. Sterne Library Reference Librarian Heather Martin and Interlibrary Loan Coordinator Eddie Luster saved my life more than once. The dean of the (former) School of Arts and Humanities generously provided a Faculty Development Grant that supported the research for this book. I also thank the Evolution, Cognition, and Culture Working Group, particularly Andrew Keitt and Marshall Abrams, for helpful clarifications and stimulating discussions (and good times!).

At the University of Massachusetts Lowell, I thank English Department Chair Anthony Szczesiul; Nina Coppens, the former dean of the School of Fine Arts, Humanities, and Social Sciences; Julie Nash, the School of FAHSS interim dean; Bridget Marshall; Michael Millner; Keith Mitchell; Jonathan Silverman; the O'Leary Library staff, particularly Interlibrary Loan; Puzzlemaster Paula Haines; and General Factotum and Front Potentate Katherine Conlon.

Early drafts of sections of this book were presented in the following venues: the International Conference on Narrative 2008 in Austin, Texas, with many thanks to respondent Jennifer Wilks; the American Literature Association 2008 Conference in San Francisco; the Modern Language Association 2009 Conference (Cognitive Approaches to Literature Discussion Group panel) in Philadelphia, with thanks to Ellen Spolsky and Elizabeth Hart; and in 2011, at the University of Cincinnati Charles Phelps Taft Research Center (special thanks to Jana Leigh) and the University of Massachusetts Lowell. I thank everyone who participated in these events for their thought-provoking questions and suggestions.

Many of the ideas in this book were discussed, debated, and developed at the 2010 Project Narrative Summer Institute at Ohio State University in Columbus, Ohio. I thank fondly my cohort in that summer's workshop and our fearless leaders, Jim Phelan and Robyn Warhol.

Thanks also go to Laura Clements for her invaluable editorial assistance and many insights into anger.

I thank the following people for their wisdom, intellectual and political camaraderie, and friendship: Gina Caison, Priyamvada Gopal, Jennifer Ho, Betsy Huang, Paul Lai, Anita Mannur, Stephen Hong Sohn, and SSG (a quarter ton!). Finally, much gratitude and all the love in the world to my wonderful family and to the cheezpets, the best writing companions anyone could ask for.

ON ANGER

INTRODUCTION

ANGER GETS A BAD RAP. Calling someone "angry" often labels that person as irrational, unstable, and unpredictable. To say "He's just angry" or "She spoke out of anger" implies something beyond reason, acting as an excuse or an indictment. Regardless of the merits of that person's reasons for anger, the characterization of "angry" can dismiss not only the content of that person's thoughts and feelings, but also the entire person, in a sense erasing subjectivity and agency. This sense of anger as pathological is often associated with women and racial-cultural Others. On the other hand, anger is also sometimes equated with violence and aggression, and this kind of anger is often associated with men. Even in these brief mentions of the ways that anger is often implicitly read, we can see the gendering and Othering work also being done. In other words, emotions are culturally and ideologically laden. As psychologist Carol Tavris writes, "Anger . . . is as much a political matter as a biological one" (47).

Anger is perhaps not well understood precisely because it is omnipresent; anger is so familiar that we assume that we know what it is. Yet we still know relatively little about how anger in its various manifestations actually works. Anger may be partly physiological, cognitive, and psychological, yet it is also deeply ideological, inseparable from factors such as race, class, gender, sexuality, ethnicity, nation, and religion. We see cultural and ideological configurations of anger in a variety of ways: People of color are either more or less angry than white people. A man's anger expresses, while constituting, his masculinity, while a woman's anger is anti-feminine. The middle class defines and identifies itself through "control" of emotions and against the uncontrolled emotions of both the wealthy and the poor. Americans' anger is more rational and just, and therefore more valid, than the anger of the rest of the world, particularly the Third World.

Antiwar demonstrators and foreign policy hawks debate over whose anger is more patriotic.

In the West, there is a long history of divorcing anger from reason. Seneca argued that one had to rid oneself of anger to achieve *apatheia*, or a state of mind not subject to the passions. Both Plato and Aristotle saw the passions as potentially dangerous to the state, although they saw art as playing differing roles vis-à-vis these emotions. Such classical notions of anger as antithetical to reason continue to today. In *Anger: The Misunderstood Emotion*, Carol Tavris critiques the dominant modern strains of thought that divorce anger from reason and choice. First is the evolutionary view, which sees anger as an instinctual survival response. Second, related to the first, is the view of anger as physiological or neurochemical; in these models, we simply have to identify the hormone or chemical that makes us angry. Third is the Freudian "hydraulic" model of emotions that build up within a person. Leonard Berkowitz "calls advocates of this view 'ventilationists,' because they believe it is unhealthy to bottle up feelings" (Tavris 43). Fourth are forms of pop psychology, variously influenced by the Freudian model, that are based on the "principle that anger, aggression's handmaiden, must not be blocked or silenced," that one must "let it out" (Tavris 43). Primal scream therapies and the like are examples of this model. In contrast, Tavris argues that cathartic models of anger neither sufficiently explain the causes of anger nor offer productive ways of dealing with anger. She is particularly critical of biological or neurochemical explanations for anger, arguing that anger is fundamentally cultural: "People everywhere get angry, but they get angry in the service of their culture's rules" (49).

I would add to Tavris's formulation that anger also reflects conflicts within a society. As cultural studies teaches us,[1] cultures are not monolithic or homogenous; rather, culture can be the site(s) of ideological contestation, where different value systems, social groups, and material interests vie for dominance. So people may become angry when different rules of different cultural groups conflict with one another, or when cultural rules about fairness or morality contradict with the material limits that society puts on certain individuals. The texts I examine in this book (novels, a film, and a television series) depict situations in which complex social contradictions and conflicts produce anger in characters, authors, and readers/viewers. We can parse anger in order to better understand both the emotion itself as well as the structural conditions that produce the emotion(s).

Two separate and still rarely intersecting arenas of scholarly inquiry have dealt most substantively with anger. The first includes the fields of cognitive psychology, cognitive philosophy, and other fields that generally approach emotion as something to be studied as a more or less universal human phenomenon. The other tradition, primarily in women's studies, ethnic studies, and postcolonial studies, deals with anger as explicitly political, if not always simple or desirable. These two discourses seldom come into contact not only because they happen in different academic spheres, but also because they have such different, often mutually hostile, fundamental assumptions about universality, reason, and objectivity. Literary and cultural studies, including fields such as ethnic, postcolonial, and gender studies, have been transformed—in both productive and problematic ways—by poststructuralism and its assault on humanism, empiricism, referentiality, and universalism. Thus, cultural studies today are often primarily concerned with difference, otherness, power, and ideology. At the same time, scholars in ethnic and postcolonial studies have challenged the premises of "mainstream," "Western," or "white" poststructuralism. In particular, the skepticism about our ability to know reality, past and present, has never sat very easily with scholars in these fields because of the political demands of recuperating lost histories, correcting official narratives, and forging better stories.[2]

Furthermore, cultural studies remains deeply skeptical of cognitive psychology and related fields for a variety of historical reasons.[3] Ethnic and postcolonial studies are leery of science and medicine in general and cognitive studies in particular because, historically, "science" writ large has been used to articulate racial and sexual difference as inferior and/or pathological. Examples range from Lothrop Stoddard's *The Rising Tide of Color Against White World-Supremacy* (1920), Madison Grant's *The Passing of the Great Race* (1916), and works by other eugenicists, to *The Bell Curve: Intelligence and Class Structure in American Life* (1994) and other contemporary arguments correlating race, innate cognitive ability, and therefore social hierarchies. In this context, then, cognitive studies can seem both dangerous and appealing to the ethnic studies scholar. But recent work in cognitive literary and cultural studies signals directions that are consonant with the concerns and aims of ethnic studies. Among such historicized approaches are methodologies that allow us to understand that human commonality *and* difference underlie human behavior, including cognition and emotion, in ways that may be compatible with accounts of political anger. As scholars working in cognitive studies in the humanities, such as Frederick Luis Aldama, David Herman, Patrick Colm Hogan, Lisa Zunshine, Suzanne Keen, Kay Young, and Ralph Savarese, have pointed out, we have to be very careful about generalizing fundamental, innate, and/or universal cognitive structures based on observable human behaviors. Cognitive studies can never fully explicate how emotions actually work in the world without the insights of cultural studies, particularly gender and ethnic studies. But by the same token, intellectually and politically, cultural studies should not ignore the ongoing "cognitive revolution," which seems to have an increasing influence on our world. This book is an attempt to bridge these two conversations while focusing on anger and race.

The study of anger is key for understanding both the possibilities and limitations of cognitive studies. On one hand, anger has been identified as one of the five or so emotions that seem to be universal (in addition to fear, happiness, sadness, and disgust), suggesting that even cross-culturally, human beings may have certain shared aptitudes. On the other hand, just like any other emotion, anger is historically situated. Just as no one is afraid, happy, or sad in a vacuum, nobody is ever *just* angry in a vacuum. In fact, I argue that the historicity of anger makes it particularly important to recognize and analyze, because its appearance is always charged. Emotions of happiness, sadness, and fear are just as socially constructed, but anger marks the *feeler* as pathological, dangerous, or ignorant more sharply than do other emotions. Thus, *On Anger* examines anger as an elastic and multivalent phenomenon that must be understood through myriad lenses, including cognitive, affective, ideological, and materialist. I focus on how particular cultural productions explore the ways in which anger, politics (particularly race and class), and narrative forms intersect; in this way, the texts themselves theorize emotion and anger. Just as narratives are one of the key ways in which anger, even as individually experienced, is culturally framed and constructed, so narratives serve as means of reflecting on not only experiences of anger, but also *how we think about anger*—its triggers, its deeper causes, its wrongness or rightness.

The central arguments of *On Anger* are as follows:

- Our individualistic conceptions of anger are insufficient to explain its collective, political, structural, and historical nature. There is a fundamental contradiction between the ways we experience and think of anger; we conceive of it individually, but anger is often produced by collective, structural phenomena, in different ways at different historical moments. *On Anger* focuses on racial anger in late capitalism, but anger is arguably just as historically situated at other times. Currently, many scientific and popular conceptions cast anger as primarily an individual and personal phenomenon. But the sources of many kinds of anger are ideological and institutional; structures of race, gender, neocolonialism, capitalism, and byzantine bureaucracies produce feelings of frustration and anger that we often do not know how to process.

- Furthermore, this individualized conception of anger exacerbates the structures that cause anger in late capitalism. That is, individualistic atomization, the distinction between reason and emotion, and other characteristics of common conceptions of anger not only fail to explain why and how many of us are angry today, but also reinforce the systemic conditions that produce our anger (and alienation, depression, confusion, etc.).
- Cultural productions (e.g., films, novels) are important sources to study in order to better understand human emotion and cognition, and, moreover, the texts themselves can be forms of theorizing about emotions. The particular texts I examine in this book repeatedly demonstrate how the subjects situated within, reproducing, and reacting to such institutions (including characters as well as viewers and readers) do not know how to respond to, articulate, or even understand their anger, because our functioning conceptions of anger and emotions in general are, again, so individualistic. Therefore, rather than recognize and change the system, various kinds of ineffectual lashings-out occur. The texts themselves take a variety of positions regarding this state of affairs—I argue that *Crash* implicitly condones it while *Wizard of the Crow* exposes and mocks it—but the pattern in the storyworld of the texts emerges again and again.
- Racial anger is and is not about race. Racial anger refers to the anger arising from racial/national formations appearing in various specific forms around the world, commonly conditioned by global capitalism, colonialism and neocolonialism, and liberal individualism.[4] Race, like anger, is ideologically and historically constructed, so many of the conflicts that seem to center on an essentialized concept of race are actually a collision of various historical-political factors; as we do anger, we fetishize race, or isolate it from the systems and structures out of which it arises (particularly economic systems). For example, in Chapter 4, I discuss how

The Wire scrutinizes the social, economic, political, and other institutional forces that produce the phenomenon of angry, urban, minority youth. All of the texts I examine, in fact, have to do with race as a nexus of issues.

- Anger is dialectical. Understanding anger as dialectical means reading anger as an affective response to subjective and material senses of embodied frustrations that are encountered when obstacles are placed directly in the way of one's attainment of goals. By "dialectical," I mean a way of thinking that incorporates fundamental contradictions and ongoing movements within a phenomenon that we may perceive to be singular. Rather than fixed, abstract, singular, or expressive of an interiority, anger can be understood as an ongoing (and not necessarily teleological) process, a combination of many historical factors that produce a certain experience and expression of a person's anger at a particular moment in time.[5] In considering anger, commonplace oppositions such as nature and nurture, cognitive and cultural, individual and collective, material and affective, and rational and emotional should also be understood as dialectical, in the sense of ongoing processes of perceived antitheses actually showing themselves to be interrelated. In other words, anger is not only physiological and cognitive but also social and historical and, therefore, ideological. Anger is not just individual but also social, collective, and historical. Even "nature" and evolution, as I will discuss below, are not purely biological; cognitive structures change in response to contexts, which are themselves continually changing.

- Just as narratives are key to shaping the subject, gender, sex, race, nationality, and other ideological formations, so narratives are central to shaping emotion. Chapters 1 and 2 explore the ways in which both cognitive and cultural studies critics are coming/have come, separately, to the conclusion that emotions (and cognition) are inseparable from narratives and context; subsequent chapters explore how narratives and emotions interact in specific texts.

- Some of the methodologies of cognitive and cultural studies can be fruitfully combined to better understand the dynamics of racial anger in late capitalism. The unconscious, the processes of the physical body, cultural norms and values, economic resources and systems, institutional formations—these all play a part in shaping emotion. To help explicate the dynamics of these things, the insights of cognitive psychology, philosophy, and narratology can be helpful. By the same token, the committed social critique and ethical element of overtly political accounts of anger are necessary to remedy the limited scope of scientific inquiry.

WHY COGNITION? WHY CULTURE?
AND OTHER PITFALLS OF COMPARISON

One question we must tackle is *why* do cognitive studies and cultural studies need to talk to one another?[6] What do these two fields have to offer each other? Although in very different ways, both cognitive and cultural studies have seen movements away from an abstract, Cartesian model of mind toward the notion of a complexly embodied subject, whose being in the world is not wholly rational, conscious, and atomistic/discrete. In other words, scholars in very different fields have been working with the general notion that a subject (as we may put it in cultural studies) or a mind (as it is often put in cognitive studies) is affected by a variety of factors—physiological, unconscious, social, and intersubjective—in often unexpected, unpredictable ways. I discuss the variety of ways that anger is treated in each of these two areas in Chapters 1 and 2, but here I outline some general reasons for even bringing cultural and cognitive studies into conversation.

Cultural studies serves as an important corrective to the lacunae within science and the social sciences. As Patrick Colm Hogan writes, "Cognitive science can hardly claim to explain the human mind if it fails to deal with such a ubiquitous and significant aspect of human mental activity as literature" (*Mind* 4). Hogan notes that some scientists and social scientists who study emotion "almost entirely ignore a vast body of existing data that bears directly on feelings and ideas about feelings—literature, especially literary narrative" (1). Cultural studies scholars bring expertise on reading texts and ideology as well as more sophisticated understandings of how identities are socially constructed. Chapter 2 deals at length with the importance of cultural studies, or the humanities, to understanding emotion and cognition, and this book deals primarily with ethnic, postcolonial, feminist, and Marxist cultural studies.

For humanists, the difficult question may be what cognitive studies have to offer. Any model or theory that projects human beings as locked into their identities, thought processes, or behaviors should be considered insufficient; people have the ability to choose, although usually not in circumstances of their own making. But complex cognitive approaches to ideology offer a number of potential benefits for cultural studies, particularly at this moment. First, cognitive theory offers us an alternative way to think about emotion in the wake of the many critiques of the relativism, skepticism, and political despair of certain strands of poststructuralism. Freudian and Lacanian psychoanalysis have hitherto been where we get most of our ideas about affect in cultural studies, and while I do not dismiss all of those insights, I would agree with Carol Tavris and others that there are other, perhaps more productive or insightful ways to think about emotion than as some elusive, uncontrollable force controlling us (psychic or linguistic). Second, cognitive studies may be a means to obtain better information about how our minds work. Even if we do not take the empirical data at face value, cognitive studies does provide material that may challenge our assumptions, or as Rey Chow puts it, interrupt our skepticism of referentiality; even if we do not know things perfectly, at least we can know things *better*. Third, it offers a way to think about sameness (cognitive capabilities shared by all humans) as well as difference (recognition of historically and socially produced differences, particularly the unequal distribution of resources). Fourth, it offers a way to recognize emotions like anger as phenomenologically real as well as a means to analyze and assess those emotions. But the most important reason to engage with cognitive studies may be political: the cognitive revolution is happening. One only needs to turn on NPR or open a newspaper to see daily references to neuroscience, cognitive psychology, and other studies of the brain. Just as narratologists working in cognitive studies have argued that humanists should be involved, I argue that interdisciplinary ethnic, postcolonial, and women's studies scholars also need to be engaged. The blind spots of the sciences need to be checked by work in the humanities, particularly fields such as these that are tied to social movements. In fact, arguably the most important reason for ethnic and postcolonial studies scholars to engage cognitive studies—particularly in terms of emotion and anger—is that without our insights, the concepts of "human" and "cognition" more than ever run the danger of becoming liberal multicultural, bourgeois, First-World fallacies. Chapter 1 further examines some of the areas of cognitive approaches to emotion that invite or necessitate intervention by cultural studies. In order to develop a truly human cognitive theory, we have to understand a variety of humans and their thoughts, emotions, experiences, cultures, and histories.

This breadth is partly why I chose to write about such a variety of texts. I recognize that covering such disparate texts and contexts runs the risks of obscuring differences; Paul Haggis, Maxine Hong

Kingston, Tsitsi Dangarembga, Ngugi wa Thiong'o, and David Simon write and work in distinct places and times (and genres). They write about issues of racialized oppression, but the specific cultural and historical contexts are very different. Comparative analyses such as mine sacrifice deeper exploration into the specifics of situation and form; one could write several books on the development of affect and realism in Ngugi's novels alone, with greater engagement with colonial and postcolonial Kenyan history, or on the depictions of anger in contemporary U.S. serial television (and I would read both books). But my project in *On Anger* is to engage and interrogate conceptions of anger in cognitive studies (primarily psychology) to work toward a more inclusive, more universal theory of anger. In other words, I acknowledge the possibility that human beings across the globe share common capacities for emotion and cognition, which is the attraction of cognitive studies. But the current state of cognitive studies leaves much to be desired in whom and what it examines and how such analyses take place. As I discuss in Chapter 1, most of the research in cognitive psychology focuses on First-World, white, upper-/middle-class, and young people. Much of the skepticism about the discourse of humanism and human rights arises from such implicit erasure of most of the human race. While I do think we share commonalities, we can only understand them if we actually study all kinds of people in a variety of situations. To this effect, I also seek to reconsider what kinds of narratives can be central to understanding human experience, in ways that attend to particularities as well as similarities and may have repercussions for all. The parallels as well as the differences in and among the cases I examine can help illuminate aspects of anger.

A number of strong commonalities exist among the texts: except for Ngugi's novels, they are all in English (and Ngugi translates his own work; I discuss this issue in Chapter 6), and both the U.S. and African texts all deal with collision of races—within and between nations—in the postcolonial, late-capitalist era. While emerging from a variety of cultural contexts, these texts (except *Crash*, which I discuss in Chapter 3) deal with racial interactions not in terms of discrete, homogenous groups confronting one another (e.g., white vs. black, West vs. East), but through the far more complicated, vexed, and realistic lens of mixed, changing cultures under unequal power relations. For instance, Tsitsi Dangarembga's *Nervous Conditions* and *The Book of Not* draw on traditional Shona culture, colonial British and Christian cultures (not always identical), white Rhodesian settler culture, and postcolonial Zimbabwean nationalism, but the specific manifestations of these cultures in the novels are never pure or singular. Indeed, both the novels are partly about the conflicts of a contemporary existence in which the quest for purity—in a variety of senses—is impossible. This complexity is one reason why, although I argue that anger is partly shaped by narratives, I do not discuss at length traditional cultural views of anger (e.g., "This is how Asian Americans/Korean Americans view anger"). For instance, in her otherwise excellent book, *Anger: The Misunderstood Emotion*, Carol Tavris draws on anthropological studies of cultures such as the Kapauku Papuans of West New Guinea (55) and the !Kung-san of the Kalahari Desert, contrasting their traditional views and customs of anger against those of Americans or the West. But one needs only to read authors such as Epeli Hau'ofa, Albert Wendt, and Bessie Head to see the complexity of modern cultures, most of it initially wrought by colonialism and neocolonialism and subsequently metamorphosed into new, unexpected formations. I am not saying that there is no difference between cultures; rather, that in the age of globalization, it is far too easy to attribute emotional narratives to cultures. As Fanon has shown us, cultures and psyches change when exposed to colonialism and neo-imperialism.

Furthermore, I agree with those who argue that what ultimately links U.S. racializations and postcolonial conditions are global capitalism and its ideologies, particularly individualism and neoliberalism. That is, capitalism does not render racial formations and racial oppressions the same across the world; rather, its systemic nature impacts people differently, in varying structures and systems, which are specific in expression and impact, but can—in the final instance— be traced back to the exigencies of capitalism. In many instances, we find that such exigencies emerge from the many forms of liberalism that inform and are informed by global capital, including, historically, the selective granting and denial of liberal individualism to certain persons and groups. As David Theo Goldberg writes, "The racially subjugated are the ghosts of slave and colonial pasts, and by extension of postcolonizing present" (26).[7]

By individualism, I refer to the basic idea that individuals, rather than communal or historical circumstances, determine their own fate and conditions. Individualism ranges from the extreme pure individualism à la Ayn Rand, which celebrates capitalism as an expression of the survival of the fittest, to more moderate notions that emphasize free agency within certain limits. The opposite of indi-

vidualism may be a number of things: collectivism, social or economic determinism, social constructionism (the individual is merely
a nexus of social constructions). In relation to social justice, moreover, the question becomes even more complicated. My own stance
is between strict individualism and constructionism, a combination
of cognition and culture. I emphasize the collective and structural elements of anger in this book because heretofore the individual aspects have been privileged, but, to quote (slightly altered) Marx's fa-
mous line from *Eighteenth Brumaire*, "[human beings] make their
own history, but they do not make it just as they please; they do not
make it under circumstances chosen by themselves, but under circumstances directly found, given and transmitted from the past" (54).
We can think of "history" here as encompassing the ways that we
feel and how we think about what we feel.

OVERVIEW OF CHAPTERS

The first chapter surveys work on emotion and anger in cognitive
studies, particularly psychology, and cognitive narrative theory. I explain both the dominant "appraisal" theory of emotion and some of
the principal challenges to it. I also explore some of the ways in which
cognitive psychology has attempted to deal with culture and history,
and some of the ways in which it falls short. This discussion leads to
the second chapter, "Anger as Culture," which describes work in cultural studies, broadly defined, on emotion and anger. In this chapter, I first outline three trends in cultural studies of emotion: 1) emotion as ideological analysis; 2) historical genealogies of emotion; and
3) explorations of gaps, fractures, excesses, and other "beyonds" in relation to defined emotions. The second part of the chapter looks at
Marxist and narratological approaches to emotion as providing useful
frameworks and tools for analyzing anger.

The third chapter, "Liberal Anger: Technologies of Anger in
Crash," examines Paul Haggis's 2005 film and its use of anger. The
film erases historical and structural reasons for racial and class conflict and advocates liberal multiculturalism as a panacea. The film's
subscription to an individualistic model of cognition, anger, and emotion in general—and its inability to perceive of histories and structures beyond the individual—ultimately ends up reinforcing racist
and exploitative systems. The fourth and fifth chapters explore how
time and space constitute important considerations for understanding anger situated in history and structures. Chapter 4, "Temporal-

ity and the Politics of Reading Kingston's *The Woman Warrior*," explores the importance of multiple layers of narrative and historical time that go into constructions, depictions, and experiences of anger. Chapter 5, "Anger and Space in Dangarembga's *Nervous Conditions* and *The Book of Not*," explores how the ideological production of spaces—and the contradictions embedded within them—also prescribes, proscribes, and produces certain bodies and emotions.

The sixth and seventh chapters consider time, space, and narrative form in order to further explore the dialectical nature of anger. Chapter 6, "Estranging Rage: Ngugi's *Devil on the Cross* and *Wizard of the Crow*," argues that constructions of Ngugi as an angry, idealistic nativist (which still continue today) and readings of his later novels as less affective than his earlier works assume that a conception of emotion is individual, separate from collectives as well as from reason and ideology. Ngugi's later novels, I argue, interrogate the division between emotion and reason in form and content. Chapter 7, "'This Game Is Rigged': *The Wire* and Agency Attribution," examines how the critically acclaimed HBO television series shows that while we still tend to search for an individual external agent to blame for our actions, to serve as the target of our anger, the actual causes of our anger and frustration are systemic. Even the debates about the political efficacy of the show, I argue, often hinge on an untenable division between individual blame/anger and structural critique/collective action.

The conclusion considers the distinction between frustration and outrage through a consideration of Stéphane Hessel's call to arms, *Indignez-vous!* The texts examined in *On Anger* repeatedly show that frustration develops not only because a person is blocked from achieving his/her goals, but also because the very conception or framework of anger is insufficient, in its notion of agency and blame as only individual, to really understand the collective, structural/institutional, and historical reasons for the anger. Outrage, however, can be a conscious ethical choice based on collectively articulated group norms, such as justice and human rights, which can also lead to political engagement with the world. Understanding various models of anger and their implications, I argue, is key to understanding how the mind, cognition, emotion, culture, and the world really work. We still have a long way to go; I believe we are just at the beginning of the enterprise, which is very exciting. This book participates in that ongoing project by looking at the emotion of anger in its cognitive and cultural human complexities.

CHAPTER I

ANGER AS COGNITION

Anger implies hope.

NICO FRIJDA, *THE EMOTIONS*

THIS CHAPTER SURVEYS CURRENT WORK on emotion and cognition, highlighting central insights and debates about anger within cognitive psychology. Despite discussion of a "warrior gene" that predisposes certain individuals toward greater aggression and violence ("Can Genes"), surprisingly little consensus exists among cognitive psychologists about what actually constitutes anger—its triggers, its manifestations, its parameters, its ontological status. To me, this lack of agreement among cognitive psychologists was most surprising, because in cultural studies our understanding of "science" writ large is that of totalization, universality, and objectivity. In contrast, scientists' and psychologists' conversations about emotions, particularly anger, often prove to be not only multivoiced but also highly (and entertainingly) contentious. Further insight into many of these questions and debates, I argue, can only be provided by cultural studies and certain cultural productions. To that end, the final part of the chapter reviews recent work done in narrative theory that seeks to integrate cognitive and literary studies.

As opposed to the tradition of psychoanalysis since Freud, modern cognitive studies of emotion has its origins in the work of William James and Carl Lange, both of whom saw emotion as a response to external stimuli via physical and visceral—i.e., somatic—bodily changes. In the classic James-Lange formulation, I see a bear or attacker, my heart rate goes up and my muscles get tense, and I interpret those physiological responses as fear.[1] Or, as Elspeth Probyn puts it:

In other words, the body perceives itself perceiving the trigger of emotion, which sets off movement (trembling), and then gets named as a cognitive state (fear). Or there is Deleuze's description of this sequence: (a) the perception of the situation; (b) the modification of the body; (c) the emotion of consciousness of the mind. (142)

Part of the turn-of-the-last-century's movement toward the scientific and systematic in the social sciences, James and Lange's approach to emotions held that "[s]ince each emotion was nothing but the mirror-feeling of some complex of bodily arousal (some pattern of physiological changes), then all you needed to know in order to distinguish and describe the various emotions was to study the physiological details of each pattern of arousal" (Lyons 31–32). In the early decades of the twentieth century, however, psychology turned from the somatic view of emotion of James and Lange toward the behaviorism of B. F. Skinner and Pavlov. Behaviorists posited emotion as a product of environment and external factors, rather than internal psychological or physiological processes. According to Lyons, J. B. Watson's 1913 "exciting and combative" paper, titled "Psychology as a Behaviourist Views It," radically altered the field: "At a stroke, from being 'the science of the mind,' psychology had been redefined by Watson as 'the science of behaviour'" (32–33).[2]

The cognitive revolution in the middle of the twentieth century arose in the historical conjunction between innovations in neurobiology, computer technology and artificial intelligence, information theory, and other new fields (Miller). The view of emotions shifted from behaviorism to one of information processing.[3] As Lyons summarizes:

For a time, from roughly 1960 to 1980, the guiding metaphor in philosophy of mind was the computer. The mind is to the body, so the slogan went, as a computer's program or software (its functioning) is to its electronics or hardware (its structure). The study of a human's mental life or psychology amounts to the investigation of the human program (or functioning). Evolution is both the programmer of the software and the designer of the software. (37)

Whereas this first cognitive revolution viewed the mind as essentially a computing machine, the second cognitive revolution of the late twentieth century began to incorporate more nuanced and com-

plex processes. David Herman discusses the fundamental difference
between these two cognitive revolutions:

> The first cognitive revolution marked a shift away from behavior-
> ism to the study of cognition, postulating that "there are mental pro-
> cesses 'behind' what people say and do, that these processes are to be
> classified as 'information processing,' and that the best model for the
> cognitively active human being is the computer when it is running a
> program." In contrast, although the second cognitive revolution also
> accepts that there are cognitive processes, it views them as imma-
> nent in discourse practices. From this perspective, *the mind does not
> preexist discourse, but is ongoingly accomplished in and through its
> production and interpretation.* ("Narrative Theory" 156, emphasis
> added)

That is, the second generation of cognitive scholars, sometimes referred to as "postcognitivists," recognizes the mind as "immanent
in discourse practices," embedded in social groups and intersubjective dynamics, rather than as a discrete input-output calculating machine. For example, George Lakoff and Mark Johnson in *Philosophy
in the Flesh* argue for an "embodied realism" that would break down
the subject-object split between self and world; they write, "What
disembodied realism (what is sometimes called 'metaphysical' or 'external' realism) misses is that, as embodied, imaginative creatures,
we never were separated or divorced from reality in the first place"
(93). This second revolution is marked by the work of scholars such
as Lakoff and Johnson, Antonio Damasio, Mark Turner, Gilles Fauconnier, John Tooby and Leda Cosmides, and others; these are also
the scholars with whose work literary and cultural critics have found
productive interface.

In this second revolution, the relationship between emotion and
cognition has been one key site of inquiry. As Joseph Forgas observes,
"Research on affect and cognition is now one of the most rapidly
growing endeavors in psychology, providing a unifying focus for researchers working in a variety of disciplines such as social, cognitive, developmental, clinical, and neuropsychology" (xiii). Many cognitive psychologists accept that all human beings are hardwired for
certain emotions, with most concurring that anger is one of the five
to eight or so emotions found in all human cultures.[4] But scholars
differ greatly on the ways that emotions play out in actual human

beings in the real world. Many cognitivists recognize that emotion is linked to cognition, but not in any simple or unilinear way. Studies of emotion focus on the relationship between reason and emotion, the origin of emotions (e.g., emotions are shaped by neurological and physiological factors, conscious evaluations of a situation, communal norms, memory triggers, etc.), the social nature of emotions, and the extent to which emotions are culturally specific.

This chapter outlines appraisal theory, or the dominant theory of emotions in cognitive psychology, as well as complications of and challenges to this approach.[5] These discussions demonstrate that, despite an emphasis on cognition, or the information-processing of the mind, an awareness of cultural context *as an integral part of the mind's processes* haunts many such accounts of emotion. Methodologically, however, cognitive psychologists have failed to deal meaningfully with multiple cultural and historical contexts, so several cognitive humanists, particularly narrative theorists, have attempted to meld the insights of cognitive and literary studies. I outline some of these developments, with special attention to anger.

WHAT IS ANGER?

PART I: APPRAISAL THEORY

In cognitive psychology, as with emotions in general, physiological indicators such as rises in blood pressure and temperature are commonly agreed upon, but there is a great deal of disagreement about the triggers, parameters, and scope of anger. What *is* anger? What distinguishes anger from its expression(s)? Are there different degrees of anger, and if so, should these be categorically differentiated: for example, are frustration and anger two qualitatively different things, or are they similar emotions on a scale of vehemence? Does the anger precede the cognitive appraisal—conscious or not—or vice versa, or is it a two-way street?

The very range of questions and issues has resulted in broad general definitions, a "wide tent" approach to studies of anger. *The Handbook of Cognition and Emotion* (1999) states, "Most authors agree that anger ranges along a dimension of intensity, from frustration and annoyance to rage," with some differentiating further between anger and "subanger," which includes irritation and frustration (Dagleish and Power 5). At the same time, whether expressed as aggression or shouting or silence, "Anger is generally held to be a negative (aversive) emotion, but one that involves an active approach, in contrast to the negative emotions of sadness and fear which involve inhibition and withdrawal, respectively" (Dagleish and Power 5).[6] In their 2008 survey of work on anger in psychology, neuropsychology, and cognitive behavioral studies, Cox and Harrison reach a similarly wide-ranging definition, writing that "the construct of anger is considered to be multidimensional with distinct affective, behavioral, and cognitive dimensions and distinct physiological elements that contribute to both the experience and expression of the emotion" (372). In fact, Cox and Harrison go on to argue against a "categorical" definition of anger altogether, instead advocating for a context-dependent conception of anger.[7]

Nevertheless, Cox and Harrison observe that although "there are numerous theories of anger within the cognitive-behavioral literature, appraisal theory, in one form or another, dominates the current cognitive-behavioral literature" (373). That is, even as there is debate about the precise role appraisal plays in producing emotion, they conclude, "most cognitive models of anger indicate that the experience of anger depends on the higher order appraisal of events" (373). Likewise, in their wide-ranging survey of the study of emotions, Keltner and Lerner claim that "emotions are rooted in appraisals" (320). Appraisal theory contends that emotion is produced by a subject's perception of success or failure in achieving a desired goal.[8] In classical appraisal theories, "emotion results from a type of evaluation in which one judges the implications of a certain situation for oneself," usually in relation to achieving some goal, and the emotion helps us to organize information and decide on actions (Hogan, *Cognitive Science* 140–141). This goal or objective, of course, must have *personal significance* affecting personal values; not all goals are equally important to an individual.

Under the rubric of appraisal, many further distinctions come into play. As the *International Handbook of Anger* notes, "There is quite broad agreement that typical triggers of anger include frustration; threats to autonomy, authority, or reputation; disrespect and insult; norm or rule violation; and a sense of injustice. Some authors subsume these various provocations under a rubric of goal blockage" (Potegal, Stemmler, and Spielberger 3–4). Discussions of "appraisal" in cognitive psychology thus include considerations of frustration; norm or rule violation, which is linked to appraisal; agency attribution; coping potential; and physiological as well as subconscious factors.

Within and across some areas of agreement, however, are also provocative questions that continue to be debated.

For instance, cognitive appraisal depends in large part on one's definitions of cognition. A restricted definition of cognition holds that, as in the first cognitive revolution, cognition requires "the transformation of sensory input into a new mental construction" (Berkowitz and Harmon-Jones 108). Berkowitz and Harmon-Jones argue that if we use this restricted definition of cognition, appraisal theory is insufficient to account for emotions because some triggers of anger are physiological and subconscious.[9] Conversely, Richard Lazarus and others argue for a broad definition of cognition, including unconscious appraisals as well as knowledge that is not necessarily a product of appraisal vis-à-vis a singular goal ("Cognition-Emotion Debate" 10). An individual may have conflicting yet simultaneous beliefs; Lazarus writes, "We can believe simultaneously, for example, that flying in an airplane is safe; at the same time, we can act as if we believed that it is very dangerous" ("Cognition and Motivation" 363). Smith and Kirby concur with Lazarus, arguing for the relevance to appraisal of "associative processing," or second-order cognitive processes that are not conscious (134).[10]

Three considerations or aspects often arise in discussions of appraisal theories: 1) illegitimacy, or violation of group norms; 2) agency attribution, or blame of another being who acts on us; and 3) coping potential, or the notion that one has some degree of power or control over the situation. First, appraisal theory is often linked to the notion that anger is a reaction to violations of norms and rules—or illegitimacy—but this proposition has wildly different implications. Violation of group norms can run the gamut from personal "disrespect and insult" to social "injustice" (Potegal, Stemmler, and Spielberger 3). For example, some theorists argue that anger reinforces hierarchical social structures by enforcing the status quo and/or preventing subordination of the self to others in a struggle for dominance (see Chapter 7 in Potegal et al.). Fessler argues that the "male flash of anger" is such a mechanism for maintaining power and/or defending the self, which bypasses more time-consuming processes of negotiation and reasoning (Chapter 21 in Potegal et al.).

In contrast, Clore and Centerbar read more optimistically the notion that group norms shape the rules for just behavior and for the criteria of blameworthy actions. Research on animals, they argue, suggests that collective group norms shape affective reactions, particularly in distinguishing simple bad outcomes from bad outcomes attributable to bad behavior. They cite Stanley Coren's 1994 *The Intelligence of Dogs*:

> [Consider] the difference between the hang-dog expression of the family dog when he does not get to go in the car and his angry growl when someone reaches for a bone in his mouth. The former reflects a disappointment-like state fueled by loss of an expected goal, while the latter reflects violation of a universal canine norm whereby food (or anything else) in a dog's mouth is the rightful property of that animal, regardless of his position in the dominance hierarchy. (quoted in Clore and Centerbar 140)

Among humans as well, appraisal in the context of group norm violations produces anger: "The elicitation of [a]nger implicates both the violation of standards and the thwarting of goals" (Ortony, Clore, and Collins 153).[11]

A second factor in considering appraisal theories of anger is "agency attribution," or directing blame at intentional beings that act on us. Hogan describes "dispositional entities" as "anything to which one attributes intent" or "objects that act on us" (*Mind* 253). Many theorists see a perceived intentional offense by an external agent as integral to the production of anger.[12] For example, Clore and Centerbar argue that "frustration becomes anger only when it becomes agent-focused" (140). For them, a "negative outcome" or goal blockage without a "blameworthy agent" would result in frustration or distress, but not anger (139). In fact, they continue, it is the *moral* aspect in evaluating an external agent's actions that gives anger its intensity and can lead to "extreme action"; they write, "One reason that anger is powerful and problematic is that it is an embodied conviction that others have acted wrongly" (141). They discuss examples of political rage, which they see as justified, as well as types of delusional and unjustified rage. Ultimately, for them, *"anger implicates agency"* (141, emphasis added).

But this criterion does not mean that the blamed agent actually exists; because cognition is not a simple, straightforward process, we may blame persons and things even if we know that they did not or could not have intended harm. For example, Ortony, Clore, and Collins argue that even in instances in which there appears to be no blameworthy agent—such as, for example, when "one's car will not start"—a person only becomes angry if "in fact, one does attribute causal agency (quite possibly, wrongly, and knowingly so) to something (the weather, the car, the garage mechanic, the person who last drove it, etc.)" (152). They suggest calling these "desperate" attributions because "they represent a desperate attempt to attribute responsibility, even when there is no culpable agent available" (152). They maintain that ultimately, even if the external agents are far-fetched and even "bizarre," "one's anger presupposes that there exists such a cause" (152).

In contrast, others do not see agency attribution as central to anger. For example, while their literature review reveals that "there is nearly complete agreement that someone or something, an external agent, must be seen as responsible for the negative event if there is to be anger" (109), Berkowitz and Harmon-Jones argue that noncognitive factors, such as physical pain and muscle memory, are just as important in producing anger. In fact, Berkowitz and Harmon-Jones hold that agency attribution and illegitimacy, while common, are not integral to the production of anger, and they argue that blame-placing can be the *result* of anger, rather than its cause: "Several researchers . . . have suggested that the blame placing found in many appraisal investigations may be an epiphenomenon, a consequence rather than an antecedent of anger arousal" (113).

By the same token, not all theorists differentiate so clearly between anger (with an external agent to blame) and frustration (without one). For example, in 1939 Dollard et al. forwarded the "frustration-aggression hypothesis," in which "(1) The occurrence of aggression presupposes the existence of frustration; and (2) the existence of frustration always leads to some form of aggression" (Power and Dagleish, 317). Dollard et al., however, did not specifically articulate anger as part of their model. In 1962's *Aggression: A Social Psychological Analysis*, however, Berkowitz inserted anger as a mediator into the frustration-aggression hypothesis: "frustration leads to anger which acts as a drive and heightens the probability of aggressive behavior. That is to say, frustration is not the immediate cause of aggression; rather, it is mediated by anger" (Power and Dagleish 317). Berkowitz differed from Dollard in that "frustration need not necessarily lead to aggression, merely to anger" (317–318), placing frustration and anger on a continuum while differentiating aggression as an expression of anger.

Illegitimacy and blame are connected to the third concept com-

monly discussed in relation to anger: "coping potential," or "the person's perceived ability to deal successfully with the eliciting event"
(Berkowitz and Harmon-Jones 110). Coping potential implies a degree of power and control in a situation, even if that power and control are thwarted. There is debate about whether some degree of control potential is necessary merely to feel anger. Some argue that if I
did not believe I had any ability to affect my situation whatsoever, I
would not become angry; rather, I would become depressed, sad, fear-
ful, and/or anxious. Frijda writes, "Anger implies nonacceptance of
the present event as necessary or inevitable; and it implies that the
event is amenable to being changed" (199).

Frijda thus summarizes the conventional appraisal view of anger,
including goal-blockage, agency attribution, and coping potential:

> [Anger's] situational meaning structure involves an obstacle that in
> principle might not have been there. The antagonist could have acted
> otherwise; *something or someone else is to blame.* This implies that
> behind the obstacle the blocked goal still exists, still is available;
> and the nature of the obstacle is such that, in principle it can be con-
> trolled and modified. *Anger implies hope.* Further, anger implies that
> fighting is meaningful; one is not reduced to mere passivity. These
> are the advantages. The disadvantage resides in the effort and alert-
> ness required and the burden of responsibility for effecting or not
> effecting the change that is possible. Efforts toward that change,
> moreover, may fail and thus produce humiliation and disappoint-
> ment. (429, emphasis added)[13]

Frijda goes on to explain that what we perceive as "bad" anger is poor
agency attribution, or blaming something/someone that is not really
the cause of the situation, whereas "good" anger is directed at the
correct problem. But the disadvantages of effort, responsibility, and
the possibility of failure result in people not only *not* being angry at
oppression, exploitation, and inequality—even and particularly when
these conditions are defined as being morally wrong—but in fact failing to acknowledge and even *actively repressing* evidence that such
injustices occur. I return to these issues in the last section of this
chapter.

Appraisal theories of anger, arguably, imply degrees of focus, direction, and reason, and theorists use this to differentiate an emotion,
such as anger, from mood. For example, Frijda argues that, in con-

trast to emotions, "behaviorally, moods are configurations of activity that are not centered around an object or event, but that in fleeting manner attach now to this object, then to that" (59). While moods can be similar to emotions such as sadness or happiness, they are less focused and more fleeting. Yet Frijda goes on to admit, "The distinction between moods and emotions, as these words are usually used, is equally unsharp" (60).

PART 2: CHALLENGES TO APPRAISAL THEORY

A different line of thought about anger puts more emphasis on non-conscious factors and conditioned emotional-physical responses. After theorizing in the 1960s that anger mediates between frustration and aggression, Berkowitz later developed a more complex theory of anger, or what he called "the neo-associationist model of anger." In 1990 Berkowitz wrote, "Associative networks link specific types of feelings with particular thoughts and memories and also with certain kinds of expressive-motor and physiological reactions . . . [and] the activation of any one of the components in the network tends to activate the other parts as well" (496). That is, rather than a linear or causal appraisal model, in which goal-blockage results in anger, Berkowitz argues that somatic and cognitive processes can work in multidirectional and unexpected ways, through parallels or associations or empathetic identifications. He claims, "There is an associative connection between negative affect and anger-related feelings, ideas, and memories, and also with aggressive inclinations" (496). So if I am experiencing one kind of bad sensation—my tooth hurts, or I am overly hot, or I smell an unpleasant odor—I am more likely to become angry, hostile, and/or aggressive because memories of somatic and cognitive processes of anger have been triggered. But because these are associations and not triggers, an aversive situation will not necessarily lead to anger. That is, initial reactions to stimuli do not immediately lead to an emotion; rather, "rudimentary fear and anger experiences" simply establish conditions that usually result in emotions of fear and anger (497).

Berkowitz argues that this neo-associationist model accounts for the heterogeneity of actual emotions that arise in different people, as well as for the differing emotional responses to a single event that a person may experience over the course of time. A "negative event" results in "basic, primary reactions," or "relatively automatic associative processes," that may or may not result in more complex emotions and "complicated thoughts of the type postulated by cognitive theorists" ("On the Formation" 497). Berkowitz thus argues, contra appraisal theory, that it is "in these later stages that the affected person makes appraisals and causal attributions and considers what feelings and actions are appropriate under the particular circumstances" (497).

In a 2004 special issue of the psychology journal *Emotion*, Berkowitz and Harmon-Jones again take square aim at appraisal theory, arguing for what they now term a "cognitive neo-associationistic" (CNA) model of anger. They argue that classical appraisal theory does not sufficiently take into account other factors that may affect and produce emotions, such as physical pain and emotional memories tied to muscle movements, including facial expressions. According to Berkowitz and Harmon-Jones, what appraisal theorists identify as the causes of emotions are actually only things that may *intensify* the experience of anger. Instead, they argue that the CNA model (because less causal and linear) can account for more of the factors that come into play in shaping emotion. Somewhat in the tradition of James and Lange, although accounting for more of the intermediate steps and less monocausally, Berkowitz and Harmon-Jones emphasize "aversive conditions," or "a state of affairs the person ordinarily seeks to escape or avoid" (117), such as pain, stress, discomfort, etc., that can affect a person's emotions. For example, they cite studies that "indicate that persons facing physically uncomfortable conditions can become angry and hostile even when it is unlikely that they made the particular appraisals often postulated as the anger-evoking emotion" (118). These uncomfortable situations have included hot or cold, cigarette smoke, and "even the presence of a stimulus associated with previously experienced pain"; such studies have found that these uncomfortable situations "can evoke stronger aggression than otherwise would have occurred" (118). Bodily movements also can shape emotion; Berkowitz and Harmon-Jones cite research by Paul Ekman and others showing that "manipulated facial expressions typical of each of six different emotions led to distinctive changes in heart rate and finger temperature," physiological indicators of a change in emotional state, and resulted in corresponding cognitive statements: "People who adopted the facial expression and bodily posture characteristics of anger made the external-agency appraisals predicted by most appraisal accounts of anger, whereas the sad pose results in more situational attributions" (121).

Thus, Berkowitz and Harmon-Jones argue for an "associative" model of emotion sources, rather than a theory of appraisal that sees emotions as a causal result of cognition: "We suggest that the various physiological, skeletal muscle, experiential, and cognitive components of an emotional syndrome are *interconnected associatively* so that the activation of any one component will spread to other components in proportion to the strength of the associations between them" (122, emphasis added).[14] In other words, an "aversive event" triggers an entire host of responses—emotions, memories, ideas, association, physiological reactions and impulses, etc.—that are discernibly associated but highly unpredictable. They use the term "syndrome" to try to capture the multidirectionality and heterogeneity of the physical, cognitive, and neurochemical processes that can shape an emotion. Moreover, they note that multiple "syndromes"—those of fear and anger, for example—can be simultaneous and mutually interactive, with one or the other dominating depending on the conditions.

The rejoinders from appraisal theorists have been vociferous. Buss argues that CNA is too broad and methodologically unviable: "Frustration-aggression is so broad—aversiveness leads to anger—and so complex that it might contain escape hatches to deal with negative evidence" (132). Roseman contends that while neurophysiological factors are undoubtedly important, perception and cognition are more important in ultimately shaping emotion: "A striking consistency in the empirical literature is that expressive movements have relatively little power to affect emotions when pitted against perceptions of events" (149). Smith and Kirby argue that Berkowitz and Harmon-Jones's definition of "cognition" is too narrow. While there are different varieties of appraisal theories, they argue, most (if not all) recognize that appraisal does not only occur in "focal awareness," or conscious thought (134). For example, Smith and Kirby "posit a second, more automatic level of *associative processing,* in which information stored in memory is activated through such processes as priming and spreading activation" (134, original emphasis); moreover, they argue that "associative processing is typically much *more* relevant than reasoning for initiating emotional responses" (134, emphasis added). Smith, Kirby, and others use a broader definition in which non-conscious, associative mental processing—including "any information that can be represented in memory, including sensory information such as visual, auditory, olfactory, and proprioceptive cues, as well as abstract representations"—are included (134).

Others also argue that Berkowitz and Harmon-Jones's account of appraisal theory is problematic because, in appraisals, cognition *precedes* emotion. That is, whereas Berkowitz characterizes appraisal as a cognitive evaluation following an event, the development of values, goals, and group norms entail cognitive processes that must occur *before* any emotion-eliciting event. Thus, appraisal is less linear than it appears. Clore and Centerbar's example is that while we may fear snakes and wild animals, we will not do so at the zoo:

> The cognitive context of the zoo changes their meaning. It would not matter if cognition were slow because most cognitive or interpretive work takes place *before* emotional stimuli appear. Most real-world experiences are contextualized in this way, so that the usefulness of the bear-in-the-woods model may be limited. . . . The point of the cognitive revolution was not that people respond to what happens by thinking a lot, but that *perception and action are automatically informed by preexisting knowledge structures.* Like other stimuli, *emotional stimuli are experienced in contexts that recruit knowledge.* Such contexts give stimuli meaning, and those meanings elicit emotions. (Clore and Centerbar 143, emphasis added)

So whereas Berkowitz and Harmon-Jones portray cognitive appraisal as a conscious thought process following an event, Clore and Centerbar argue that emotion as appraisal relies on an already-existing cognitive architecture into which a stimulus enters. In other words, emotions only make sense in cultural contexts, regardless of the neurological and physiological processes taking place within an individual.

Similarly, Power and Dagleish add that Berkowitz's notion of "aversive" stimuli—physical or mental—already implies a level of appraisal. Since nothing is inherently "bad," they argue, "something is bad because it is appraised with respect to models of the self, world, and other, and more importantly as a function of goal structures" (320–321). Moreover, Clore and Centerbar charge that the CNA model is overly mechanistic in attributing emotion to muscular movements and neurochemical processes; physiological processes go hand-in-hand with appraisals because the meanings of each depend so much on context. They claim, "Our experiments suggest that perceptions of events, including [facial] expressions, are always embedded, situated, and contextualized" (142).[15] They continue,

> Appraisal theory is not an alternative to a neurochemical account of anger. It concerns what situations and interpretations trigger and modulate the neurochemistry of anger. . . . Not only might some-

thing like testosterone be chronically elevated but also reflexive attributions of blame and an insistent *narrative* that necessitates externalizing behavior toward the villains and fools in their lives. Probably both of these fingers must be on the trigger for anger to fire. The same *ideation* in a different person might result in sadness or even humor, and the same hormones without relevant *mental constructions* might simply yield quirkiness, accident proneness, or impulsiveness. (Clore and Centerbar 141, emphasis added)

So the physiological processes of anger and/or muscular movements (facial expressions, body movements), while perhaps fairly consistent, only take on meaning as an emotion in the context of certain narratives, "ideations," and "mental constructions." Thus, cultural productions and cultural studies, which are centrally concerned with narratives and mental constructions, become crucial to understanding emotion.

Appraisal theories of emotion assume that cognition precedes emotion, not necessarily in a specific temporal order for every specific emotion, but in that a perceiving being must first exist in order to have emotions. That is, a configuration of goals, values, narratives, and the like must exist in order for phenomena—external stimuli, neurochemical processes, muscular movements, etc.—to be evaluated by and via a mind.[16] So as recent work suggests, the relationship between emotions and cognition is not only bi-directional but multi-directional. Because we are emotional beings in history and in social groups, emotions help shape and inform beliefs just as cultural norms shape our emotions.[17] Cultural narratives, therefore, are important indicators of what we feel and why—and perhaps if and how things should be changed.

The upshot of all this debate about appraisal theory is that—sometimes explicitly but more often implicitly—context, culture, and collectivities are integral to understanding emotions, particularly anger. For instance, Cox and Harrison conclude not only that "all four divisions of the brain . . . [are] involved in some part of the perception, experience, and expression of anger" (379), but also that language and memory play some role in nearly every account of anger. They write:

Virtually in every explanation of cognitive appraisals there is an element of applying a personal world view or attitude to the interpretation of stimuli that is inherently linked to the language and memory at some level, suggesting that appraisals are necessarily associated with significant memory processes and some verbal or subverbal process. (379)

In other words, if language, memory, and "personal world views" are components of every account of cognitive appraisal, then culture, ideology, and history must play a role in the production of anger.

By the same token, collectivities also play a crucial role in shaping our emotions. Because we are all always members of various groups, our relations to others, real and imaginative, also play a role in cognition and emotion. For example, as discussed above, groups establish norms of acceptable behavior. Furthermore, as we know from reading books and watching films, our emotions are not only triggered by things that actually happen to us; our imagination and empathy make us respond to the situations of others as if we were in those situations. Hogan argues that "in approximating emotional egocentrism, such evolutionary mechanisms [such as empathy triggered and/or increased by proximity] actually avoid emotional egocentrism" (*Mind* 217). In other words, while the appraisal accounts of emotion tend to focus on one's *own* survival, safety, and/or achievement of goals, the phenomenon of empathetic emotions induced by someone else's suffering or joy suggests something about our ability to move beyond a purely egocentric survival mode. Such empathetic capabilities coincide with findings about how altruism not only helps us survive but also makes us feel good physiologically.[18] In other words, as Greg Smith echoes Berkowitz and Harmon-Jones, "an associative model of emotions" must deal with "multiple sources of input" ("Local Emotions" 111).

But while cognitivists return repeatedly to issues of context and culture, what exactly do they make of these things? The next section examines some of the ways that culture has or has not come into discussions of cognition, emotion, and anger, while the next chapter explores how cultural studies can intervene in these debates about appraisal, cognition, and emotion.

CONTEXTS, CULTURES, AND COLLECTIVES

So in the debates about what constitutes anger—particularly over the sufficiency of appraisal theory—context, culture, and collectives are central. Culture shapes not only the expressions, or "output," of emotions but also the input, including the biological and chemical processes that are sometimes thought beyond or before the realm of culture. For instance, the basic distinction between the emotion itself and its expression comes about due to cultural differences in conventions for displaying emotion. For example, while aggression is most commonly associated with anger, it is usually clearly distinguished from the cognitive, affective, and somatic processes that go into the emotion of anger per se. Just as "it is certainly possible to be aggressive without being angry," Dagleish and Power note, "conversely, anger without overt aggression is the norm in many cultures" (4). The distinction between the emotion of anger and its expression is found to be necessary because of the *cultural* differences in how it is expressed. Similarly, the *International Handbook of Anger* summarizes: "There is also general agreement that the expression of anger very much depends on target and social circumstance, governed by display rules that are learned in childhood" (Potegal, Stemmler, and Spielberger, 4). Paul Ekman's work on the facial expressions of basic emotions across cultures has been hugely influential, spawning scores of studies. While his models have developed over the decades, the basic notion that emotions can be read via facial expressions has remained the same. Other researchers, however, have argued that "display rules" of emotion are culturally produced (see Matsumoto, Yoo, and Chung; and Safdar et al.). Similarly, other researchers have argued that women are not "more emotional" than men; rather—not surprisingly to anybody who works in gender studies—the ways in which men's and women's emotions are read are quite different, and just as importantly, differently expressed and interpreted.[19]

But culture does not shape only the expression of emotions; culture and history—individual and collective—can also shape *physiological* processes that are involved in emotion and cognition. Some researchers have argued that even the meanings of muscular movements and chemical responses—things we generally think of as biological, not cultural—are socially conditioned. For example, Shinobu Kitayama and Hazel Markus, two psychologists examining emotion in cultural contexts, argue that

> emotions are not *just* private properties of the heart and mind, not *just* consequences of individual attempts to make meaning and adapt to their specific environments. . . . Expanding the scope of this focus, we can see that the physiological and neurochemical patterns that

accompany private feelings can also be construed as *the bodily elements of habitual tendencies of subjective emotional experience and expression*, and that *these habitual tendencies are themselves part of the vast repertoire of individual and collective social practices that make up a culture*. (340, emphasis added)

That is, even biology and chemistry can be shaped by culture. First, in that certain "bodily elements" are privileged over others, and second, echoing Clore and Centerbar, in that we only give meaning to physiological processes in the context of cultural narratives, mental constructions, and "ideations."

Similarly, Jesse Prinz argues for an "embodied appraisal theory" that takes into account both evolutionary *and* social constructionist insights into emotion by including both physical, visceral responses to stimuli and socially learned appraisals of them: "Every emotion that we have a word for bears the mark of both nature and nurture. Each is built from biologically basic emotion, but its conditions of elicitation, and hence its content, is influenced by learning" (85). Thus, these researchers' findings reflect what Sara Ahmed, Robyn Warhol, and others in cultural studies have argued: that bodily sensations—what is written on the body and *how the body is written as being felt*—tie together embodiment, emotions-as-cognition, and cultural narratives.

Recognizing that cognition, emotion, cultural context and history, and ideology are inextricably related, a few researchers have started examining the production of anger and/or the lack of it in the context of social injustice. For example, psychologists Wakslak, Jost, Tyler, and Chen investigate why, given the increasing rates of inequity, more people do not advocate for social and political change—or, to put it another way, why are more people not angry about injustice? For example, in 2007 they noted, "One eighth of Americans, for example, live below the poverty line, while the combined net worth of the 400 wealthiest Americans exceeds $1 trillion. A CEO now earns in a day and a half what the typical employee takes home in a year" (267). They find that a key indicator of individual political engagement is the bidirectional relationship between affect and ideology; they cite findings that suggest "that the emotional reactions individuals have when confronted with inequality are strong predictors of whether or not they will commit to helping the disadvantaged. Certain forms of distress, most especially moral outrage, are important motivators of action designed to help the underprivileged" (Wakslak et al. 268). In other words (and again, not surprisingly), "moral outrage," or anger at the perceived violation of group norms of justice and equality perpetrated by particular agents (e.g., the wealthy, capitalists, neo-imperialists, etc.), is often found in people who are active in social justice movements. But by the same token, the vast numbers of people who are neither angry nor politically active are so because their ideology—what the investigators refer to here as "system justification"—enables them to either deny a problem exists and/or blame the victims in order to avoid bad feelings. Here again, not only cultural studies but also cultural narratives of all forms can impact our feeling and thinking. As I discuss in later chapters, certain narratives may promote a quietist view of the world (e.g., "There is no reason to feel bad"), while others may help to spur outrage at injustice.

Not surprisingly, this tendency to use ideology to avoid acknowledging mass injustices and its attendant bad feelings can be mapped across race. Rankin, Jost, and Wakslak (2009) find that "system justification was associated with [psychological] benefits only for European Americans and may even be detrimental to the well-being of low-income African Americans" (328). That is, although they found that "low-income African Americans exhibited levels of system justification that were comparable to those exhibited by their low-income European American counterparts, they did not appear to benefit from the same ideological illusions that appeared to comfort European Americans" (330). In other words, as this book argues, racial formations, gender, class, and culture are central to how we experience emotions, particularly anger, cognitively and culturally. Psychologist James Smith writes, "Race does matter, and it is correlated with emotion and behavior in numerous ways, positive and negative, conscious and unconscious" (94). I concur with Smith's argument that "if any meaningful change and growth is to occur across the broad spectrum of human intrapersonal and interpersonal interaction, if social and economic justice is to be a reality, there must be increased acknowledgement of the role our emotional nature plays in all forms of expression and behavior" (94).

Nevertheless, despite the conclusion of many researchers in emotion and cognition that culture and context is integral to understanding anger, the actual parameters of most studies in psychology fall woefully short of cultural diversity or even any meaningful cross-sampling of research subjects. For example, surveying articles published between 2003 and 2007 in the top journals in six subfields of psychology, J. Arnett found that the vast majority of test subjects in psychology journals were twenty-something undergraduate college students in Western industrialized nations, particularly the U.S. That is, 68 percent of subjects were from the U.S. and fully 96 percent were from "Western" industrialized nations (European, North American, Australian, or Israeli). This means that 96 percent of the studied subjects were drawn from 12 percent of the world's population (Heinrich, Heine, and Norenzayan 63). Heinrich et al. argue that despite the often "broad claims about human psychology and behavior," the sample subjects most scientists rely on are actually behavioral "outliers." They dub this population "Western Educated Industrialized Rich Democratic," or W.E.I.R.D. Their pointed acronym highlights the *non*-representativeness of this subject population for making overarching claims about human cognition and behavior. Greg Downey, reporting in *Neuroanthropology.net*, summarizes their findings: "To put it another way, you're 4000 times more likely to be studied by a psychologist if you're a university undergraduate at a Western university than a randomly selected individual strolling around outside the ivory tower." Yet, Downey continues, "despite the skewed sampling, psychologists seldom offer cautionary notes about the source of their data or its potential cultural boundedness." Likewise, studies that argue for the evolutionarily advantageous traits of certain successful people in the West neglect the entire history of imperialism that undergirds the entire edifice of First-World capitalism's wealth (Hogan, *Cognitive* 198–199). *On Anger* is certainly one attempt to address such shameful lacunae.

Another problem with some cognitive approaches to emotion is methodological; some researchers, including some discussed above, tend to assume (implicitly or explicitly) that junctural (short-term) emotions as observed in lab experiments and surveys function the same way as emotions in the real world. Yet, as Patrick Colm Hogan notes, "there is an interpretive component to emotional experience, and that component is at least a matter of relating a raw feeling to eliciting conditions and actional/expressive outcomes" (*Mind* 242). In other words, as literary and cultural critics well know, emotions and cognition are deeply overdetermined by ideology, history, identity, memory, embodiment, and innumerable other factors. In order to attempt to isolate specific emotions, scientists and psychologists tend to focus on immediate and individual emotional responses, as

self-reported or measured according to some pre-existing scale. But as
Lisa Zunshine writes, "Cognitive *literary* analysis . . . continues beyond the line drawn by cognitive scientists—with the reintroduction
of something else, a 'noise,' if you will, that is usually carefully controlled for and excised, whenever possible, from the laboratory settings" (*Why We Read* 39).

To summarize, cognitive approaches to emotion, particularly appraisal theory, tend to leave out the different historical-social loca-
tions of subjects, the varying cultural narratives of subjects that go
into constituting those subjectivities and emotions, the wider cultural contexts in which different subjects experience things *as well
as* the specific cultural contexts that conflict with one another and
create emotions, and the histories that constitute cultural contexts.
To put it another way, in terms familiar to cultural studies scholars,
the relationships between nature vs. nurture, mind vs. brain, individual vs. collective, and even paradigmatic and syntagmatic must
be understood as dialectical, as informing one another through time
and space, in conjunction with the various other ongoing, changing
developments of history. Such findings in the fields of cognitive psychology evince less biological determinism than attempts to discover
how emotions actually work in mind, body, and culture/history. At
the same time, this recognition of the impact of context and culture
on emotions is not the same thing as behaviorism, which attributes
everything to socialization. Rather, a productive cognitive approach
to emotion recognizes the processes of an individual embodied mind,
the role of history and culture, *and* the inextricability of individual
and collective, the particular and the general.

COGNITIVE NARRATIVE THEORY:
MINDS, PROTOTYPES, EMOTIONOLOGIES

Before moving on, it may be helpful to readers new to cognitive studies to briefly outline the ways that some narrative theorists have engaged with this growing body of cognitive studies. As I hope has become apparent, cognitive studies—at least in the realm of cognitive
psychology and emotion—does not see the human being as simply
an input-output calculating machine, at the mercy of deterministic
biological or neurological processes. Rather, while recognizing the
importance of physiology and neurochemistry, many of the debates
about emotion hinge on *what we do* with the combination of physi-

cal, chemical, and cognitive processes in the context of complex relationships with other human beings. The problem, however, is that many studies tend to be very limited in scope, both methodologically as well as culturally. This book therefore seeks to participate in the ongoing process of broadening the studies of emotion and cognition, focusing on anger, because this area is still very much in its initial stages; we still know so little about emotion in all its complexity.

In this ongoing project, many humanists point out that not only are literature and narrative relevant for understanding cognition and emotion, they are *necessary*. Spolsky argues that stories, as prime shapers of cognition, are evolutionarily vital: "Narratives are themselves the processes that human beings have evolved to understand, express and meet the need for revised and revisable behavior in an unstable world. . . . The indirections of narratives . . . allow us to be flexible in the face of the new, and flexibility is by definition the most valuable survival mechanism" (181). Given the importance of stories, Hogan argues that it is deeply problematic that "empirical researchers in the social sciences . . . almost entirely ignore a vast body of existing data that bears directly on feelings and ideas about feelings— literature, especially literary narrative" (*Mind* 1). As Hogan puts it, the goal is not simply about "applying cognitive science to literature" (*Cognitive* 2); rather, "the arts are not marginal for understanding the human mind. They are absolutely central" (*Cognitive* 3).

In the recent turn to narrative, scholars from many disciplines emphasize the importance of narrative. Philosophers of the perceptual theory, such as Amélie Rorty and de Sousa, argue that emotions are crucial for navigating the confusing welter of information and stimuli with which we are constantly bombarded, and are therefore not only complementary but in fact necessary for cognition. De Sousa argues in *The Rationality of Emotion* that "emotions are among the mechanisms that control the crucial factor of salience among what would otherwise be an unmanageable plethora of objects of attention, interpretations, and strategies of inference and conduct" (xv). Emotions are also basically dramatic and narrative in structure; de Sousa writes that "our emotions are learned rather like a language and that they have an essentially dramatic structure" (xvi). Scholars such as Mark Turner and Martha Nussbaum have argued for, respectively, the cognitive and ethical importance of literature. But as David Herman notes in his review of Turner's *The Literary Mind*, even humanists outside literary studies tend to talk about narratives in relatively simplistic terms. The special tools of literary and cultural critics are needed to talk more specifically and technically about narratives themselves.

Since the 1990s, a growing number of literary and cultural critics have, as Alan Richardson and Francis Steen write, "steadily been producing work that finds its inspiration, its methodology, and its guiding paradigms through a dialogue with one or more fields within cognitive science: artificial intelligence, cognitive psychology, post-Chomskian linguistics, philosophy of mind, neuroscience, and evolutionary biology" (1). Just a few examples of this trend can be seen in special issues of the journals *Poetics Today* (1998, 2002, and 2003), *Style* (2002 and 2008), *Philosophy and Literature* (2001), *SubStance* (2001), *College Literature* (2006), and *Image and Narrative* (2010). Just in the year 2010, books published in cognitive approaches to literature and culture include *Theory of Mind and Literature*, edited by Leverage et al. (Purdue UP); *Intermediality and Storytelling*, by Marina Grishakova (De Gruyter); *The Neural Sublime: Cognitive Theories and Romantic Texts*, by Alan Richardson (Johns Hopkins UP); *Literary Reading, Cognition and Emotion: An Exploration of the Oceanic Mind*, by Michael Burke (Routledge); *Imagining Minds: The Neuro-Aesthetics of Austen, Eliot, and Hardy*, by Kay Young (Ohio State UP); *Toward a Cognitive Theory of Narrative Acts*, edited by Frederick Luis Aldama (2010); and *Introduction to Cognitive Cultural Studies*, edited by Lisa Zunshine (2010). In film studies, the work of David Bordwell, Ed S. Tan, Carl Plantinga, Greg Smith, and others has also drawn extensively on work in cognitive studies to forge an alternative path to psychoanalytic film theory.[20] In the rest of this chapter, I examine the work of three cognitive narrative theorists—Lisa Zunshine, Patrick Colm Hogan, and David Herman—that helps concretize how the cognitive approaches have been and can be useful for literary and cultural studies.

Lisa Zunshine draws on the work of evolutionary cognitivists Tooby and Cosmides to discuss "theory of mind" (ToM) in our reading practices. "Theory of mind," or "mind reading," refers to our ability to read others' behavior to surmise their underlying states of mind: "Mind-reading is a term used by cognitive psychologists to describe our ability to explain people's behavior in terms of their thoughts, feelings, beliefs, and desires" ("Theory" 271). Mind reading includes abilities such as "metarepresentation," or figuring out who is talking/narrating, in what situation, at what point in time, and what they are saying; and "source-tagging" (*Why We Read* 47), or attributing ultimately who is speaking (given levels of narration and embeddedness). For example, Zunshine examines how we understand a passage in Woolf's *Mrs. Dalloway*, given the multiple and multilayered levels of "embedded intentionality" (of the characters, of characters speaking of and to other characters, of the narrator and implied author) (*Why* 32–33). Her point is that we do this all the time without even realizing it, and cognitive science can, in part, help us understand what we are doing when we read. At the same time, Zunshine challenges literary scholars to use our skills in order to historicize the sometimes universalist assumptions of scholars studying the mind. She calls attention to what is outside the laboratory because cognition and emotions do not happen in a vacuum. Zunshine writes, "There is no such thing as a cognitive ability, such as ToM, free-floating 'out there' in isolation from its human embodiment and its historically and culturally concrete expression" (*Why* 37).

In this sense, cognitive narrative theory often seeks to balance the universal and the particular, the common and the different. So, for example, Zunshine argues that mind-reading is "greedy"—we seek ways to exercise it—and this desire for mind-reading explains the universal appeal of stories (*Why* 163): "Theory of Mind is a cluster of cognitive adaptations that allows us to navigate our social world and also structures that world. Intensely social species that we are, we thus read fiction because it engages, in a variety of particularly focused ways, our Theory of Mind" (*Why* 162). But although she sees ToM as a universal human capability, she also adds that texts, of course, work differently for different people at different times. Zunshine writes, "In spite of our evolved cognitive ability to attribute states of mind to ourselves and other people and to store information metarepresentationally, there is no predicting what cultural forms, literary or otherwise, these cognitive abilities can take" (*Why* 155). Thus, she concludes, "we are at present a long way off from grasping fully the levels of complexity" of our ToM's engagement in novel reading (164).

ToM has applicability to emotions because although we know that fictional characters are not real, we still become emotionally invested in them as if they were real. This paradox, when our "evolved cognitive architecture indeed does not fully distinguish between real and fictional people" (19), causes some unease. So,

when cultural representations push our mind-reading adaptations to what feels like their limits (with particular historical milieus, that is), we might find ourselves in rather emotionally suggestive moods. Depending on the context and genre of the representation . . . a momentary cognitive vertigo induced by the multiple mind-embedment may render us *increasingly* ready either to laugh or to quake with apprehension. (*Why* 31)

In other words, ToM, in reading and in real life, is inextricably bound up with emotions. In fact, Zunshine argues, "ToM gives meaning to our emotions and is in turn given meaning by them" (*Why* 164). That is, to return to anger, ToM is necessary to figure out an external agent's intentions, our coping potential among particular group(s) of people, and even, to some degree, the viability and legitimacy of individual goals—ours and others'—vis-à-vis group norms.

While Zunshine is primarily interested in ToM, Patrick Colm Hogan's *Cognitive Science, Literature, and the Arts: A Guide for Humanists* is a useful and readable introduction to cognitive approaches in general. Hogan describes the basic model of cognition that informs cognitivists, and then explores the complexities that arise from the conjunction of the cognitive studies with the study of history and culture. First, according to the cognitive model, the mind "encodes" information as it receives it:

We encode any incoming stream of sensations when we provide those sensations with structure. We do not experience the world as it is in itself. We experience a structured version of the world. Certain details, certain properties, certain relations enter our minds while others do not. Technically, some details and the like are encoded, and others are not. (*Cognitive* 11)

Cognitivists seek to discover and describe the "cognitive architecture" of the mind in its full variety. For instance, Hogan outlines three broad components or aspects of cognitive architecture: (1) *structures*, or "the general organizational principles of the mind"; (2) *contents*, or "representations or symbols"; and (3) *processes*, or "operations that run on contents" (*Cognitive* 30). He explains that several different levels and models of cognitive architecture come into play in considerations of the brain and mind, ranging from the neurophysiological, which tends towards the physical and mechanical and is concerned with "neurons and synapses"; to intentionalism, which focuses on subjective experiences and "how we feel, what we would like to accomplish, what we believe, and so on" (*Cognitive* 31). So, for instance, most of the appraisal theories of anger I discussed in previous sections would be more on the intentionalist end of the spectrum of cognitive architectures (see also Chapter 2 in *Cognitive*).

Despite the range of approaches to cognition, however, Hogan does not see the intentionalist and neurophysiological views as incompatible; rather, like other cognitive scholars, he argues that the physical and the mental shape one another: "Neuroanatomy does not fix psychological structure, though the laws of neuroanatomy place limits on psychological structure. Rather, patterns that appear at the level of psychology themselves define certain structural relations in neuroanatomy" (*Cognitive* 207). For example, as Shinobu Kitayama and Hazel Markus argue, the physiological is not self-evident; culture and history can shape which physical stimuli we respond to or even register. In another example, Hogan warns that studies that attribute different beliefs and abilities (e.g., notions of beauty, gendered ways of communicating) often move too quickly. He writes, "We cannot simply assume that a difference of this sort is part of primary structure— thus biologically innate (with all that this entails socially, politically, and so on)—rather than a contingent feature of secondary structure" (*Cognitive* 207). That is, we have to be very cautious and skeptical about attributing specific beliefs, practices, and worldviews onto biology; while biology puts limits on what is possible (e.g., we cannot literally read other people's minds, we cannot fly without help), it in no way determines or predicts what we actually think or feel. As Hogan puts it, cultural practices have "partial autonomy" from biology (*Cognitive* 207).

In his work on emotions, Hogan draws on Oatley and Johnson-Laird's appraisal accounts of emotion to argue that emotions are bound up with prototypical narratives and therefore fundamentally ideological. To understand his argument, it is necessary to understand his distinction between "schema," "prototype," and "exemplum." A "schema" is a "hierarchy of principles defining" a category or genre, in which "the hierarchy is based on 'definitiveness' or 'centrality' of properties" (*Mind* 57). For example, a rise in blood pressure is more central to the definition of anger than aggressive action; I can be angry without being aggressive, but it would be difficult to categorize my emotions as anger without some kind of physiological change. A "prototype" is "a sort of concretization of the schema with all default values in place," both the central and less important elements (*Mind* 58). So, for example, the appraisal theory of anger, in which an external agent violates group norms to block my achieving a goal, would constitute a kind of prototype.[21] An exemplum is "any specific instance of a category"; so, for example, any of the texts I discuss in Chapters 3 through 7 include exempla of different kinds of anger.

Prototypes are the important concept here; as do some psychologists and other cognitivists, Hogan argues that "*emotions are prototype-based in both eliciting conditions and expressive/actional consequences*" (*Mind* 83, original emphasis). That is, our appraisals are based on narratives that are not simply open-ended; we have prototypes of how things should be and unfold in the world, how our lives should be, how other people should act, how we should respond.[22] In other words, "emotions are embedded in stories" (*Mind* 83). Prototypes, then, are both universal as a possibility or potentiality, as well as historically and culturally particular. We could argue, for example, that prototypes are gendered, raced, classed, sexed. Hence, Hogan argues that "the relation of emotion to politics and ideology" lies in the fact that "emotions and standard plot structures are particularized in socially functional ways. Specifically, they tend to be defined and organized to preserve social structure" (*Mind* 250). He cites the romantic plot as an example of patriarchal societies seeking to preserve hierarchical social structures (*Mind* 251). In this way, he argues:

> not only cultural particulars, but cultural universals are imbued with ideology from the start. The division of emotions, the definition of emotion prototypes (including eliciting conditions and expressive/actional outcomes, even to a certain degree the raw feel of the emotion itself), and finally the prototype narratives . . . are the product, not only of cognitive structures (and human biology), but of *socially functional categories and relations*. Thus ideology is not simple. It is continually troubled by contradictory ethical and empathic impulses. But it is nonetheless functional and pervasive. (*Mind* 251–252; emphasis added)

In other words, Hogan explores the functioning of the mind as situated in a social world in order to investigate both the nature of narratives and emotions *as well as* ideology and history.

David Herman, in his pioneering book *Story Logic*, also seeks to bring together cognitive studies and narrative theory via a complex model of how we as readers construct "storyworlds." He defines "storyworlds" as "mental models of who did what to and with whom, when, where, why, and in what fashion in the world to which recipients relocate—or make a deictic shift—as they work to comprehend a narrative" (*Story* 5). He coins the term "storyworld" in order to better capture "the ecology of narrative interpretation," because

> in trying to make sense of a narrative, interpreters attempt to reconstruct not just what happened—who did what to or with whom, for how long, how often and in what order—but also the surrounding context or environment embedded existents, their attributes, and the actions and events in which they are more or less centrally involved . . . this surrounded environment, which is always perspectivally filtered . . . , is not just temporally but spatially structured. (*Story* 13–14)

That is, when we read, we do not read just content or a story; we also create three- and four-dimensional worlds that are fuller, more fleshed out than what the simple words on the page may imply. We do not simply "piece together bits of action into a linear timeline," and we do not just incorporate information "additively or incrementally" (*Story* 14); rather, "narrative understanding requires determining how the actions and events recounted relate to what might have happened in the past, what could be happening (alternatively) in the present, and what may yet happen as a result of what already has come about" (*Story* 14). We constantly negotiate multiple states, temporalities, characters, levels of story, filling in gaps as needed and making connections. That is, rather than "reconstructed timelines and inventories of existents," the storyworlds we create when we read "are mentally and emotionally projected environments in which interpreters are called upon to live out complex blends of cognitive and imaginative response, encompassing sympathy, the drawing of causal inferences, identification, evaluation, suspense, and so on" (*Story* 16–17).[23]

This process of creating worlds is, Herman argues, important for understanding how we think, feel, and live. Against what some critics have dubbed a mechanistic "cult of cognition," Herman argues that mental models must always understand individuals as located in place and time:

I assume that the mental models supporting narrative comprehension require interpreters to construe storyworld entities and individuals *as situated*—i.e., as embroiled in a space-time context that is at once physically, historically, and socially or interactionally constituted. Hence a commitment to studying the cognitive dimensions of story logic does not, in my view, entail blind obedience to a cult of cognition. (*Story* 374, original emphasis)

Moreover, the relationships between textual cues and the story-worlds that we construct are variable, probabilistic, and preference-based (i.e., cultural, historical, collective, cognitive, ethical) (*Story* 12). That is, although texts include indicators that limit reasonable readings (e.g., Humbert Humbert is not a reliable narrator), the actual ways in which we construct meanings out of texts are variable and historical.

Herman follows up *Story Logic* by examining how we think and feel in groups, or thinking of the mind as "distributed":

From this perspective, cognition should be viewed as a supra- or transindividual activity distributed across groups functioning in specific contexts, rather than as a wholly internal process unfolding within the minds of solitary, autonomous, and de-situated cognizers. Hence, instead of being abstract, individualistic, and ratiocinative, thinking in its most basic form is grounded in particular institutions, socially distributed, and domain-specific, that is, targeted as specific purposes or goals. ("Storytelling" 319)

If we think of cognition as not a purely individual phenomenon—as is implicit in the cognitive psychology above and explicit in my argument—we can also think of emotions as not purely individual. Herman draws on a concept from discursive psychology, "emotionology," or "the collective emotional standards of a culture as opposed to the experience of emotion itself," as key to understanding any particular instance of emotion ("Storytelling" 322). Herman continues, "Every culture and subculture has an emotionology, a system of emotion terms and concepts, that people deploy rhetorically in discourse to construct their own as well as other minds. . . . Stories provide insight into a culture's or subculture's emotionology—and also into how minds are made sense of via this system" ("Storytelling" 322). But it is not just a question of decoding stories to determine the emotions of a culture; the relationships between narratives, cultures, and emotions are bidirectional and multivalent: "Hence stories do not just emanate from emotionologies but also constitute a primary instrument for adjusting systems of emotion terms and concepts to lived experience—whose broader profile is configured, in turn, through collaborative discourse practices" ("Storytelling" 324–325). We may add also that if culture can be a field of ideological struggle, then the emotionologies (collective) and specific emotions (individual) also constitute part of those ideological struggles. Many of the ensuing chapters of this book focus on how particular episodes of anger are more complex than they may initially appear, involving histories, ideologies, structures, various collectivities, contentions, contradictions, etc.

The work of cognitive narrative theorists, which I have only touched upon here, represents forays into negotiating cognitive studies and literary and cultural studies to try to gain a fuller, richer understanding of how our minds, bodies, and emotions work in history. This book participates in this attempt by similarly drawing together conversations and approaches. To do so, the next chapter surveys some of the ways in which literary and cultural critics have theorized anger, particularly in terms of ideology and textuality.

CONCLUSION

While earlier conceptions of cognition were limited to the input-output model, more recently scholars have conceptualized cognition as situated, embodied, collective, narrative, and intimately tied to emotion. Although there are several models of emotion and anger, "appraisal theory" is dominant in cognitive psychology. Appraisal theory posits that emotions are based on a cognitive analysis of events in relation to a goal; hindrances tend to cause negative emotions, and assistance produces positive emotions. Three considerations in discussion of appraisal include group norms, or a collective agreement of what constitutes legitimate behavior; agency attribution, or blame of an external dispositional agent; and coping potential, or the sense that one has at least some ability to affect the situation. Against critiques that appraisal theory is too linear and causal, proponents of appraisal theory respond that rather than thinking of appraisal as a single linear thought process, a host of complex cognitions must precede emotion. In other words, emotions and cognitions relate not just bidirectionally but in multiple ways, because human beings exist, produce, and are produced by complex histories and collectives. Emotions, therefore, are complexly related to cognition; in fact, emotions can themselves be seen as a form of cognition.

But despite the developments and insights of the "second cognitive revolution," which places more emphasis on contexts and discourses, cognitive studies of emotion still remain methodologically limited. A vast majority of psychological studies have focused on a very small, non-representative sample of humanity (rich, educated, white Westerners), and have yet to engage substantively with both other cultures as well as other disciplines, such as cultural studies (which I discuss in the next chapter). Cognitive narrative theorists have been attempting to meld the insights of cognitive and literary studies, but a great deal of work still remains to be done.

CHAPTER 2

ANGER AS CULTURE

We are talking about characteristic elements of impulse, restraint, and tone; specifically affective elements of consciousness and relationships: not feeling against thought, but thought as felt and feeling as thought: practical consciousness of a present kind, in a living and interrelating continuity.

RAYMOND WILLIAMS, *MARXISM AND LITERATURE*

THE PREVIOUS CHAPTER SUMMARIZED key debates in cognitive psychology about anger; this chapter surveys some approaches to emotion and anger in cultural studies, broadly defined. That is, by "cultural studies" here I refer not only to cultural studies in the Frankfurt or Birmingham School tradition or the more contemporary poststructuralist, post-Marxist approaches to culture; rather, as will become clear, I am referring to these strands of cultural studies as well as various other approaches to studying culture. In other words, "cultural studies" in this chapter should be understood as an umbrella term, just as "cognitive studies" is a general term for a wide variety of disciplines and approaches. In particular, I focus on approaches that I argue can be productively brought into conversation with cognitive approaches and/or that intervene in some of the problems and/or lacunae in cognitive approaches. In fact, as I hope became apparent in the previous chapter, inquiry into emotion as cognition is just beginning; research into the unconscious, collective emotions, emotions over long periods of time, and culturally different conceptions of emotions have all been noted as needing further study.[1] As I hope was also apparent by the end of the previous chapter, the division between cognition and culture is illusory and, in fact, untenable. Therefore, the kinds of insights into ideology, culture, emotion,

and experience enabled and produced by cultural studies are crucial
for a better understanding of how emotion and cognition work in the
real world. I realize that in separating the chapters this way, I run
the risk of reinforcing the very division that I am trying to question,
but I use this organizational scheme for these first two chapters because, even as heterogeneous fields within themselves, cognitive and
cultural studies approach things very differently. In order to explore
where they can coincide, we must first examine where they are.

The first part of this chapter surveys major trends in the ways that
emotions have been examined and theorized in cultural studies. Contemporary cultural studies work on emotions generally takes three
forms, all of which, I argue, are important complements and corrections to the clinical parameters of most cognitive studies of emotion. The first two historicize and contextualize emotions, although
in different ways. The first, particularly in the wake of second-wave
feminism and cultural nationalist movements of the 1960s and '70s,
depicts anger as the result of an ideological explanation (anger as resulting from a political analysis) and has much in common with
the concept of cognitive appraisal. The second, more characteristic
of studies in the twenty-first century, explores the historical genealogy of an emotion, how it is ideologically shaped, deployed, and pro-
scribed. The third approach, also characteristic of later studies, explores the fractures, gaps, excesses, and other emotions beyond the
bounds of conventionally recognized and/or sanctioned emotions.
The second approach obviously draws on Foucault (implicitly or explicitly), while the third tends to draw from Derridean deconstruction and Lacanian psychoanalysis. Surprisingly, however, several
scholars in this category also draw on the work of Silvan Tomkins,
who throughout the twentieth century challenged the cognitivist
concept of emotions as appraisal, arguing that affects constituted a
physiological system distinct from cognition. These three general approaches overlap to some extent, but they constitute distinct projects.
All three approaches, however, take as their objects of study a wide
variety of literary and cultural productions, which, as Hogan writes,
are "a ubiquitous and significant aspect of human mental activity"
(*Mind* 4). And while I do not necessarily agree with all of the assumptions and conclusions of these studies, I would argue that such
work nevertheless contributes to our understanding of emotions and
should inform our approach to anger.

The second part of the chapter explores in greater detail two approaches that I see as most potentially productive—yet relatively unexplored—for the study of anger in culture: Marxism and narratology. While these may seem like odd bedfellows, I argue that, in conjunction with a third odd bedfellow, cognitive studies, the work on emotions in Marxism and narrative theory can provide useful frameworks and tools for more fully explicating how anger works in texts and in the world, on both macro and micro levels, historically and individually.

ANGER AS POLITICAL

FEMINIST ANGER

In many popular and scholarly discussions of anger and politics, anger is often equated with violence, aggression, or at least shouting. In such discussions, anger is not really theorized; rather, it is an index of political conflict and violence. For example, in its examination of the ways that globalization creates, mobilizes, and exacerbates ethnic differences, Arjun Appadurai's *Fear of Small Numbers: An Essay on the Geography of Anger* equates anger with violence, both by the state and by non-state formations of various ideological valences.[2] Implicit in many such discussions is the opposition of anger to reason; for example, comedian Jon Stewart's 2010 "Rally to Restore Sanity" was meant to counteract the anger of the increasingly vitriolic right-wing movements, exemplified by the Tea Party and Glenn Beck's "Rally to Restore America" earlier in the same year. Against the irrationality, aggression, and resistance to knowledge of this right-wing anger, Stewart's rally posed reason, even-temperedness, and ironic distance. But the liberal separation of reason from emotion is as problematic as the conservative privileging of emotion and "the gut" without regard to reason and reference, or what comedian Stephen Colbert facetiously, but quite accurately, calls "truthiness."

Feminist theorists have long argued for the validity of anger not only politically but also epistemologically. As Kathleen Woodward observed in 1996, "Anger is the contemporary feminist emotion of choice" ("Anger" 74). Feminist critics such as Naomi Scheman, Elizabeth Spelman, and Alison Jaggar argue that not only is anger cognitive, evaluative, and political—political anger is angry *about* something—but so is the ability to identify and articulate that emotion as anger. As Brenda Silver argues, feminine and feminist anger is often pathologized and thereby dismissed; she writes, "Reigning discourses in [the twentieth] century, whether political, critical, or psychological, have constructed truths that condemned anger, at least women's anger, and with it feminist critique as destructive of truth" (341).[3] Spelman writes, "There is a politics of emotion: the systematic denial of anger can be seen in a mechanism of subordination, and the existence and expression of anger as an act of insubordination" (270; quoted in Woodward, 89). Woodward concurs, "In terms of a cultural politics of the emotions, angry women have long been labeled irrational or hysterical. The strategy was—and still is—to demean those women" ("Against Wisdom" 206).[4] Thus anger is gendered; while male anger "generates assurance and definition," feminine anger "conjures anxiety and abstraction" (Helal 81).[5]

Another central claim of feminist theorists is that anger is collective rather than wholly individual. From Aristotle's implicit notion of emotion as something that wells up from within, can become "bottled up," and must therefore be "purged," to Freud's notion of emotions as produced by internal drives that must be repressed and controlled, the traditional notion of emotions in the West has been that of an individual, internal substance. In contrast, feminist theorists argue that emotion is something that is produced socially, politically, discursively, and collectively. Woodward notes that the most immediate context for feminist theorists in the '80s is the consciousness-raising group: "Thus from a feminist perspective, it is not the Freudian case that the emotions are located inside us, repressed, as if they were highly idiosyncratic personal property only waiting to be discovered. Rather, they are created *in the group*" ("Anger" 89, emphasis added). In other words, "Anger is generated, sustained, and strengthened through discourse" (89).

And not only is anger produced in the collective; emotions—particularly strong political, ethical, and evaluative emotions like anger—can *create collectivities*. Woodward writes:

> If Freudian guilt is isolating and individualizing, feminist anger is conceived in precisely the opposite terms. It is presented as an emotion that will not only be the basis for a group but will also politicize the group, as an emotion furthermore that is created in a group, as an emotion that is enabling of action, not inhibiting of it. The weight of his work is on containing and regulating violent anger, and de-authorizing male anger. Conversely, the work of feminists appro-

priates male anger, using it to establish the authority with which to challenge patriarchal culture. ("Anger" 85–86)

While Woodward is focused on feminist anger, implicit here in Woodward's depiction is a politically ambivalent model of anger that is both individual and collective, formed in/by as well as helping to form, in constant mutual interchange, the individual and the collective. "Male anger" is related to the maintenance and violent regulation of patriarchy, suggesting that the anger of patriarchal men is formed in and by the patriarchal system that demands regulation. To put it in cognitive terms, patriarchal systems dictate a group norm in which men have authority—angry women not only threaten the male's privilege within that system but also violate those group norms (agency attribution); and coping potential, or the ability to control the situation, depends on suppression of feminist anger via male violence. Or, to put it dialectically, anger is produced in and by, and produces, the ongoing interchange between individual men and the collectives that they produce and that produce them.

Thus, a feminist notion of anger as cognitive and ideological contends that "the paradigm of oppressor-oppressed is key" and "oppression can be identified by anger . . . and should be responded to by anger" (Woodward, "Anger" 91–92). Woodward, however, raises "two major objections to the advocacy of [feminist] anger" ("Anger" 90), which we could describe roughly as synchronic and diachronic in nature. First, Woodward points out that "anger as a 'political' emotion does not exist in a pure form. Emotions come in clusters" ("Anger" 91). In other words, feminist anger is, of course, not inherently progressive or correct; our emotions and politics can be affected by "unconscious components," contending ideologies and demands, greed, ignorance, error, etc. Moreover, I would add to Woodward's formulation that not only do emotions not come singly (i.e., they come with other emotions), but emotions also come in and with clusters of many things that are not—or not only—emotions. These "extras" include both "affects" that are ill-defined—which I will discuss further below—as well as institutions, structures, economies, systems, and collectivities that inform and are informed by emotions. In other words, if we think synchronically, any one feeling or event at any one point in time is informed by and in dialogue with a multitude of different factors. Woodward's second objection to a valorization of feminist anger is diachronic; the valence of a particular kind of feminist anger may change over time, particularly as structures and systems change. For example, she cites feminists "who entered the academy under the banner of politics of anger find themselves today in positions of authority, responsible to many others" ("Anger" 92). In this context, Woodward argues, "'righteous,' habit-forming anger, once understood as a 'right,' can take on the shape of abusive arrogance" ("Anger" 92). That is, emotions are *historical*: "Thus we need a historical perspective on the uses of anger" (92).[6]

I would add to Woodward's objections the problems of reference and evaluation. Because, in the paradigm of the oppressor-oppressed, just because a person self-identifies as oppressed and becomes angry, does not necessarily mean that this view of affairs is *accurate*. One need only look at the example of the Tea Party and right-wing anti-government militias to realize that *believing* oneself to be oppressed by the godless tyrants of science, the government, and the liberal media—and being angry about it—does not necessarily mean that it is so. The component of evaluation based on reference—even as what we reference is critically scrutinized—is crucial for differentiating the valences of anger.

Here, Alison Jaggar, Nancy Hartsock, and other feminist standpoint theorists' contention that emotions have "epistemic potential" is useful (Jaggar 163). Like philosophers Martha Nussbaum and Ronald de Sousa, Jaggar argues that emotions are "helpful and even necessary rather than inimical to the construction of knowledge" (146). Although anger is an "outlaw emotion" that is "conventionally unacceptable" (160), Jaggar argues that anger is not only deeply political, but she goes on to link knowledge and external reference to evaluation and error, to emotion as a kind of appraisal.[7] Jaggar and others' account of anger as a cognitive appraisal based on an interpretation of and active engagement with the world is helpful in accounting for the possibility for *error*. That is, if emotions are in part based on some kind of evaluation or proposition, there exists the possibility that those evaluations and propositions may be wrong, or that evaluations may be in conflict with one another, even within one person. Different propositions or evaluations may be partial, self-contradictory, and undergoing transformation. On the other hand, Jaggar's account of emotion as epistemic does not account for bad faith, or when anger and other emotions are used strategically to manipulate a complex affective and political landscape. Nevertheless, the notion of

emotions, particularly a "negative" emotion such as anger, as reveal-
ing important knowledge about the world is a crucial contribution of
feminist theorists.

RACIAL (AND FEMINIST) ANGER

Just as second-wave feminism and feminist theory privileged anger
as an epistemologically valid and politically insightful appraisal, U.S.
ethnic studies reclaimed anger in the wake of cultural nationalist
movements in the 1960s and '70s. For instance, the title of *Aiiieeeee!
An Anthology of Asian American Writers* (1974), the first anthology
of Asian Americanist literature, refers to "Asian America, so long ig-
nored and forcibly excluded from creative participation in American
culture, is wounded, sad, angry, swearing, and wondering, and this is
his AIIIEEEEEE!!! It is more than a whine, shout, or scream. It is fifty
years of our whole voice" (Chin et al. xii).[8] Audre Lorde wrote in 1984
that "my response to racism is anger" (124). The reclamation of political anger occurred, somewhat ironically, alongside the challenges to
the pathologizing of brown bodies as irrationally, pathologically angry. Work on anger in ethnic and postcolonial studies has largely involved reclaiming and exploring the ideological validity of emotion,
as well as interrogating characterizations of minorities in the West
and Third World peoples as pathological, volatile, and irrational in
their anger. The project largely involves examining how "emotions
shape the 'surfaces' of individual and collective bodies," as well as
how "'being emotional' comes to be seen as a characteristic of some
bodies and not others" (Ahmed, *Cultural* 1, 4).

Just as with women's anger, the fear and dismissal of black rage,
particularly black *male* rage, is ubiquitous and longstanding.[9] Any
critical discussion of gangs, inner-city poverty, "at-risk youth," incarceration, the Black Muslims, the Black Panthers and black power, rap
music, etc., must take anger into account in two ways: first, as expression of protest against continuing structural racism and injustice; and second, as an externally imposed blanket characterization
of poor people of color that evacuates the anger of validity and insight. This black rage exists despite class and privilege—sometimes
because of it. For example, critical race theorist Patricia Williams fa-
mously wrote about being barred from a New York City clothing bou-
tique, in the middle of a Saturday afternoon, by a white employee.
Journalist Ellis Cose's 1993 book, *The Rage of a Privileged Class*, sub-
titled *Why Are Middle-Class Blacks Angry? Why Should America*

Care!, examines how even wealthy, elite African Americans were affected by and angry about structural racisms, manifested in the disproportionate number of African Americans impoverished and/or incarcerated as well as in the "glass ceiling" and paternalistic tokenism of the corporate world. This anger, Cose argues, is an index of those continuing structural racisms.[10] But the anger of poor African Americans, particularly young men, continues to be among the most pathologized and feared in American culture.

In dialogue with white feminists, black cultural nationalists, and allies in general, in 1981 Audre Lorde was one of the first feminists of color to explicitly discuss the "uses of anger" in an essay of that same name in *Women's Studies Quarterly*. She recounts speaking in anger at a conference, when a white feminist tells her, "Tell me how you feel but don't say it too harshly or I cannot hear you" (*Sister* 125). This book, then, is in part an attempt to heed Lorde's conclusion that "any discussion among women about racism must include the recognition and the use of anger" (*Sister* 128). Against the fear of or guilt in response to the anger of the racial other, Lorde argues for the importance of the intellectual and political analyses that produce anger. Lorde writes, "Anger expressed and translated into action in the service of our vision and our future is a liberating and strengthening act of clarification" and a "painful process of . . . translation"; she continues, "Anger is loaded with information and energy" (127). In casting anger as having "vision" and "information" and being oriented toward the future, Lorde suggests that anger is an assessment of a problematic situation, and the rejection of this situation implies an imagined alternative. The expression of anger itself helps to change the situation, and the psychological and physiological intensity of anger can help propel this change. In other words, Lorde's description of anger resonates with that of appraisal theory, in which the "group norm" of justice is violated, and suggests that "coping potential," or the belief that one can affect the situation, is historical and ideological; her claim to and even advocacy of anger can be read as an argument that women of color *do* have agency and can intervene in the situation.

But Lorde also discusses the fallibilities of anger: "In the 1960s, the awakened anger of the Black community was often expressed, not vertically against the corruption of power and true sources of control over our lives, but horizontally *toward those closest to us who mirrored our own impotence*. We were poised for attack, not always in the most effective places" (*Sister* 135–136, emphasis added). Here

Lorde indicates that emotions can be evaluated as more or less appropriate and/or accurate in terms of situational assessments, targets, and outcomes. That is, rather than understanding that capitalism, patriarchy, racism, homophobia, and other interactive exploitative systems trap and limit all of us, we might run the risk of incorrect "agency attribution," or blaming the wrong agent, *particularly* one whose lack of power within these systems mirrors our own powerlessness. The one whom we choose to blame may be constructed in any number of ways, such as emasculated men of color perpetrating domestic violence on women of color in order to reclaim some sense of power.

Lorde's point here is critical because it indicates a fundamental contradiction in how we think and feel about anger. The error she describes is not only that we blame the wrong external agents, *but also* that, even before we find a target, we think in terms of a *person* to blame, rather than a *system*. Seeking an external agent to blame suggests that anger is individual, but as Lorde points out, political anger is *systemic*—and the lack of ability to think *and feel* systemically masks and exacerbates the conditions that make people angry. That is, systems such as capitalism and patriarchy are constituted by people,[11] but we are not likely to interact with many of the other people embroiled in our systems, and we certainly cannot meet *all* of them. Not only will we *not* interact personally with corporate executives, politicians, and other bureaucrats whose decisions shape our lives, but also many of us will never meet or even know who else is involved in global flows of trade of, for example, clothing, food, and most other consumer goods. Venting anger at *one* sexist person does not necessarily change the values and structures of patriarchy. The texts I examine in Chapters 4 to 7 all explore the contradiction between agency attribution, which looks for an individual to blame, and the exploitative, oppressive, bureaucratic, and other systems that produce anger.

In *Killing Rage: Ending Racism* (1996), bell hooks also elaborates on the necessity and pitfalls of anger. She writes that while colonizers do not want to see anger—in the same way that Lorde speaks of white feminists who cringe at women of color's anger—it nonetheless poses a kind of threatening presence that makes it unavoidable. She writes:

> In the graduate seminar I teach on Toni Morrison we pondered
> whether black folks and white folks can ever be subjects together if

white people remain unable to hear black rage, if it is the sound of
that rage which must always remain repressed, contained, trapped in
the realm of the unspeakable. In Morrison's first novel, *The Bluest
Eye*, her narrator says of the dehumanized colonized little black girl
Pecola that there would be hope for her if only she could express her
rage, telling readers "anger is better, there is a presence in anger." Perhaps then it is that "presence," the assertion of subjectivity that colonizers do not want to see, that surfaces when the colonized express
rage. (hooks 12)

Particularly in the context of the poststructuralist assault on the
metaphysics of presence, hooks suggests that a visceral emotion like
anger can force a sense of presence of the Other, despite the colonizer's desire to suppress/repress that presence. At the same time,
hooks warns that because "rage can be consuming . . . it must be
tempered by engagement with a full range of emotional responses to
black struggle for self-determination" (19). She continues:

> Renewed, organized black liberation struggle cannot happen if we
> remain unable to tap collective black rage. Progressive black activists
> must show how we take that rage and move it beyond fruitless scape-
> goating of any group, *linking it instead to a passion for freedom and
> justice that illuminates, heals, and makes redemptive struggle possi-
> ble.* (20, emphasis added)

In other words, while hooks identifies anger as productive and liberating, she also implies that it must be tempered by other emotions—empathy, grief, anxiety, relief—as well as *linked* to struggles
for justice, which rely on many other things, including getting more
information, forming solidarities, and finding ways to heal and redeem. In other words, hooks here highlights both the potential political dangers of anger ("fruitless scapegoating of any group") as well as
its political possibilities ("linking").

Drawing on the work of Audre Lorde and bell hooks, Sara Ahmed
observes that despite the tradition of feminist theorizing of anger,
the anger of women of color is still read as the "truth" behind political critique, enabling dismissal of not only the critique but also the
critic. Ahmed writes:

> The figure of the angry black woman is also a fantasy figure that
> produces its own effects. Reasonable thoughtful arguments are dis-

missed as anger (which of course empties anger of its own reason), which makes you angry, such that your response becomes read as the confirmation of evidence that you are not only angry but also unreasonable! To make this point in another way, the anger of feminists of color is attributed. So you might be angry *about* how racism and sexism diminish life choices for women of color. Your anger is a judgment that something is wrong. But in being heard as angry, your speech is read as motivated by anger. Your anger is read as unattributed, as if you are against x because you are angry rather than being angry because you are against x. You become angry at the injustice of being heard as motivated by anger, which makes it harder to separate yourself from the object of your anger. (*Promise* 67–68)

Political critiques from certain bodies (e.g., women of color) are read as being "really" about anger, and therefore such critiques can be dismissed as unreasonable and/or be feared. Moreover, as Ahmed explains, the awareness that such dismissal is occurring *and* that such dismissal happens to similar bodies (gendered, raced, sexed, etc.), exacerbates the anger of the critic. This exacerbated anger further frustrates the feeling person because she has become indistinguishable from the emotion. As Ahmed puts it, "You become entangled with what you are angry about because you are angry about how they have entangled you in your anger," and "in becoming angry about that entanglement, you confirm their commitment to your anger as the truth 'behind' your speech" (*Promise* 68). In other words, the social location of the feeler, the structures of power (here race and gender but also a particular culture of "politeness"), and the valuation of the emotion are bound together, rendering both the feeling and the feeler illegitimate within that system.

In such discussions of political anger, cognitive theories of anger can be productive. Ideas like appraisal, group norms, coping potential, illegitimacy, and intentionality reinforce the notion that anger is a cognitive act with social, contextual reasons. On one hand, cognitive psychology can help us understand the processes by which humans react to the world around them (and themselves); on the other hand, cultural studies brings to cognitive studies a heightened awareness of the historical processes that do not produce all subjects and their emotions in the same way. Moreover, in examining the historical systems that differently subjugate and repress subjects, ethnic, postcolonial, and feminist approaches to anger show the contradiction between the conception of anger as a purely individual phenomenon, and the lived reality of anger as a collective, systemic, and ideological product.

ANGER AS HISTORICAL: GENEALOGIES OF EMOTION

In addition to the accounts of anger as resulting from a political appraisal, another approach to studying emotion constructs genealogies, in the Foucauldian sense of tracing the origins, history, and effects of a concept, and how that concept is shaped by while also shaping hegemonic social formations. Such studies draw on the insights of feminist, ethnic, and postcolonial studies; more than "intersectional," contemporary cultural studies not only crosses but also often challenges the very boundaries between former disciplines and fields. Cultural critiques also tend to reject the universal or abstract in favor of the historical and contingent, and studies of emotion are no different. So while political and genealogical accounts often work together, the former tends to see the emotion as a political good (e.g., reclaiming feminist anger), and the latter seeks to critique, deconstruct, and denaturalize what is too often seen as positive or simple. Moreover, sometimes the genealogical approaches have been in critical conversation with the political analyses. Such historical, ideological investigations of discursive constructs are important, as Kathleen Helal puts it, "because the discourse of anger constructs and organizes social reality . . . understanding the way it works can alter that reality" (80).

Lauren Berlant's work on "sentimental politics" and compassion exemplifies work that scrutinizes a purportedly positive emotion. Berlant examines how certain emotions help to delineate and police national identity by determining which subjects are "worthy" of empathy and compassion. She defines "national sentimentality" as "a rhetoric of promise that a nation can be built across fields of social difference through channels of affective identification and empathy. Sentimental politics generally promotes and maintains the hegemony of the national identity form, no mean feat in the face of continued widespread intercultural antagonism and economic cleavage" ("Subject" 128). That is, despite the exacerbation of economic divides, a sentimental nationhood maintains unity and suppresses those divisions, even as those same emotions mark others as outside the unity. But Berlant saves her strongest indictment for compassion, or a display of sympathy that has no structural or political consequences. She argues that compassion constitutes a "technology of belonging" in which the proper objects of compassion are articulated/demarcated (*Compassion* 5). For example, "By insisting that society's poorest members can achieve the good life through work, family, community participation, and faith, compassionate conservatives rephrase the embodied indignities of structural inequality as opportunities for individuals to reach out to each other, to build concrete human relations" (*Compassion* 3–4). Combined with the popular conception of emotion as individual, particularly in a liberal individualist society, the notion that "good intentions" are not only ineffectual but actually may be harmful is anathema: "We do not like to be held responsible for consequences we did not mean to enact. We can feel bad about it; we can feel compassionately toward those who suffer: why isn't it enough to have meant well, or not to have meant badly?" (*Compassion* 5–6). Both compassion and sentimental politics, she argues, "[are] too often a defensive response by people who identify with privilege yet fear they will be exposed as immoral by their tacit sanction of a particular structural violence that benefits them" ("Subject" 153).

What I want to highlight here is that Berlant implicitly distinguishes between the abstract emotion in itself and its operation in history, i.e., its genealogy. She writes that while compassion may be "a simple emotion ideally, intending a clear program of amelioration for justice to follow, in context its power involves myriad anxieties about who among the sufferers deserves to be positively or negatively judged, and why, and whether there is any adequate solution to the problem at hand" (*Compassion* 6). In other words, to unearth how compassion works historically and ideologically, Berlant and other cultural critics are interested in "creat[ing] new genealogies and archives of compassion, seeking to understand the concept as *an emotion in operation*" (*Compassion* 4, emphasis added). Studies such as Elspeth Probyn's *Blush: Faces of Shame* (2005); Suzanne Keen's *Empathy and the Novel* (2007); Kathleen Woodward's *Statistical Panic, Cultural Politics and Poetics of Emotions* (2009); and Sara Ahmed's *The Promise of Happiness* (2010) similarly investigate the historical developments and ideological deployments of an emotion, examining how ideology shapes our emotions and our attitudes about emotions, and how those emotions function within and against ideology. Such historical genealogies of emotions are important because they unpack what is taken for granted. For instance, Elspeth Probyn argues that while other "negative emotions, such as anger or rage or guilt or sadness, are regularly discussed in both popular and academic accounts" (2), we are ashamed even to talk about shame. Her investigation, "an attempt to follow the different lines that lie coiled within shame" (4), reveals great complexity in what seems to be unitary and self-evident. In many ways, such studies are a response to Woodward's concerns that emotions, such as anger, are less clear, unchanging, and unitary than some feminist and ethnic studies theorists may have acknowledged. *On Anger* seeks to draw on such studies by exploring how, although anger is apparently understood and "regularly discussed," we still have much to learn about how it works in terms of narrative, ideology, and cognition. In other words, as Probyn puts it, many different things "lie coiled" within the thing that we call anger.

ANGER AS AFFECT: INTERROGATING BOUNDARIES

In the third vein of cultural studies of emotion, the distinction between "affect" and "emotion" becomes important. Brian Massumi, Elspeth Probyn, Eve Sedgwick, and other cultural critics follow Silvan Tomkins in seeing affects as a distinct set of bodily processes separate from cognition. In this model, *emotion* is generally understood to be a socially, narratively, and therefore ideologically constructed product, whereas *affect* is pre-digested, pre-expressed emotional energy at work in a body, even preceding and/or outside of the self-narration and self-delineation necessary for subjectivity. According to Brian Massumi,

> an emotion is a subjective content, the sociolinguistic fixing of the quality of an experience which is from that point onward defined as personal. Emotion is qualified intensity, the *conventional, consensual* point of insertion of intensity into *semantically and semiotically formed progressions*, into *narrativizable* action-reaction circuits, into *function and meaning*. It is intensity *owned and recognized*. (Massumi 28, emphasis added)

Massumi associates "intensities" with all the bodily stimuli and drives that are constantly at work, which are unfiltered in babies and entirely filtered in adults. So emotions are "subjective" (i.e., implying that an articulated, defined subject exists), "semantically and semiotically formed" intensities that are shaped into "progressions" and narratives of behavior produced by "convention" and "consensus." In contrast, affect is "unformed and unstructured," abstract, preconscious, physiological (Massumi 60). Elspbeth Probyn summarizes: "A basic distinction is that emotion refers to cultural and social expression, whereas affects are of a biological and physiological nature" (11). Several recent studies of affect have joined this notion of affect as eluding conventional definitions, categories, and narratives, reflecting poststructuralism's general emphasis on incommensurability, fractures, slippages, intersubjectivity, etc.[12] For instance, Teresa Brennan's *The Transmission of Affect* argues that affect is produced socially and can move from person to person; she writes, "By the transmission of affect, I mean simply that the emotions or affects of one persona . . . can enter into another" (3). And while the transmission of affect is "social in origin," it is "biological and physical in effect." For Brennan, emotions and affects are distinct; the former is narrative and cognitive—feelings have "found the right match in words"— while the latter is physiological: "When I feel angry, I feel the passage of anger through me. What I feel with and what I feel are distinct" (5). The notion of transmission seeks to undermine "the dichotomy between the individual and environment and the related opposition between the biological and the social" (7). In undermining the dichotomy, however, Brennan does *not* mean to collapse the two; she writes, "That does not mean, I stress again, that there is no distinction between the individual and the environment. That is evidently absurd" (7). Rather, in good dialectical fashion, Brennan works with the oppositions while also examining how the two must actually be understood together. Brennan notes that while we "accept with comparatively ready acquiescence that our thoughts are not entirely independent, we are, nonetheless, peculiarly resistant to the idea that our emotions are not altogether our own" (2); such "containment is constructed, rather than given" (12). Although she does not develop this line of thought, she implies that bourgeois liberalism, in its privileging of reason and individualism, recognizes that thought is socially and ideologically constructed, yet retains a public/private divide by relegating emotions to the realm of the individual.

By the same token, Sianne Ngai's *Ugly Feelings* focuses not on "grander passions," such as anger, but examines negative affects such as "envy, anxiety, paranoia, irritation . . . 'animatedness' [a racialized affect], and a strange amalgam of shock and boredom that [she] call[s] 'stuplimity'" (2–3). Ngai reads these "affective gaps and illeg-ibilities, dysphoric feelings, and other sites of emotional negativity in literature, film, and theoretical writing" (1) as emotional expres-sions of bourgeois art's sense of its political ineffectuality, or its "sus-pended agency," particularly when late capitalism appropriates bour-geois art's "disaffection" into its own logic. Again, what I find useful about her approach is her examination of these "ugly feelings" as, citing Rei Terada, "unusually knotted or condensed 'interpretations of predicaments'—that is, signs that not only render visible different registers of problems (formal, ideological, sociohistorical) but conjoin these problems in a distinctive manner" (quoted in Ngai 3). That is, emotions are not only *not* individual, but also unique convergences—"unique" at a variety of levels—of many factors.

Like Ngai, José Muñoz explicitly reads certain uncategorized/-able affects as being socially inflected and "deeply relational" ("Feeling Brown: Ethnicity" 71), particularly in terms of race. If we think of race and ethnicity as performative (in the Austinian and Butlerian senses as *constituting* by doing) rather than fixed, then part of how we can understand race and ethnicity is through the performance of certain kinds of feelings. Muñoz describes this "affective difference," or "brown feeling," as "the ways in which various historically co-herent groups 'feel' differently and navigate the material world on a different emotional register" ("Feeling Brown: Ethnicity" 70). Muñoz seeks to "theorize affective particularity and belonging" ("Feeling Brown, Feeling Down" 676–677) as demonstrated in, for example, the depressive affects found in the work of some Latina performance art-ists. He reads this particular form of depression as "racial performa-tivity generated by an affective particularity that is coded to specific historical subjects who can provisionally be recognized by the term *Latina*" ("Feeling Brown, Feeling Down" 679). While I would contend that Muñoz's concept of "normative affect" is too homogenous, I take his point that certain emotions and affects are deemed "normal" (i.e., white, male, straight, First-World—the unmarked dominant term) and that certain historical groups feel and are seen as feeling in par-ticular ways. Here, we can see a link to political readings of emo-tion, although Muñoz couches his analyses in more antifoundation-alist terms.

Likewise, in her last book, *Touching Feeling*, Eve Kosofsky Sedg-wick seeks to move beyond Derrida and Butler's work, which, al-though "in service of an antiessentialist move," still demands totalization, because "the move from *some* language to *all language* seems required by their antiessentialist project" (6).[13] Instead, Sedgwick explores the myriad relations between texture, touch, and affect/emotion inherent in the word "feeling" in order to move away from such drives for totalization and truth. She writes, "Texture seems like a promising level of attention for shifting the emphasis on some interdisciplinary conversations away from the recent fixation on epistemology . . . by asking new questions about phenomenology and affect" (17). In other words, she is less interested in unearthing the truth and/or arguing about the knowability or unknowability of truth—in bracketing the notion of epistemology—than she is in asking "what motivates performativity and performance, for example, and what individual and collective effects are mobilized in their execution?" (17).[14]

The advantages of such approaches are summarized by Adam Frank in his review of several recent works on affect, including Berlant's and Sedgwick's:

This insistence on relationality is one of several promising things about the recent interest in affect . . . If symptomatic explanations and repressive hypotheses produce objects and subjects negatively by way of prohibition, then attention to affect theories, by beginning from middle or medium spaces, permit emergences of more contingent, even practical subjects and objects . . . Affect theories offer tools for specifying relations between the aesthetic and the political, and between the psychic and the social, that are not only linguistic. (522–523)

Frank's characterization is typical of several assumptions of this third trend in the cultural studies of emotion, including a deep skepticism about totalizations and articulations, seen as inherently and always running the risk of prohibition in the very act of enunciating; a preference for "contingent" and "fine-grained" readings that resist incorporation into any totalization; "continuities," resonances, and affinities without totalities; and ways to link critical work with "everyday lives." Despite my tendency to critique the privileging of contingency and rejection of totalization, a typical critical move of poststructuralism (as a reaction to the Enlightenment), I must admit that there are things to be learned from this approach to emotion, particularly its attention to detail and specificity. Take, for example,

Frank's contention that affect can help specify "relations between the aesthetic and the political." I agree with Brecht, contra Lukács, that there is no inherent relationship between aesthetics and politics, so affect can be one of the ways that we can approach the ideological valences of art.

In contrast to the desire of cognitive psychologists to define and delimit the characteristics of anger, this book seeks to show that *even if* we agree that certain individual physiological and cognitive processes come into play in anger, those considerations are insufficient to understand how anger actually works in any given situation, including, and in many ways especially, in literature and film. As with any historical phenomena, a whole host of political, cultural, interpersonal, and other factors come together in a unique way, and the sussing out of that uniqueness requires a mental flexibility and sensitivity. Attention to particularity does not mean, however, that larger frameworks and totalizations are impossible—in some ways they are even necessary. I also question the notion that emotions are necessarily better understood than affects. Many of the elements that "lie coiled" within anger are not fully accounted for and exceed the definitions, both because the definitions themselves are insufficient (particularly in being too individualistic) and because any given situation (real or fictive) contains its own configuration of elements. In other words, emotions such as anger may be as misunderstood as less well-articulated affects; in some ways, anger may even be more obscured because we believe that we understand it and therefore do not interrogate it further. In the subsequent chapters of this book, then, I attempt to negotiate the interplay between, on the one hand, specificity, detail, and sensitivity to particularities and, on the other hand, the larger collectivities, institutions, and abstractions in which we are all enmeshed.

ODD BEDFELLOWS? MARXISM AND NARRATOLOGY

In this last section (as in the last section of Chapter 1), I discuss some of the specific theorists whose work incorporates (or in Williams's case, founded) many of the insights above, constitutes the most productive ways to investigate emotion, and informs the readings in this book. I first revisit the work of Raymond Williams, and what he does and does not say about "structure of feeling," which will be useful for thinking about emotions in actual people in constantly changing historical formations that, while consisting of many historical parts, still should be understood as part of larger historical processes, particularly capitalism. I then discuss the work of some narrative theorists who provide useful directions and tools for studying emotion in cultural productions and their meanings for us.

All three threads of cultural studies of emotions discussed above draw on, explicitly or implicitly, the work of Raymond Williams. The political analyses utilize the Marxist concept of the proletariat's epistemic, affective, and existential knowledge, which comes not from immediate experience but via the collective struggle and articulation through which they come to know and make history. The genealogical approach to emotions resonates with Williams's claims that culture, "through variation and complication, embodies not only the issues but the contradictions through which it has developed" (11). "The most basic concepts" are not historical products, and under examination they "are suddenly seen to be not concepts but problems, not analytic problems either but historical movements that are still unresolved" (11). Moreover, the investigation of affects as beyond the articulated recalls Williams's important distinction between reduced "fixed explicit forms" of the social (articulations, definitions, categories, etc., including ideologies), and "living presence" (128), or "all the known complexities, the experienced tensions, shifts, and uncertainties, the intricate forms of unevenness and confusion" (129).[15] We should not confuse the limited, in-process, "fixed forms" that we use as heuristic tools with the reality itself: "The mistake . . . is in taking terms of analysis as terms of substance" (129).

Here, I would like to revisit Raymond Williams's oft-cited concept of "structure of feeling," because I think it can help bring these different strands of cultural studies together. In order to better articulate these different parts of society, Williams coins the phrase, in addition to the concepts of traditions, institutions, and formations, as well as dominant, residual, and emergent. As Sianne Ngai points out, "structure of feeling" does not apply to what we generally think of as emotions, which are already named, defined, and overdetermined.[16] Rather, Williams describes it as an unnamed-while-lived set of experiences, feelings, thoughts, values, etc.—emergent or pre-emergent formations—that characterize a particular generation in a given historical moment. A structure of feeling is a "particular quality of social experience and relationship, historically distinct from other particular qualities, which gives the sense of a generation or of a period"

(131). Individual experiences are not merely "personal" but *social* in the sense of "change of presence"—i.e., *change* lived in experiences, bodies, social structures, etc.—and, although the structure of feeling is not yet articulated, it nonetheless "exert[s] palpable pressures and set[s] effective limits on experience and on action" (132). But it is not simply ideology or hegemony, because the lived experience exceeds anything that is yet articulated; it is "a structured formation which, because it is at the very edge of semantic availability, has many of the characteristics of a pre-formation, until specific articulations—new semantic figures—are discovered in material practice" (134)

Williams's discussion of why he chooses this specific phrase is important to understanding the concept itself. He uses the term "feeling" "to emphasize a distinction from more formal concepts of 'world-view' or 'ideology'" (132). What falls into "social forms" includes but goes beyond formal definitions.[17] He continues that while "structures of experience" might be a better phrase because the term "experience" encompasses more than "feeling," "experience" is so associated with "that past tense which is the most important obstacle to recognition of the area of social experience which is being defined" (132) that he chooses the term "feeling." Yet, his discussion is not limited to emotions or affect; rather, he is interested in "characteristic elements of impulse, restraint, and tone; specifically affective elements of consciousness and relationships" (132). In other words, he presages both cognitive and cultural studies approaches to emotion and reason in advocating "not feeling against thought, but thought as felt and feeling as thought: practical consciousness of a present kind, in a living and interrelating continuity" (132). Moreover, he uses the term "structures" because the elements involved should be conceived of "as a set, with specific internal relations, at once interlocking and in tension" (132). While the "social experience" is still *"in process"* and "not yet recognized as social but taken to be private, idiosyncratic, and even isolating," nevertheless "analysis" can show how a structure of feeling "has its emergent, connecting, and dominant characteristics, indeed its specific hierarchies" (132, original emphasis).

Methodologically, then, to *talk about* a structure of feeling is to pose a "hypothesis of a mode of social formation" (135), centered around a "set of specific historical questions," such as "relations between this quality and the other specifying historical marks of changing institutions, formations, and beliefs, and beyond these the

changing social and economic relations between and within classes"
(131). Williams writes,

> Structures of feeling can be defined as social experiences *in solution*,
> as distinct from other social semantic formations which have been
> *precipitated* and are more evidently and more immediately avail-
> able. . . . Methodologically, then, a 'structure of feeling' is a *cultural*
> *hypothesis*, actually derived from attempts to understand such ele-
> ments and their connections in a generation or a period, and needing
> always to be returned, interactively, to such evidence. It is initially
> less simple than more formally structured hypotheses of the social,
> but it is more adequate to the actual range of cultural evidence. (132–
> 134, emphasis added)

And one of the key places to identify emerging, changing experiences
is art and literature; structures of feeling are "explicit and recognizable in specific kinds of art, which is distinguishable from other social and semantic formations by its articulation of presence" (135),
and art is "often among the very first indications that such a new
structure is forming" (133). Literary and cultural productions bear a
particular relationship to structures of feeling because they can capture a certain lived experience without explicitly articulating or defining it.[18] This process is not simple at any level; art can depict a
wide variety of relations between "fixed forms" and lived experience.
Historically speaking, structures of feeling are not necessarily reduc-
ible to a single group or class; structures of feeling may relate "to the
rise of a class" and "at other times to contradiction, fracture, or mu-
tation within a class" (134). Williams's project here, as with the en-
tirety of *Marxism and Literature*, is to broaden the scope of materialist critique while also preserving the historicity and dialecticism of
historical materialism.

In following Williams, *On Anger* is not necessarily about articulating an abstract structure of how anger works; rather, it takes Williams's methodology for examining late twentieth/early twenty-first
century ideas about, experiences of, and depictions of anger, in and as
a network of relations, definitions, and associations, that, although
apparently straightforward and widespread and ahistorical, yet remain to be articulated. Most importantly, these *relations* and *structures* are key for thinking about anger, because the various cognitive
and cultural definitions still cast anger as individual and/or fairly ho-

mogenous, rather than as deeply, multiply, and complexly *dialectical* in nature. Williams's approach also helps us to work with the "fixed forms" about anger—e.g., the various definitions of anger in cognitive and cultural studies—while not being limited to them. To paraphrase Williams, even if we could list *all* the possible definitions of anger, they would still not capture emotions as produced in "social consciousness" as lived. Rather, social forms "become social consciousness only when they are lived, actively, in real relationships, and moreover in relationships which are more than systematic exchanges between fixed units. Indeed just because all consciousness is social, its processes occur not only between but *within the relationships and the related*" (130, emphasis added). That is, we must examine not only the thing itself but also the contradictions and tensions within and between the various social elements.

So if we try to account for one instance of anger in its full complexity, we need not limit ourselves to appraisal, biochemical, political, epistemic, or transmission of affect explanations, although we should not discard them either. We can examine not only instances in which we think of anger as individual but also why we think of anger as individual. The individualism of anger doubtless has to do with the general ideology of liberal individualism and the concomitant compartmentalization of the emotions into the "private" sphere, even while emotions are commodified and made public. But surely, even if true, this explanation is not *sufficient* for every instance. For example, when we think about anger, we can look not simply at the persons involved, the events and various narratives, and/or the structure or institution against which he/she is angry, but also the relationships between and among each of these. Most importantly, because the dialectical relationship between the individual and the collective is suppressed, anger becomes the way to register contradiction within cognition, between the individual's understanding ("fixed form") of emotion as individual, irrational, private, and *not* knowledge, versus the individual's lived experiences of a deeply interrelated system.

On Anger thus seeks to examine the relations and conditions of anger through examination of texts in the context of late capitalism. While I draw on existing theories of anger, I also argue that *the texts themselves* have much to teach us about anger. As Williams writes, in art and literature the true social content is in a significant number of cases of this present and affective kind, which cannot without loss be reduced to belief-systems, institutions, or explicit general relationships, though it may include all these as lived and experienced, with or without tension, as it also evidently includes elements of social and material (physical or natural) experience which may lie beyond, or be uncovered and imperfectly covered by, the elsewhere recognizable systematic elements. (133)

In order to delve into what these texts can show us, I draw on narrative theory, which constitutes a set of heuristics for talking about form. As Williams writes, "the problem of form is a problem of the relations between social (collective) modes and individual projects" (187). While literary and cultural studies have become quite proficient in talking about the ideological and thematic relations between individual texts and various kinds of collectivities, for a variety of historical and disciplinary reasons, our vocabulary for talking about literary form has been less developed. Narrative theory offers a precise and yet flexible set of tools for dissecting aesthetic form. While philosophers such as Ronald de Sousa and Martha Nussbaum have written about the importance of reading and narratives in the formation of emotions, narrative theory can help us more precisely identify *how literary narratives work*. As in the last chapter, I will survey the work of some narrative theorists whose work productively mobilizes many of the concepts discussed in this chapter.

Robyn Warhol and Suzanne Keen's feminist works on narrative theory, emotion, and aesthetic texts provide excellent models. In *Having a Good Cry: Effeminate Feelings and Pop-Culture Forms* (2003), Robyn Warhol examines how narratives are central to constructing our emotions. In talking about emotions, Warhol advocates moving beyond a psychoanalytic discourse of desire and examining and identifying what she calls "technologies of affect," or narrative forms and conventions, the "textual machinery" that works to elicit certain emotions on the part of readers (8). She writes, "Narratives mark readers' bodies with these effects, and if the cry, the laugh, the gasp, the yawn is only ephemeral in any given instance, certain genres invoke these physical responses in predictable, formulaic patterns" (7). She examines in particular how such technologies of affect work to create and regulate gender: "We should think of narrative structures as another of these instruments, as devices that work through readers' bodily feelings to produce and reproduce the physical fact of bourgeois subjectivity" (8). At the same time, lived experience always exceeds these regulations. For instance, Warhol examines how serial novels by Anthony Trollope and Patrick O'Brian differently configure place, characters, repetition and recapitulations, and plot—that is, each of these and the relations between them—and produce different gendered effects.

By the same token, Suzanne Keen's work on empathy, with equal recognition of both biological processes as well as social forces, focuses on narrative structures that, historically, elicit certain affective responses—and yet do not do so all the time. Echoing the balance advocated by Herman, Hogan, and Zunshine in the previous chapter, Keen writes, "It is important not to confound underlying structures with outcomes that may express cultural assumptions rather than biological fact" (7). She examines why, despite the nearly universal view of philosophers and psychologists that empathy should produce moral growth and "prosocial action," it does not necessarily do so. In fact, as Keen (like Berlant) shows, empathy—or the idea that one is being empathetic—can actually be problematic and harmful. After a historical survey of the development of the concept of and attitudes about empathy, she examines narrative features that tend to elicit readerly empathy (e.g., the use of "internal perspective," or narration from the point of view of a character, whether in first or third person) as well as different narrative strategies an author may choose to invoke empathy in different groups (e.g., "bounded," or in-group, empathy vs. "broadcast," or universal, empathy).

The work of James Phelan in narrative theory and ethics is also important in considering emotions and narratives. Echoing Raymond Williams's contrast between definitions and experience distilled in literature, Phelan writes that literature's advantage over philosophy of ethics is that "it can get beyond the abstract meanings and black-and-white implications of ethical categories to the complexities and nuances of ethical choices within the detailed contexts of human lives" (*Experiencing* 93–94). Against the trend of privileging ideologically non-linear narrative forms, Phelan argues that narratives of all kinds, including and especially those with an "emphasis on judgment and progression," have important ethical value. But in writing about emotions and ethics, he notes that we still have much to consider. First, our vocabulary for talking about affect in reading—"*sympathy,*

desire, hope, disappointment, sorrow, happiness, expectation, antic-
ipation," etc., or *"uncertainty, puzzlement, understanding"* (*Experi-*
encing 91–92)—is still "preliminary and partial," because it is "insufficiently precise" and insufficiently comprehensive (*Experiencing*
92). When we talk about these affects in a text, whose feelings are we
talking about? The characters'? The reader's? The reader's in relation
to the characters'? The author's as encoded in the text? The author's
as gleaned from beyond the text? For instance, as I discuss in Chapter 4, one scene of anger in *Woman Warrior* can be approached from
many different angles, including narrative structure and time. Likewise, in Chapter 5, I explore how anger is linked to the contradictions
embedded in spaces. In other words, moments of anger are not simply expressions of individual characters' interiorities; they can be in-
dexes of complex, multilayered social, political, and narrative topog-
raphies. As Phelan puts it, "I see improving this vocabulary as one of
the important future tasks in the rhetorical theory of narrative" (92).
Second, our ethical judgments have affective consequences and, vice
versa, our emotions have ethical consequences; moreover, the two—
emotions and ethics—are in constant historical and dialectical relationship, just as they are with innumerable other factors. *On Anger*
seeks to participate in this process of articulating the "technology of
affects" that produce various kinds of anger, drawing on the tools of
narrative theory; the historical and ideological approaches forged by
the work discussed in this chapter; and the cognitive approaches outlined in Chapter 1.

CONCLUSION

To summarize the insights of the various approaches outlined in this
chapter:
   Anger is cognitive, because feeling and thinking are inextricably
interlinked.
   Anger is individual as well as collective and intersubjective. As
the work of Brennan, Woodward, Spelman, Jaggar, and other theorists
shows, not only are emotions produced in and by a group, but also
groups are produced by emotions—just as individuals are produced
by groups, and groups are produced by individuals. Another way to
put it would be that individual emotions and groups are dialectically
related. Just as Kathleen Woodward distinguishes between an *"emo-*
tional experience (what an individual feels) and *emotional standards*

or ideals (what a culture demands in terms of emotional behavior or etiquette)" (190, original emphasis), anger is both individual *and* collective in complex, multiply determined ways.

Anger is gendered, raced, sexed, classed.[19] In most cases, the anger of the privileged group is seen as justified, while the anger of a subordinate group is often seen as hysterical, irrational, and/or dangerous. In the West, the differential characterization of anger according to social power has to do with the relationship of the emotion to the feeling person's cognition, reason, or "intellect," which is often linked to the person's body. That is, male anger is more often linked to reason and is not located in his/her body as a kind of neurotic symptom, whereas women's anger is seen as hysterical and located in her instability as a body (e.g., premenstrual syndrome). This pattern is changing, of course, in the context of late capitalism's changing demands for "sensitivity" and "flexibility," indicating again that the constructions of anger, and how those constructions of anger construct us, are always *historical*. For example, the valences of male anger are raced, classed, and sexed: black male rage is seen as just as irrational but more threatening than female anger; working-class male anger tends to be read by the middle class as irrational, ignorant, and/or threatening; and gay male anger is seen as just as hysterical and physically neurotic as women's.

Anger is historical, and thereby ideological and political. Therefore, genealogies, histories, and other studies of the ideological work of the production and regulation of emotion—defined as "emotion," or less articulated like "affects"—give us crucial insight into the dynamics of power and subjectivity.

And in being collective, ideological, and historical, *anger is also related to systems*. We tend to think of anger as individual, but its causes and effects are really *systemic*—and our lack of ability to think *and feel* systemically exacerbates the conditions in which many people are angry. As Lorde points out, if we do not recognize the vertical, or power, relationships that produce our situation, we may take out our anger on those horizontally related to us, or in the same position as we are in. In other words, it is *because* the dialectical relationships between the individual and the collective are suppressed that anger becomes the way to register contradiction within cognition, between the individual's understanding, via the existing terms we have, of emotion as individual, irrational, and private, versus our lived experiences of emotions as also collective, cognitive, and public, part of complexly interrelated systems.

Anger, then, is really a "problematic," or a related cluster of issues that generates as many questions as answers, and that is related to many other considerations beyond the realm of emotions. Just as Probyn, Ngai, and others reveal that many "different lines . . . lie coiled within" what we consider to be relatively simple emotional states, anger is much more complicated than it appears at first glance. It is in this expansive, complex sense of anger that we can explore what Williams calls a "structure of feeling," or a hypothesis about the conditions in which we not only experience anger but feel and think about anger in this historical moment, as demonstrated— beyond our extant terms for it—in literature and art. In the chapters that follow, I explore how various texts produce "technologies of affect" that represent, configure, and manipulate anger in myriad ways with ideological, ethical, and aesthetic implications.

CHAPTER 3

LIBERAL ANGER:
TECHNOLOGIES OF ANGER IN *CRASH*

Do you wanna hear something funny? . . . You're the best friend I've got.
JEAN CABOT TO HER MAID, *CRASH*

WHY WAS THE 2005 FILM *Crash* so popular? Critics have discussed how *Crash* actually exacerbates the racial problems that it strives to critique. Directed by Paul Haggis, the film spans two days in Los Angeles, focusing on characters of various races whose lives intersect to varying degrees of calamity. *Crash* was lauded for its unflinching portrayal of race relations; Roger Ebert called it "a film about progress," and Oprah encouraged everyone to go see it (Glaister). The film won numerous awards, including the Academy Award for best picture in 2006, and is used in schools and institutional "diversity training" programs (Ahlquist and Milner). But ethnic studies scholars and others have repeatedly pointed out that the film actually reinforces racial and gender hierarchies; *Crash* characterizes "racism" as an individual failing, rather than a product of histories, structures, and practices of power that give shape to our current racial formations. As Hsuan Hsu writes, the film's "reduction of racism to the scale of individual characters [attitudes and practices] occludes crucial and harmful institutional, legal, and historical aspects of racism" (144). Lundegaard adds that today *covert* racism, rather than the overt kind displayed in the film, is the real problem.[1] The liberal multicultural model of race is limited and ultimately harmful because it contradictorily relies on notions of individual attitudes and "stereotypes," while also flattening group differences into discrete, relatively homogenous racial and/or ethnic categories, unsituated in space and time. In other words, the dominant model of race relations in the

U.S. naturalizes racial formations and encourages all parties to stay within those lines, rather than critically historicizing and challenging such formations.

Critiques of the film point out crucially important conflicts in ideological framings and constitutive histories, but the question remains, why do audiences have such strong but varying emotional responses—rather than consciously political ones—to this film? This chapter explores how we can understand the film and reactions to it by thinking in terms of ideology as a cognitive tool that produces emotions. Although there are a lot of angry people in the film, why and how does the film try to make us feel good? The film uses representations of the characters' anger to elicit certain reactions in viewers, whose emotions have ideological effects in the contemporary U.S. In short, the film's technologies of affect justify and naturalize a liberal multiculturalist and neoliberal worldview that ultimately exacerbates racial oppression.

Robyn Warhol defines technologies of affect as popular "established conventions for inspiring certain feelings at particular junctures of the story" (7). Such narrative structures can be ideological instruments, "devices that work through readers' bodily feeling to produce and reproduce the physical fact of bourgeois subjectivity" (8). She explores the conventions producing Western gendered experiences, and in this chapter I focus on how *Crash* reproduces liberal multicultural views of race, at the level of the storyworld (i.e., the universe of the characters), the viewers (our world), and the interactions between them. Although the film purports to be about race and racial anger, it actually obliterates the structures that produce race. The kinds of reactions the film seeks to (and does) produce are emotions that assuage guilt and elicit relief from culpability and responsibility. Viewers are supposed to judge negatively characters' racial anger because the film presents racial anger as ubiquitous (everyone is angry), structurally equivalent (everyone's anger is as personal as everyone else's), and ahistorical. By rendering racism a personal failing rather than a structural condition, the film assuages white guilt while also maintaining white supremacy.

The film manages this feat through the racial ideology of liberal multiculturalism. Although there are different models of multiculturalism,[2] liberal multiculturalism is the version based on a notion of cultures as homogenous, discrete, and equal—as E. San Juan describes it, "plural cultures of ethnicities coexisting peacefully, without serious contestation, in a free play of monads in 'the best of all possible worlds'" (*Racism* 6). Liberal multiculturalism, San Juan writes, may "grant cultural autonomy but hide or ignore structural inequalities under the umbrella of a refurbished humanist cosmopolitanism" (*Racism* 7), and therefore it serves as the "official policy designed to solve racism and ethnic conflicts in the North" (*Racism* 9). This form of multiculturalism, somewhat paradoxically, homogenizes groups by races and ethnicity while also being perfectly compatible with individualism. On one hand, each "group" is seen as distinct and uniform: African Americans, Latinos (or "Hispanics"), Asian Americans (sometimes distinguished from Arab Americans, sometimes differentiated by nationality or region), and Native Americans. "Whiteness" is usually not seen as a particular racial formation.[3] "Change" is seen not as structural changes but as individual advancement within existing structures; thus, liberal multiculturalism is perfectly compatible with and even appropriated by reactionaries. Logically, such abstract, fossilized racial equality leads to arguments *against* structural changes and targeted policies, such as affirmative action, to redress historic and systemic problems. David Theo Goldberg describes this multiculturalism, compatible with individualism and capitalism, as "racial neoliberalism"(361).[4]

Liberal multiculturalism is the language of "tolerance," in which we endure other cultures, rather than understanding the historical relations between groups and the systems—capitalism, colonialism, neo-imperialism—that conditioned and even created some groups. For instance, the storyworld of *Crash* shows groups who are not produced by anything, who do not come from anywhere and have no historical or structural relationships to one another.[5] There are simply Asians, Latinos, blacks, and whites, all of whom are angry.[6]

"I'M REALLY HOPING THAT I'M WRONG ABOUT YOU"

One of the film's most discussed scenes involves a confrontation between a white police officer, John Ryan (played by Matt Dillon), and an African American HMO administrator, Shaniqua Johnson (played by Loretta Devine). Ryan, suspecting that his father has prostate cancer but has been misdiagnosed, wants permission to see a doctor outside the HMO network. The night before his face-to-face meeting with Johnson, Ryan is frustrated by the bureaucratic obstacles and makes a racist comment to her on the phone. When they do meet in person, he apologizes for his comment, explaining that he has not been sleeping well and that his father is in a lot of pain. When Johnson refuses to help him, Ryan becomes angry and says, "I can't look at you without thinking about the five or six more qualified white men who didn't get your job." As she calls security, he continues:

I'm saying this 'cause I'm really hoping that I'm wrong about you. I'm hoping that someone like yourself, someone who may have been given a helping hand, might have a little compassion for someone in a similar situation . . .

You don't like me, that's fine. I'm a prick. My father doesn't deserve to suffer like this. He was a janitor. He struggled his whole life. Saved enough to start his own company. Twenty-three employees, all of them black. Paid 'em equal wages when no one else was doing that. For years he worked side by side with those men, sweeping and carrying garbage . . .

Then the city council decides to give minority-owned companies preference in city contracts. And overnight, my father loses everything. His business, his home, his wife. Everything! Not once does he blame your people. I'm not asking you to help me. I'm asking that you do this small thing for a man who lost everything so people like yourself could reap the benefits. And do you know what it's gonna cost you? Nothing. Just a flick of your pen.

Johnson remains steadfast, saying, "Your father sounds like a good man. And if he'd come in here today, I probably would've approved this request. But he didn't come in."

This event is pivotal to the film's plot, starting a chain of events that will lead to the central car crash/rescue scene, a still from which was featured in most publicity about the film.[7] Ryan's resulting impotent anger leads him to stop a black couple in their SUV and sexually assault the woman, Christine Thayer (played by Thandie Newton). Later, however, Ryan heroically saves an injured Thayer from her overturned, burning Jeep, despite her initial revulsion when she realizes who is trying to save her. Ryan's action is meant to redeem him; according to the film's script, "Ryan looks into [Thayer's] face and sees her pain and humiliation, and knows he was the cause of it" (scene 66), and Dillon and Newton effectively portray this exchange. The film ultimately depicts Ryan as someone who, despite making bad decisions regarding race in a confusing world (as does pretty much everyone in the film), is essentially a good person. While Ryan is not the clear protagonist, he is one of the central characters and emotional centers of the film.

We can parse the emotions of characters and viewers to understand the political ramifications. First, the anger of Dillon's *character*, John Ryan, can be understood in terms of appraisal *within* contending social-ideological systems, or what Herman terms "emotionologies," or "the collective emotional standards of a culture" ("Storytelling" 322). John Ryan is angry about a number of things: his father's ailing health, the intractability of the health insurance system, the African American woman's apparent indifference to his plight and implicit anti-white racism. His immediate goal is to alleviate his father's suffering, which suggests that since this motive is not merely selfish but empathetic, he is not an irredeemable character. At the same time, since his father's suffering makes him suffer empathetically, alleviating his father's pain will help alleviate his own pain. His goal is initially balked by the implacable bureaucratic hurdles of HMOs, but his frustrated anger is channeled into a different narrative that informs a collective concept of anger, the narrative of "reverse racism," in which white people—men in particular—are victimized by the preferential treatment given to people of color. Note that with John Ryan, we are given reasons to partially identify and empathize with him.

But his individual experience of emotion does not just draw on this emotionology; his emotion is intensified by the immediacy of his father's suffering and informed by his father's past actions. In liberal multiculturalism, in which groups of people are organized socially and institutionally by a naturalized notion of race ("your people"), he assumes his father's work must have helped Johnson. So for Ryan, Johnson represents not only the balking of Ryan's current goals, but also a betrayal of his father by the "people" whom he went through so much to help. Not only do painful memories stir Ryan's current response, but he also has a sense that in the division of labor to achieve communal goals (good white people like his father sacrifice, so black people should be properly appreciative), Johnson is not doing her part. And Johnson responds in kind; she acknowledges that although Ryan's father is a "good man," because Ryan falls into the category of "white racist," her anger leads her to deny Ryan's father's request. Ryan can only see the health insurance problem in terms of race, and Johnson, while recognizing Ryan's father's merits and needs, refuses to help because she sees Ryan as a racist. Although Ryan and Johnson are ostensibly equally racially angry, the *viewer* has more information about and emotional investment in the character Ryan. Furthermore, the film's presentation of an African American woman with more power than a white man implies that racial and gendered hierarchies no longer exist; rather, we simply have interracial hatred that is personal.[8] As the 2010 flap over Shirley Sherrod and the USDA demonstrates, Johnson is a fantasy of "post-racial" equality in which minorities have achieved legal, economic, and political parity and practice reverse discrimination.[9]

So despite the apparently neutral *content*—everyone's point of view is shaped by race—the film overall and this scene specifically invite sympathy for Ryan's anger rather than Johnson's anger. When the Ryan-Johnson scene begins, we see that Johnson's secretary is a white woman, and then the film cuts to Ryan sitting in the waiting room. Again, this juxtaposition shows Johnson's relative power in relation to Ryan; she confers with her secretary while he sweats in the waiting room. The stylistic cues in the film invite us to empathize with Ryan without realizing it; the lighting, staging, and camera angles in the film are "realistic," and thereby apparently neutral, not making obvious use of music or other indicators of the goodness or evilness of a character.[10] The stylistic realism is meant to reflect the film's thematic realism, but the style cues do subtly guide our responses. Ryan's body language indicates his anxiety and defensiveness; he sits in the waiting room on the edge of his seat, hunched over, tapping his feet, and twiddling his fingers, and he walks into Johnson's office with his arms crossed. In contrast, when she learns who is waiting to meet with her, Johnson's face displays a look of angry pleasure: "Send him in," Johnson tells her secretary, with a smile on her face. Her mannerisms and speech are all sardonically polite, while he is apologetic, wary, and diffident. The window behind Johnson backlights her while throwing stronger light on Ryan; Matt Dillon, the bigger star, has more lines and screen time. As Ryan tells the story of his father, Johnson physically indicates her sympathy by nodding and waving away the (black) security guard, but she ultimately still refuses him.

The scene suggests that her racism causes his, which makes his anger and frustration seem justified. His later sexual assault of Christine Thayer may be horrific, but it is "just" an emotional response of an individual in frustrating and painful circumstances. In the "ventilationist" or "bottling" view of emotions, he simply transfers his hostility from Johnson to Thayer (rather than consciously choosing to participate in the systemic sexual abuse of women). He is simply racist because someone was racist to him; as we see later when he saves Thayer, it is not because he is a bad person, and it certainly has nothing to do with the police, the class system, and other structures (for instance, the health system in the U.S. itself is *not* indicted by the film—Johnson *chooses* not to help Ryan).

We can understand responses to the film in ways that reveal ideological contestation in the heart of emotional responses.[11] Most of the film's viewers will tend to distance themselves from the racial elements of Ryan's anger, incorporating this particular event into the "everybody is racist" logic of the film. A viewer may share Ryan's frustration over his inability to help his father, but the goal both for the viewer and for the character Ryan is to *not be racist*. In contemporary liberal multiculturalism, one of the most central fears of (particularly white) liberals is to be called racist, and everything is done to prevent the *perception* of being racist.[12] Given this racial anxiety, the appeal of *Crash*'s liberal multiculturalism makes complete sense. When John Ryan saves Christine Thayer, he is redeemed. His courage, fear, remorse, and generally confusing welter of emotions after the rescue suggest that he is *not simply* an angry racist. Whatever mistakes he may have made in the past, the film implies, whatever he may have said out of irrational anger, he is not fundamentally a racist because he values all human life and is willing to risk his own life to save a black woman. The viewer's goal for the character has been fulfilled, and in wishing that Ryan learn the error of his ways and then having that wish fulfilled, the viewer feels successful in his/her goal of not being a racist. Viewers are told that it is simultaneously acceptable to live vicariously through these characters and to be angry, but also that in the simple act of going to see the film, one has done some kind of anti-racist ethical action. Whatever mistakes viewers may have made in their own lives, whatever disconcertingly non–"politically correct" memories are triggered by earlier scenes in the film, they can be reassured that they, like John Ryan, will be excused and redeemed. In other words, racist feelings are resolved and absolved by the film while leaving structures of racial domination intact. Such viewers find the film *emotionally* satisfying because it fulfills and reinforces the cultural scripts and narratives of liberal multiculturalism.[13] It is at this level, with such a reaction elicited by such a film, that the whole *Crash* phenomenon is most problematic and dangerous.

"DOPEY FUCKING CHINAMAN"

In cognitive terms, John Ryan sees Shaniqua Johnson as a dispositional entity purposely obstructing his goal. The fact that he reacts to her as a dispositional agent means that at least he credits her with intentionality. Given the historical context, this is problematic because this individualized, liberal multiculturalist model of "we are all racist" ignores the structure inequalities that continue to disproportionately disenfranchise and impoverish women and people of color. However, the Ryan-Johnson interaction pales in comparison to the depiction of the minds of Asian/Asian Americans, as played out in scenes with Anthony (Chris "Ludacris" Bridges) and Peter Waters (Larenz Tate). In the film, these Asian/Asian American figures are erased of intentionality and agency; they are simply "nondispositional" objects to be acted upon.

A scene that is meant to be one of the funniest in the film also is one of the most disturbing. While driving an SUV, Anthony and Waters realize that they have run over an Asian man (whom we later learn is Korean American). As the man lies under the truck, they panic while trying to figure out what to do. The structure and pacing of the scene is geared for maximum slapstick comedy.

PETER: Man, we done ran over a Chinaman.
ANTHONY: You're saying there's a Chinaman under this truck?
PETER: What part don't you understand? There's a Chinaman stuck underneath the fucking truck.

Eventually, despite the potential risk to themselves, they decide to drop him off at the hospital. At this point, the "Chinaman" is never a real human being; he is just a comic device to show the essential humanity of carjackers Anthony and Waters.

Later in the film, however, we discover that, in essence, the "Chinaman" deserved to be run over. His name is Choi Jin Gui (Greg Joung Paik), a Korean American man, and the van he was driving contained chained and ragged Southeast Asian immigrants.[14] Choi was apparently going to sell them, and while he recovers in the hospital, he gives his wife a check to cash, telling her to do so quickly.

In other words, although he has lost the van with the immigrants, he still wants the money for their sale; he is more concerned about the money than his own welfare. In contrast, Anthony, now without Waters, finds the abandoned van, and although the owner of a chop shop offers him $500 for each of the prisoners in the van, Anthony sets them free. In the last scene of the film, Anthony opens the door of the van and unchains them, saying to one of the men, "Look, here's forty bucks. Buy everybody chop suey. You understand? Dopey fucking Chinaman."

The film obviously seeks to portray the plight of smuggled, exploited illegal immigrants, and to complicate the white, middle-class, dehumanized notion of carjackers, but it does so at the expense of the "Others" to whose minds we have less or no access. In other words, the film attempts to humanize the young black male carjacker, Anthony, at the expense of both the Korean slave dealer and the Cambodian immigrants, all inscrutable, alien beings. By the same token, although the film establishes Ryan's racist remarks as a cause for Johnson's anger, the scene of their face-to-face confrontation (and his later rescue of Thandie Newton's character) implicitly attempts to locate viewer empathy on the side of Ryan. In this sense, the film's structural "equality" is doubly deceptive; it privileges some minds over others in utterly typical ways—white over black, citizen over foreigner—while wrapping itself in the rhetoric of pluralism and impartiality. The episodic, decentered structure of the film is meant to not foreground any of the central cast any more than the others—everybody is equally prey to prejudicial anger and racial redemption—and in doing this the film seeks to convey a sense of the equality implied in the model of liberal multiculturalism. Despite the ensemble cast, the central characters are white and the minority characters are given depth and complexity according to the level of liberal guilt currently afforded to that group: in order of guilt, African American, Asian (Middle East), Latino, and Asian (East Asia and Southeast Asia). The film's faux equality centralizes certain characters and represses others while pretending not to, thereby reinforcing certain notions of who counts as "citizens" in an American liberal multicultural, "melting pot" model, while normalizing and hiding its own suppression of others. In these ways, the film reflects a liberal political model of equality that obscures structures of raced and classed (and gendered) power. Ironically, in this way the film's approach to characters reflects the ways in which a global late capitalism that relies on difference/change/flexibility/movement espouses this notion of free-floating, decentered, structurally equal consumer-citizens, *while also* suppressing the exploitation, stratification, and differentiating that capitalism as a value-extracting system relies upon.

Take, for instance, the opening scenes of the film, which showcase angry collisions involving the principal characters, which the film ostensibly goes on to complicate. The very first words of the film are spoken by Detective Waters, musing on the alienation of life in LA. He says, "It's the sense of touch. . . . Any real city, you walk, you know? You brush past people. People bump into you. In LA, nobody touches you. We're always behind this metal and glass. I think we miss that touch so much that we crash into each other just so that we can feel something." This sense of isolation that the film purports to and perhaps actually believes itself to be critiquing is actually structurally, cognitively, and emotionally *reinforced* by the film's portrayal of how race works. For instance, in the first scene, Detective Ria (played by Jennifer Esposito) confronts Kim Lee (Alexis Rhee), who has rear-ended Ria and her partner Detective Graham Waters's car. Kim calls Ria "Mexican," and Ria mocks Kim's pronunciation of "brake" as "blake." In casting this scene as two individuals basing their reactions to one another on the basis of the crudest ethnic stereotyping, the film completely ignores the history of interethnic communities, organizing, and cultural productions.[15] Moreover, it suggests that people of color are "just as guilty" of stereotyping as white people, while ignoring structural or systemic inequities (both women are visibly middle-class). Kim Lee, we learn later, is also the wife of Choi, who has been trafficking in human slaves, further showing that she is just as bad a person as everyone else. The second scene shows Iranian American shop owner Farhad (Shaun Toub; the character has no last name) and his daughter Dorri (Bahar Soomekh) trying to purchase a gun; as they confer in Farsi, the gun store owner (Jack McGee) says to Farhad, "Yo, Osama! Plan a jihad on your own time," and orders them out of the store. When Farhad leaves in anger, the daughter completes the purchase while being subjected to the threatening sexual innuendo of the store owner.

The film then cuts to Anthony and Peter Waters leaving a diner, with Anthony angrily asking, "Did you see any white people waitin' an hour and thirty-two minutes for a plate of spaghetti?" Peter laughingly protests that the waitress was black, but Anthony replies, "And black women don't think in stereotypes? You tell me. When was the last time you met one who didn't think she knew everything about your little lazy ass before you even opened your mouth, huh?" Anthony's words again reinforce the notion that *everyone* is racist. Anthony then becomes angry at a white woman, Jean Cabot (Sandra Bullock), who expresses fear when she sees the two black men. It turns out, however, that *her fear is justified*, because they in fact have guns and steal the Cabots' SUV.

The fourth scene revisits Detectives Graham Waters (Don Cheadle) and Ria as they arrive at a crime scene in which a white police detective, Conklin, has shot an off-duty black police officer, William Lewis; Conklin claims it was self-defense. Waters's anger is palpable as he observes, "Looks like Detective Conklin shot himself the wrong nigger." This apparent racial episode, however, proves to be false; Waters later says that, having found three hundred thousand dollars in the trunk of Lewis's car, it was likely that Lewis was on drugs. In other words, ultimately it appears the shooting of the black police officer *was justified*. Moreover, the white detective, Conklin, will be scapegoated by the white DA, Rick Cabot (Brendan Fraser), who wants to appeal to liberal voters by coming down hard on a white man. In a fantasy of reverse discrimination, Detective Waters is shown agreeing, albeit reluctantly, to cover up evidence of Lewis's guilt and allow Conklin, a potentially innocent man, to be indicted for racial shootings. Waters does this, in part, in return for the DA's waiver of the warrant for Waters's troubled younger brother, the carjacker Peter, indicating for the viewer that, again, *each individual* is self-serving and complicit in racism.

Then we cut to the home of the Cabots, where Jean becomes angry at the young Latino locksmith, Daniel Ruiz (Michael Peña), who is changing the locks on their house in the wake of their carjacking. She suspects Ruiz of being a gang member who is going to return to rob their house, and she becomes angry at her husband for questioning her desire to have the locks changed again in the morning, and for questioning her fear. She is actually angry at feeling guilty about feeling afraid of the black male carjackers as well as the young Latino man:

> JEAN: Do not patronize me. I want the locks changed again in the morning. . . . You know, didn't I just ask you not to treat me like a child? . . . I would like the locks changed again in the morning. And you might mention that we'd appreciate it if next time they didn't send a gang member . . .
>
> RICK: A gang member? You mean that kid in there?

JEAN: Yes. The guy with the shaved head, the pants around his ass, the prison tattoo.

RICK: Those are not prison tattoos.

JEAN: Oh, really? And he's not gonna sell our key to one of his gangbanger friends the moment he is out our door?

RICK: We've had a really tough night. I think it'd be best if you just went upstairs . . .

JEAN: And wait for them to break in? I just had a gun pointed in my face.

RICK: You lower your voice!

JEAN: And it was my fault because I knew it was gonna happen. But if a white person sees two black men walking towards her, and she turns and walks in the other direction, she's a racist, right? Well, I got scared and I didn't say anything. And ten seconds later I had a gun in my face! Now I am telling you, your amigo in there is gonna sell our key to one of his homies. And this time it'd be really fucking great if you acted like you actually gave a shit!

Jean's liberal-guilt dilemma is very telling. Ostensibly, she is angry because her goal is to not be seen as a racist. The emphasis here is on perception: she does not regret feeling afraid; she regrets not being able to show it. The problem is not her racial or class privilege or structural racism and poverty; the problem is that liberal etiquette requires that she not be afraid of black people. She is angry at the agents to whom she attributes malicious intent, the young black men and the Latino locksmith; they have violated the rule of liberal multiculturalism in which all people of color act like middle-class white people. But as we can sense in this conversation and confirm over the course of the film, we find out that Jean is *really* angry about not feeling loved by her husband and not having real friends. She just wants Rick to "g[i]ve a shit." In other words, Jean is not really racist or overly privileged; the problem is not structural racism, urban blight, commodity fetishism, or the 1 percent: she just needs a hug.

And, outrageously, the person to give her that hug is *her maid*. Frankly, this scene, which is meant to evoke sentimental good feelings, compassion and empathy, enrages me. An ostensibly chastised Jean Cabot says to her maid, Maria, who is not even given a last name, the words of this chapter's epigram: "Do you wanna hear something funny? . . . You're the best friend I've got." Jean then hugs Maria in what is meant to be some kind of redemption or atonement for her earlier (unwarranted) racial profiling of Ruiz, but Maria in the scene is more akin to an updated Mammy figure; the woman-of-color maid serves as a vehicle for the emotional and ethical development of the white protagonist. Maria has no backstory or emotional depth. In fact, throughout the film, real emotional and cognitive "understanding" is reserved for *individuals*, at the cost of depthless others, rather than the structures and histories that produce particular racializations, classes, etc. The notion that Maria or Daniel Ruiz might be angry at structural oppression (race and class but also the division of resources between countries and the *histories* of colonialism and neo-imperialism that produced those differences) never enters the pictures. Rather, they are simply saintly ciphers, ready to patiently bear with abuse and then absolve and comfort white people when needed.

Thus, despite the film's formal and thematic claim to equality of racial anger, the film—formally and thematically—erases the historical and structural differences between groups *and* implicitly privileges *white* people's feelings. That African American characters get slightly more complexity in the film (Graham Waters and Cameron and Christine Thayer, although she is quickly reduced to needing rescue by the white man who sexually assaulted her) reflects the racial hierarchy of white liberal guilt. The film's popularity speaks to the emotional desire for emotional absolution by a disturbing number of film viewers. E. San Juan's scathing critique of liberal multiculturalism resonates perfectly with the project of the film:

This hegemonic pluralism operates most effectively in the guise of multiculturalism, alias ethnic diversity, within the parameters of a unifying national consensus that privileges one segment as the universal measure: the Euro-American elite. To secure its reproduction together with its basis in existing property relations, the hegemonic racial formation elides the conflictive relations of domination and subordination. It substitutes parallelism, synchrony, or cohesion of interests. It negotiates the acceptance of a compromise, a homogenous national life-style (innocent of gender or class or racial antagonisms) into which other generalized cultures—Asian, American Indian, Latino, African American—can be gradually assimilated. This liberal approach fails to recognize that the reality of U.S. institutional practices of racism is grounded in the unequal possession of wealth. (*Racial Formations* 115)

The "parallelism" of racial anger in *Crash* effaces the structural and historical (and global) conditions that produce racism, reducing it to simply problems of irrational emotion bursting forth due to the lack of "touch." In other words, people are angry because they, like Jean, need a hug.

This conception of racism, as individual and irrationally emotional, is what David Theo Goldberg describes as "born again racism," or "a racism purged of historical roots, of its groundedness, a racism whose history is lost," a racism as "individualized faith, of the socially dislocated heart, rather than as institutionalized inequality" (23). It has "no precedent, no intent, no pattern, no institutional explication" (23). This version of racism resonates with dominant ideas of anger; both emerge from the individual heart and are not related to reason, history, or structures. This racism, moreover, is as acceptable to the Right as the Left. As George W. Bush said to the NAACP in 2006, "I understand that racism still lingers in America. It's a lot easier to change a law than to change a human heart" (quoted in Goldberg 23; see also Silva). Bush's message is essentially that of *Crash*.

The storyworld of *Crash*, an LA where everyone is both victim and victimizer, all equally racist, depicts an affective equality in which everyone is equally angry in their racism not because of histories and structures but simply because everyone else is also racist and angry. The emotional response invited by the film is even more insidious; viewers may feel not only justified and reassured in their belief that racism is simply a personal failing, but they may even feel proud or satisfied that they simply watched the film. The liberal good feelings produced by *Crash* are a perfect example of what Lauren Berlant describes as the insidious politics of compassion, when it serves as "a defensive response by people who identify with privilege yet fear they will be exposed as immoral by their tacit sanction of a particular structural violence that benefits them" ("Subject" 153). *Crash* erases the structural violence that produces racism; rather, like the characters' anger, the film renders it private, individual, and a product of "the human heart." This erasure produces rage in other viewers of the film—such as myself—precisely because its triumphant liberalism epitomizes the problem with our discussions of both race and anger today.

CHAPTER 4

TEMPORALITY AND THE POLITICS OF READING KINGSTON'S *THE WOMAN WARRIOR*

We had been in this lavatory forever. . . . It seemed as if I had spent my life in that basement, doing the worst thing I had yet done to another person.
NARRATOR, *THE WOMAN WARRIOR*

WHEN I TEACH *THE AUTOBIOGRAPHY OF MALCOLM X* and Maxine Hong Kingston's *The Woman Warrior* in my American literature survey, students invariably tend to do two things: they evince surprise that *Malcolm X* is so much *less* angry than they had expected, and they want to read *The Woman Warrior* as being about the cultural differences between China and the U.S. These tendencies—the readerly expectations that are disrupted by the actual text of *Malcolm X* and the expectations that fail to be disrupted in their reading of *Woman Warrior*—are intimately connected. Both have to do with readers' desires to equate the complex literary productions of Alex Haley and Maxine Hong Kingston with not only the actual experiences of Malcolm X and Kingston, but also the entire group they are seen to represent within a liberal multicultural framework. The students' racialized and gendered ideological expectations are channeled into the desire for a static iconographic image that can serve as a convenient handle: the fist-raised Malcolm or poor little Maxine struggling against (Chinese) patriarchy.

These readerly tendencies, products of simplistic and regressive forms of multiculturalism, run counter to the increasing theoretical sophistication and anti-essentialism of literary criticism of marginal texts.[1] Yet even in literary criticism, debates about representation and aesthetic form continue, as evinced by conversations about anger and aggression in *Woman Warrior*. Critics do read the text as

angry, and many feminist and Asian American literary critics cele-
brate the angry figure of the title, the mythical Fa Mu Lan transfig-
ured into Asian American feminist warrior. Others argue that the
text, in its valorization of the woman warrior figure and myth, actually reinforces patriarchy and Orientalism.[2] But many such readings,
while compelling in details, are still based on the assumption that
the texts must be evaluated in terms of literary and political representation. The notion of representation may be couched in more complex terms: for example, that contradictory ideological and economic
structural pressures on a community give rise to counterhegemonic
cultural productions that must then be interpreted differently, or that
the nontraditional memoir form of Kingston's *Woman Warrior* captures a uniquely feminine and/or minority experience.[3]

The question of representation of collective experience is clearly a
complex one. On the one hand, the endeavor to fill in the blank spots
of human experience—and the ideological structures that create and
are supported by such lacuna—and to write of new human experiences is unquestionably important. At the same time, the dangers of
the simplistic multicultural approach *and* the more complex repre-
sentational approaches include not only the suppression of the actual
heterogeneities of experience, but also the under-reading of particular
marginal aesthetic texts. As Sau-ling Wong wrote twenty years ago:

> We have, then, two apparently contradictory claims on the ethnic
> writer: one, a fundamental human need to affirm the specificities of
> one's personal experience, however "atypical," especially when the
> redemption of a painful past is at stake; and the other, a no less com-
> pelling imperative to express solidarity with those whose sufferings
> take similar forms from similar causes, such that one's gift of writing
> becomes more than a tool for individual therapy or gratification. (5)

But even given the exigencies of the marginal writer, Wong eloquently defends the right of marginal artists to be free from narrow
identity politics that limit human possibilities: "To demand ortho-
doxy in the treatment of ethnic experiences is to subscribe to a narrowly utilitarian theory of literature, and the price one pays for this
simplification is . . . a reduction in the fullness of life, a shrinking
of the self to meaner if more manageable proportions" (24). Yet even
Wong's moving argument is couched in terms of the ethnic *experience*. That is, while arguing that literature should not be judged in

terms of a narrow notion of communal representation, she still ties it to experience.

Although an apparently simplistic statement, in the case of marginal writers, it bears repeating: *literary* productions—including the genres considered creative nonfiction—are conscious (and subconscious) artistic productions that can and do draw on aesthetic tools from any and all cultures in often unexpected ways. In other words, as Frederick Luis Aldama and David Treuer have pointed out, an identity-politics notion of literature as a verifiable representation of a group's—or even an individual's—experience relies on the conflation of literary creation with ethnography and ontology. Moreover, I would argue that critics' conflation of ontology and history with literary productions provides for society at large the intellectual justification to conflate them; students repeatedly evince the understanding that this reading mode is expected of them. An alternative way to approach ethnic texts might be to see what they can teach us *not only* about the communities with which they are associated, *but also* about various other issues of content, form, and context. For instance, *Woman Warrior* and its reception raise intriguing questions for us to consider in theorizing emotion in general, and anger in particular. Why does the text strike critics as angry but not readers? What can the case of *Woman Warrior* show us about the ways anger unfolds *both* in this specific context *and* in general?

This chapter delineates the ways in which Maxine Hong Kingston's *The Woman Warrior* explores the multiple valences of anger in terms of time, both in form (narrative temporality) as well as context (history). As with *Crash*, reading *The Woman Warrior* itself as well as analyzing reactions to the text can help reveal the relations between ideology, cognition, narrative, and anger, particularly in terms of time, both narrative and historical. I argue that the text demonstrates how, in a singular scene of anger, various social contradictions can be embedded in layers of narrative temporality folded into one event. The temporal and emotional layering suggests that emotions are not just tied to *linear* narratives but also more multifarious configurations of emotions and narratives, for more complex processes than an appraisal based on one narrative. For instance, *Woman Warrior*, published during the height of the Asian American and women's movements, productively encapsulates the tension between identity as individual and/or collective as well as concomitantly contending conceptions of anger.

ANGER, TEMPORALITY, AND NARRATIVE

As reviewed in Chapters 1 and 2, emotions are inseparable from narratives. The narratives discussed in the scholarship are usually the linear kind.[4] In *The Rationality of Emotion*, philosopher Ronald de Sousa discusses the relationship between emotions and narratives, or original situations that he calls "paradigm scenarios." According to de Sousa, "the stories characteristic of different emotions are learned by association with 'paradigm scenarios,' [which] . . . are drawn first from our daily life as small children and later reinforced by the stories, art, and culture to which we are exposed" (182). The temporal progressions in such narratives are key to emotions in both the stories themselves and in their repetition over time. Furthermore, the rationality of emotions also has to do with attitudes toward, relationships to, and ideas about the past and the present, inculcated in us by those paradigm scenarios and other cultural narratives.[5] Anger arises when we attribute malicious intent to agents who somehow disrupt the narratives we have written for ourselves, and/or we create narratives for and about those agents we perceive as hostile.

In terms of modern literary genres, the bildungsroman and traditional autobiographies have been responsible for most of the popularizing and normalizing of certain paradigm scenarios, not only in content but also through form. Although distinct genres, bildungsroman and autobiography tend to share a linear pattern in which early life events shape later ones. For example, Franco Moretti notes how what he calls the "classical bildungsroman" shapes modern subjectivity through a renegotiation of age progression. Moretti, focusing specifically on the urban, secular Western European bildungsroman—beginning with Goethe and Austen and ending with Eliot and Flaubert—argues that modernization and modernity rendered youth problematic. By redefining youth, the classical bildungsroman "symbolically legitim[izes]" modernity by bringing together the boundlessness of possibility while imposing limits on that same fearsome boundlessness. That is, while youth represents "boundless dynamism," the bildungsroman portrays youth as bounded by its very nature: "youth 'does not last forever'" (6). In this way, Moretti sees narrative collaborating with history writing to suggest "that reality's meaning is now to be grasped solely in its historico-diachronic dimension" (6); life events only gain meaning by finding a place in a linear historical development. In this sense, we can think of Moretti's classical bildungsroman as participating in the development of modern paradigm scenarios, and perhaps an overall framework for a number of such scenarios via "a life," molding subjectivity as cognition and emotion in both characters and readers.

In contrast to the classical bildungsroman or autobiography, *Woman Warrior* exemplifies what has sometimes been referred to as postmodern autobiography or anti-bildungsroman, which is neither linear nor individual.[6] Rather than giving meaning to events by placing them within a linear chronological progression, the *Woman Warrior* again renegotiates the relationship among past, present, and future as well as among the protagonist/narrator, other characters, and even the author. Sidonie Smith and Julia Watson, in writing about postcolonial novels that draw on autobiographical elements, note that by rejecting individualistic subjectivity, "marginal" texts complicate the subject formation of the classical bildungsroman. They write that postcolonial novels "employ the strategies and complex relationship of narrated and narrating 'I's to embed the individual subject in a collective identity overwritten by the process and legacies of colonization" (363).[7] Such "collective identities" also often include an immanent temporality, in which notions of past, present, and future may exist but are not separate and ordered in a particular way. In general, *Woman Warrior* certainly presents such a communal identity and temporal immanence. As Marilyn Yalom writes, "Kingston has to be found obliquely, in the interstices, *in relation* to the female figures that people her work" (111). While it is important not to ontologize the text (in other words, the literary text is a product of a particular author in a historical moment, not the direct transcription of experience or identity), elements of a collective experience and various formal strategies can complicate a wholly individualistic reading of a text.[8]

But beyond this general notion of collectivity and immanence, how is a moment of anger produced in the text, and how is it read in such a text? If not limited by linearity or individuality, then how is a life portrayed, and how do such representations relate to the subject's states of mind and emotions? We can consider such questions by considering temporality not only in terms of the linearity of the text, but also by the various "folds" or multiple times embedded in a given moment in the text. While most criticism on aggression and violence in *Woman Warrior* focuses on the Fa Mu Lan figure, I would like to examine another key "angry" scene that occurs toward the end of the book, in which the sixth-grade narrator confronts another Chinese American girl in the school lavatory. This confrontation scene from *Woman Warriors* captures some of the possible dynamics of literary representations of anger, including such issues as the dangers of problematic propositions, or group norms, as the basis for emotions (e.g., the sixth-grade narrator); the sources of and reasons for internalization of social norms-as-evaluations; and the histories and structures that produce emotions, beyond a single person's subjectivity, not only in characters but also readers.

This particular scene follows a long passage in which the narrator, after complaining about the loud voices of Chinese immigrant women, tells us, "We American-Chinese girls had to whisper to make ourselves American-feminine. Apparently we whispered even more softly than the Americans" (172). The narrator focuses her rage on this other girl because they are similar—they are both picked last for sports teams and both are too quiet in American school—and because the girl is silent. The narrator corners the girl in the bathroom of their school and verbally and physically attacks the other girl, saying, "You're going to talk. . . . I am going to make you talk, you sissygirl" (175). The narrator tells us, "I looked into her face so I could hate it close-up" (175); "I hated fragility" (176); "I hated her weak neck"; and even "I hated her clothes. . . . I hated pastels" (176–177). The narrator begins to hurt the girl, pinching her cheeks and pulling her hair. When the other girl maintains a stubborn, if teary, silence, the narrator's abuse turns to exhortations, couched in terms of the girl's own interest. She says,

"Say, 'Ow' . . . Just 'Ow.' Say, 'Let go.' Go ahead. Say it. I'll honk you again if you don't say, 'Let me alone.' Say, 'Leave me alone,' and I'll let you go." (178)

"I don't like you. I don't like the weak little toots you make on your flute. Wheeze. Wheeze. I don't like the way you're the last one chosen. I don't like the way you can't make a fist for tetherball. Why don't you make a fist? Come on. Get tough. Come on. Throw fists." (179)

Clearly, the narrator's actual rage is directed towards the injunction of silence imposed on her as a woman and an Asian American. The text demonstrates these complex emotions by folding together several moments in time. She tells us, "That year I was arrogant with talk, not knowing there were going to be high school dances and college seminars to set me back" (173–174). Her future of stumbling to speak is distinct from the present, yet at the same time, the narrator's sixth-grade rage is inseparable from those secondary and post-secondary school trials. So the present, future, and the past (particularly when we consider the various women's stories necessary to the narrator's subjectivity and narrative) are distinguishable but not necessarily separate in linear chronology. During the encounter itself, the narrator loses track of time, feeling as though "we had been in this lavatory forever" (179), and she tells us, "It seemed as if I had spent my life in that basement, doing the worst thing I had yet done to another person" (181). Different moments in time combine to produce the effects of this particular moment, and in this literary text, their mutual relationship informs the emotion produced at any given moment.

The narrator's anger at the other girl's silence, which reflects her own silence, is based on an implicit understanding of their interchangeability in gendered and racialized social formations (e.g. Chinese American girls, Asian American pan-ethnicity, etc.) and a desire *not* to be identified with the silent girl. We can explore the implications of this identification and dis-identification by examining the various narrative levels of the text. If we focus on the experiencing-I, the narrator as young girl, the narrator's anger toward the other girl can be seen as a reflection of her internalization of the patriarchal correlation of silence with weakness, stupidity, and lack of initiative/aggression. As King-Kok Cheung points out, the narrator's anger indicates "her indoctrination [that] silence equals a zero IQ" (88). At the same time, the sixth-grade narrator is angry not only at the other girl but also with herself, even at that moment, while she does not fully understand her own motivations. Her projection onto the other Chinese girl displays her sense of frustration with her own situation, inculcated in her by dominant cultural narratives. Her anger and scorn reflects in part her successful integration into a particular dominant culture and her intuitive sense of the ways in which the system she perpetrates traps herself as well. At this level, we can see that the narrator's anger reflects both her implicit adoption of patriarchal and racist ideologies *and* her inchoate frustration with it. As Anne Cheng writes, this scene is one of "collapsed intersubjective and intrasubjective conflict" (18), in which "the disgust provoked by the other girl bespeaks an anxiety about a racial body that is also her own" (74).[9]

On another level, if we read this passage in terms of the narrating-I, the person telling this story in hindsight (usually associated with the author), the emotional landscape becomes more complicated. What becomes clear at this level is an explicit anger about the situation and what Cheung refers to as the narrator's "intense desire to explode the stock image of the quiet Oriental damsel" (88). At the same time, the narrating-I expresses not only anger but also sadness that such situations exist that produce such anger.[10] This sadness resonates in the statement immediately following the confrontation scene: "The world is sometimes just, and I spent the next eighteen months sick in bed with a mysterious illness" (181–182). The narrator describes the illness as "just" because her younger self's treatment of the other girl was "the worst thing I had yet done to another person."

Moreover, the narrating-I conveys a sense throughout the confrontation that the silent girl is stubbornly defying her attacker; the silent girl's silence is, as Cheung has pointed out, "articulate" (3). Her silence angers the narrator not only because it defies her immediate wishes, but also because it defies two distinct narratives of power. From the vantage point of the sixth-grade narrator, the girl's silence disobeys direct and repeated orders; she offers direct resistance to power. Furthermore, the silent girl complicates notions that resistance itself must be violent and aggressive, that resistance itself must follow hegemonic notions of aggression and anger. In this way, she offers an alternative to dominant models of resistance. We receive this impression from the hindsight of the more mature narrator; as Yuan Shu points out, the sixth-grade narrator tries to resist power by wielding it over another person, thereby reinforcing that power. A good deal of her anger and frustration stems from this impossible and fruitless contradiction.

In fact, we learn that, to a certain extent, the silent girl ends up having been justified. We are told that a year and a half later, when the young experiencing-I narrator returns to school, "She [the silent girl] had not changed. She wore the same clothes, hair cut, and manner as when we were in elementary school, no make-up on the pink and white face, while the other Asian girls were starting to tape their eyelids. She continued to be able to read aloud" (182). While the young narrator embraces dominant notions of aggression and loudness, the silent girl resists hegemonic notions of femininity and political resistance. While the other girls tape their eyelids to make their eyes look bigger, accepting Western notions of femininity and patriarchy, the silent girl continues on a different path (while also distinct from the dominant model, her path would still be culturally and socially constructed and located, and thus is not necessarily "good" in and of itself; nevertheless, she does pose challenges to the narrator and her assumptions). While the narrator is struck down by illness and later struggles to speak in college seminars, the silent girl continues to "read aloud."[11]

On this level, the narrator experiences emotions—guilt, regret, sadness, anger—about having had emotions—anger, hostility, jealousy, sadness—that arose from certain evaluations or propositions (e.g., that silence is bad, regardless of circumstances). In this case, the text presents both the narrator's and the stubborn, silent girl's subjectivities as temporally multilayered, rather than in terms of their underlying evaluations or propositions at one moment. The scene constructs a complex, multilayered, historically constructed ideological and cultural topography. Exploring these contending levels of and reasons for anger—including the array of readers' possible responses—illuminates the range of ways emotion can function.

For instance, we see that emotions do not necessarily correlate one-to-one with cognitive evaluations, although they nevertheless have some propositional and evaluative content. Historical-social forces shape and inform emotions, and emotions respond to, tell us about, and help us to affect the world around us. Furthermore, emotions are not only individual but also communal, shared among members of groups with shared historical experiences *and* between readers, textual voices, and authors; I will return to the latter group below. For groups with shared historical pasts, emotional responses can be shaped not only by past events in an individual's life, but also by *communal* historical pasts. This communal history, which may be as emotionally powerful as the present, works in conjunction with individual histories in a myriad of unpredictable ways. Moreover, emotions are not only based on linear time progression, like paradigm scenarios, in which prior events condition the understanding of later ones. Rather, as Greg Forter suggests in his work on collective historical trauma, *future* events can condition our understanding and experience of past events. In fact, some emotions can only be experienced—and made sense of—through the interaction of multiple moments in time.[12]

Considering the emotions evoked between readers and figures in the text further illuminates the ways that being, thinking, and feeling interact. In Asian American and women's studies, this scene can be said to provide a paradigm scenario or stock narrative that produces certain emotions in certain readers. In countless classrooms over the decades, the scene has been read as a paradigmatic moment of anger against stereotyping and silence. In this sense, a canonical reading of this scene has accompanied the inclusion of *Woman Warrior* in the American canon. But as I have discussed, the axes of identification and the production of emotion in the text are not simple; some things that the narrator thinks and does are justified, while others are portrayed ambivalently or even critically through the textual layering of times, places, and people. Therefore, the kinds of identificatory and/or relational emotions evoked are important in the text's social function. For example, if readers identify with the sixth-grade narrator's explicit evaluative assumptions, such identifications would be problematic, because readers would be sharing her disdain for silent others. If readers share the sixth-grade narrator's *emotions*, however, why do they do so? Readers may identify with the narrator because they condemn the silencing of women, but such identifications run the risk of ignoring that the sixth-grade narrator's conscious reasons for attacking the silent girl are not liberatory but complicit. The text's critique of silencing is tied to an implicit critique of the narrator's embrace of aggression and violence *and* a concomitant notion of Westernized femininity. Built into the form of the text is a warning about an unproblematic emphasis on coming to voice and resistance to silence that does not examine its own assumptions.

In other words, readers may identify with the figures in the text, but this identification is not the only or even the primary reason for its continuing relevance despite the changing theoretical orientations of Asian American and women's studies over the decades. The complexity of *Woman Warrior*'s depiction of emotion helped theorize Asian American and female subjectivity by exploring the ambivalence of historically specific, politically necessary collective identity. This scene from *Woman Warrior* captures the narrator's anger about the ambivalence of collectivity, or at least identification. If the girls are interchangeable, they lose individuality in a world in which they are constantly told to be individuals explicitly (American culture) or implicitly (for example, Brave Orchid, the narrator's mother, makes demands of the narrator to do certain things that require her own agency). But historically, culturally, and politically, the girls also need to identify with one another in order to have a sense of community. Their collectivity arises from a situation in which the choice between the individual and communal is not wholly voluntary. The kinds of identification explored in the text—gendered and racial/cultural—are cultural and familial, and can be a source of strength and communion, but identifications are also imposed on them by others in oppressive and dehumanizing ways. Alternately, these external groupings often demand that the collectives rearticulate themselves and band together even further. Such groupings preexist and shape the individual, even as the groups themselves are in process and can become the foundations for new collectivities.[13] Published in the post–civil rights 1970s, at the height of second-wave feminism, *Woman Warrior* served not necessarily to resolve this individual-community contradiction, but rather to help the Asian American and feminist subjects work through and appropriate that contradiction for their own use, within cultural contexts with contending and contradictory messages about individuality and collectivity (e.g., "us versus them" American individualism that nevertheless demands conformity).

In contrast, if some readers do not so much empathize with the narrator as they *sympathize*, in the sense of feeling things *about* another person's emotions rather than sharing the initial emotion, then do those readers not share the narrating-I narrator's anger about the structures that would produce such a situation in the first place?[14] Say, for example, that an American reader (of any race) does not share the older narrator's anger about the entire situation, but rather only feels sorry for the younger narrator and her inability to understand the situation. I would contend that, given the text's explicit situation in contemporary *American* society, such a reading infantilizes the cultural Other and distances the reader's Self and responsibility from a problematic situation that *includes* the reader. Such distanced sympathy, rather than empathy, characterizes the reading mode of liberal multiculturalism, in which texts like *Woman Warrior*—regardless of their intent—function as Asian American representatives in a buffet-style approach to discrete, exoticized cultures. Such readings produced initial reviews of the text as an "East meets West" tale, as Kingston discusses in her response essay, "Cultural Mis-readings by American Reviewers." In such cases, readers' non-identification results from the assumptions indoctrinated in them by liberal multiculturalism, which blocks off part of the reading of a text by designating a certain reading—distance and difference from the Othered figures in the text—as the politically correct one. As such, readers want to do the right thing, but the separation of otherness hinders readers' potential to identify not only with figures in the text but also with emotions elicited by situations and structures.

This point is tricky but important. On one hand, it is almost impossible to stress too much or too often the importance of avoiding unproblematized, ahistorical appropriation. At the same time, the notion that an outsider can only read the author's work as a privileged recording of experience that cannot be accessed or empathized with by the reader risks blocking off understanding a large part of the potential and actual ways the text functions. In this way, emotions produced in readers are significant and telling. Both Martha Nussbaum and Lisa Zunshine emphasize the importance of identifying with and feeling things about characters and texts. Nussbaum argues that readers' emotions towards characters, authors, and the possibilities in readers' own lives are crucial for developing moral reasoning (238–248). Such emotions are not merely "playacting" but genuine responses that evince and effect cognition. Similarly, Zunshine notes that despite our conscious distinction between fictional and real characters, "*on some level* our evolved cognitive architecture indeed does not fully distinguish between real and fictional people" (*Why We Read Fiction* 19). Identifying with racial, cultural, and gendered "others" in literature—and the structures that implicate all of us— is deeply correlated to our ability to see those others as real human beings. And just as Zunshine notes that reading is "never completely free from the danger of allowing the 'phantoms of imagination' too strong a foothold in our view of our social world" (*Why We Read Fiction* 19), we could say the reverse is also true: our views of the world around us can—and often do—overpower a text, determining and delimiting how it can be read.

THE CONTRADICTIONS OF ANGER

Franco Moretti explores the *social function* of the classical bildungsroman at the advent of modernity to argue that it was not simply "intolerant, normative, monologic," but also enabled subjects to interiorize the contradictions of modernity (10). In fact, Moretti claims that "in our world socialization itself consists first of all in the *interiorization of contradiction.* The next step being not to 'solve' the contradiction, but rather to learn to live with it, and even transform it into a tool for survival" (10). Taking the European bildungsroman as one of the numerous literary traditions and social contexts in which *Woman Warrior* intervenes,[15] we see that while *Woman Warrior* does make a specific, historically located intervention through its form and content, it also serves a social function, similar to Moretti's earlier bildungsroman. *Woman Warrior* enables readers to work through the contradiction between ideologies of individuality and collectivity, at a historical moment when racial/ethnic collectives were invested anew with political and cultural significance. The 1960s and '70s saw social movements foreground the issue of an individual's purposeful choice to make a collective political identification. Seen in this sense, *Woman Warrior* becomes a pivotal text not only in the margins, but also the "mainstream," in which "white" takes on a meaning as historically constructed and particular as "Asian American."

In terms of anger, however, the text does not so much help resolve a contradiction as capture the continuing contradiction between individualized conceptions of anger—including aspects such as villain, victim, cause, and solution—and systemic causes of injustice. We are repeatedly presented with a contradiction between, on the one hand, a notion of anger as individual, discrete, and punctual, and on the other hand, a conception of anger as systemic, collective, and durative. In the section "White Tigers," the fabulous Fa Mu Lan vengeance narrative is contrasted with the confusion and uncertainty of the narrator's contemporary reality. After her training and war victories over the corrupt old emperor, the mythic warrior goes home "where one more battle awaited me" (43). The narrator tells the local baron, "who drafted my brother," stole "my childhood," and robbed the people, that "I want your life in payment for your crimes against the villagers" (43). She exacts penance and contrition; she tells him that she is "a female avenger" and that she wants him to "[r]egret what you've done before I kill you" (43), and then beheads him (44). In this narrative, blame, agency attribution, the solution (i.e., coping potential), and the nature of the harm are all clear. It is also clear that the woman warrior has to rid the populace of the bad rulers, punishing them for their crimes, and then install new ones.

But, as the narrator puts it dryly, "my American life has been such a disappointment" (45). In also dealing with the sufferings of her family in Communist China, however, the chapter reveals that it is less about specific place than a specific *time*. Rather than contrasting "America" to "China" in the myth, the text contrasts the specificity and clarity about the nature of anger in a mythical past with the confusion of systemic and decentralized causes of anger in the late twentieth century. As the narrator says, "I could not figure out what was my village" (45). The culprits include both Chinese and American patriarchy, American racism, and the Chinese communist state. For instance, the narrator recounts her rage at Chinese sayings like "Feeding girls is feeding cowbirds" and "Better to raise geese than girls" (46); she says, "I minded that the emigrant villagers shook their heads at my sister and me. 'One girl—another girl'" (46). When her brother is born, people stop remarking on the girls, but "I learned new grievances":

"Did you roll an egg on *my* face like that when *I* was born?" "Did you have a full-month party for *me*?" "Did you turn on all the lights?" "Did you send *my* picture to Grandmother?" "Why not? Because I'm a girl? Is that why not?" "Why didn't you teach me English?" "You like having me beaten up at school, don't you?" (46)

The narrator's attempts to respond to patriarchy are individual, however, and therefore insufficient. She screams, "I'm not a bad girl" (46), realizing "I might as well have said, 'I'm not a girl'" (46). In other words, there is nothing she as an individual can do to change her inferior status; it is not a question of individual actions to constitute herself as a "good" or "bad" girl. Rather, patriarchy systematically represses *all* women. Against her great uncle who refused to take girls on shopping trips, shouting "No girls!" the narrator says, "At my great-uncle's funeral I secretly tested out feeling glad that he was dead—the six-foot bearish masculinity of him" (47). But her great-uncle's death does not alter the oppressive system that produces her anger. The novel points to the social movements of the '60s, which in other ways did emphasize the importance of systemic change, but also points out the blind spots, the systemic oppressions that still remain: "I went away to college—Berkeley in the sixties—and I studied, and I marched to change the world, but I did not turn into a boy" (47). Implicit in this sentence is the notion that "changing the world" must be collective and systematic, because there is little that certain individuals, in certain kinds of bodies, can do *individually* to change their oppression.

American patriarchy, racism, and capitalism are indicted as oppressive systems that produce anger, but the narrator continues to think in terms of individual victims, villains, and solutions. As the narrator recounts her anger at Chinese patriarchy, she also notes her performance, in the Butlerian sense, of American femininity: "And all the time I was having to turn myself American-feminine, or no dates" (47). Later in the novel, she describes the silence, in an American classroom, of the same Chinese girls who have no trouble shouting and roughhousing in Chinese school. This silence is not only a racial-cultural issue but also one of femininity: "We American-Chinese girls had to whisper to make ourselves American-feminine" (172). In contrast, the Chinese immigrant women, particularly the narrator's mother, Brave Orchid, are too loud for the narrator's comfort. Similarly, the narrator says, "When urban renewal tore down my parents' laundry and paved over our slum for a parking lot, I only made up gun and knife fantasies and did nothing useful" (48). The narrator tells us, "From the fairy tales, I've learned exactly who the enemy are. I easily recognize them—business-suited in their modern American executive guise, each boss two feet taller than I am and impossible to meet eye to eye" (48). Here the sources of injustice include late capitalism, race, gender, and culture, but the narrator's framework for anger does not quite fit the scope of the problem. She learns from myths that she should identify "the enemy" and punish them, but those individuals that she does identify as culprits—her racist bosses—are not the sole villains, whose removal, like that of the baron, will right the wrongs. As with her great uncle, the removal of *individuals* would not necessarily change the *system* of racism. Moreover, race is inextricably tied with patriarchy and capitalist exploitation; the narrator observes, "It's not just the stupid racists that I have to do something about, but the tyrants who for whatever reason can deny my family food and work. My job is my own only land" (49).

The sources of anger, moreover, are not limited to the U.S. The narrator describes the anger and sorrow produced by the news from Communist China, where landowning relatives are being tortured and executed, suffering poverty and disappearing, and appealing to her parents for aid. The narrator recounts, "My parents felt bad whether or not they sent money. Sometimes they got angry at their brothers and sisters for asking" (50). Here, the parents' anger demonstrates frustration, or anger without a clear external agent to blame or coping strategy, as well as outrage at the violation of norms. Yet, the narrator tells us, "it is confusing that my family was not the poor to be championed. They were executed like the barons in the stories, when they were not barons" (51). Despite the atrocities committed on the narrator's family in China, she admits that they were not the poor; like the barons, they were landowners while others were poor. At the same time, her relatives are also not villains, the sole cause of all the injustice in the land whose punishment would alleviate those problems. Again, the narrator attempts to use the model of individual retribution from the myths and finds it insufficient as well as impossible: "To avenge my family, I'd have to storm across China to take back our farm from the Communists; I'd have to rage across the United States to take back the laundry in New York and the one in California. . . . A descendent of eighty pole fighters, I ought to be able to set out confidently, march straight down our street, get going right now" (49). She learns from both the mythic and popular conceptions of anger that the solution is individual vengeance, but she outlines a situation in which that model of anger is inadequate, both for comprehending and fixing the situation.

Ironically, however, the same Fa Mu Lan who supplies the problematic individual model (solutions, culprits, actions/paths, victims) that is insufficient for the frustration and outrage produced by the class exploitation, racism, and patriarchy of the modern world, including both the U.S. and China (and cultures in between and across), also provides some of the passion, energy, and commitment. In other words, although the novel does not really resolve the contradiction between individual and collective conceptions of anger—instead capturing the inadequacy of the individual to grasp the systemic—it does, however, note what is useful and necessary about that individual form of anger: its clarity, passion, and commitment. The novel maintains that at least seeking the causes of anger and maintaining a kernel of anger is still necessary, and was particularly so in the late twentieth century, when systemic exploitation and injustice too often produced a widespread sense of despair and/or cynicism. In fact, *outrage*, a particular kind of anger borne out of a sense of injustice, animates *Woman Warrior*. The novel illustrates the oppression and erasure of individual women—including the No-Name Woman of the first section, Brave Orchid, Moon Orchid, and the narrator herself—by systemic patriarchy (Chinese *and* American), racism, capitalism, and political ideologies, and envisions itself as a retributive act: "The reporting is the vengeance" (53). As the narrator's mother, Brave Orchid, tells her sister Moon Orchid, whose husband left her behind in China while he lived a separate life in the U.S., "He *deserves* your getting angry with him" (125, emphasis added). That is, while Moon Orchid's individual anger at her husband would most likely not change anything, and while she could certainly not feel and exhibit the same kind of anger that Brave Orchid wields, there is also an implicit sense of outrage at a system that normalizes Moon Orchid's abandonment and dependency, and then drives her mad. In fact, even Brave Orchid herself, when faced with the power of patriarchy in the guise of Moon Orchid's husband, fails to be sufficiently angry.

The text depicts the contradiction between systemic forms of injustice and individualized conceptions of solution and blame. In doing so, *Woman Warrior* depicts the historical shift in the kinds of outrage—Who is the target? What is the crime? What is the solution?—from an individualized conception of agency and hierarchical/pyramid model of power, to systemic and decentralized, flexible notions of power. Just as the text explores how multiple layers of narrative time may function in one moment of anger—with simultaneous conflicting emotions based on different layers and worldviews—the text also considers how conceptions of anger can be multiple, ideological, and historical. In particular, *Woman Warrior* theorizes the tensions between contending notions of anger and subjectivity during the Asian American and women's movements, but we can also use this insight to consider how anger may be an arena where differing ideologies and histories collide for people in other situations.

Against liberal multicultural readings of the novel, *Woman Warrior* challenges us to ask, what would it mean to use the analysis of such shared contradictions to find common ground to critique and challenge the divisions and hierarchies that implicate all of us? How would the landscape of literary studies change if we truly interiorized particularity and universality not as a mutually exclusive binary but as a central and productive contradiction, which informs our current existence and can be used to change that existence for something better? To return to Sau-ling Wong's words, all this would involve not reducing "the fullness of life" to "meaner if more manageable proportions," but rather embracing the kinds of complex challenges offered to us by texts, like *Woman Warrior*, that delve into the historical and ideological complexities of different kinds of anger.

CHAPTER 5

ANGER AND SPACE IN DANGAREMBGA'S
NERVOUS CONDITIONS AND *THE BOOK OF NOT*

This perpetual rage was unbearable for me. I considered myself a
moral person. In fact, as a moral woman I did not intend to harbour
such uncharitable, above all, angry, emotions.
TAMBU, *THE BOOK OF NOT*

WHILE TSITSI DANGAREMBGA'S acclaimed first novel, *Nervous Conditions*, is characterized by what we might think of as "large anger," the sequel, *The Book of Not*, consists of what we might dub "small angers." That is, while the anger experienced and expressed by the women in *Nervous Conditions*—particularly Nyasha, but also Lucia, Maiguru, and Mainini—is grand, explosive, and raging at structures, *The Book of Not* shows the narrator, Tambudzai, experiencing minor rages, at offenses over apparently trivial things. These apparently quotidian outrages, however, are components of larger systems of injustice. The terms of size—large, small—also refer to how the novels explore how *spaces* are generated by and generate ideological formations and implications of emotions, or "technologies of affect" that write the body and subjectivity, particularly women's bodies. *Nervous Conditions* opens with Tambu acknowledging but refusing to apologize for her lack of proper sorrow for her brother's death, her "lack of feeling" (1). We are then introduced to the story of Tambu and her female relatives in terms of space: "My story is . . . about my escape and Lucia's; about my mother's and Maiguru's entrapment; and about Nyasha's rebellion—Nyasha, far-minded and isolated" (1). The spatial terms "escape," "entrapment," "far," and "isolated" indicate the ways in which the production of space also produces certain behaviors, logics, and subjectivities as acceptable or aberrant.

Whereas the previous chapter examined how anger and emotions can be linked to time—historical time and narrative time—this chapter looks at how space can likewise be important to the production and perception of anger. In *Nervous Conditions* and *The Book of Not*, spaces such as bathrooms, kitchens and dining halls, and other private spaces are charged battlegrounds, particularly for women, sparking anger that arises from their inhabiting of clashing ideologies and structures. The dynamics are not as simple as colonizer vs. colonized; although elements of Shona culture, Christianity, and westernization come into the mix, modernity and tradition get deployed in all sorts of ways in very contemporary struggles, sometimes over clear issues of class, race, and social status, but sometimes over harder-to-define, overdetermined, very intimate power struggles. Thus, without losing their particularity, domestic spaces are conditioned by national and international political struggles. *The Book of Not* ends by taking these private dynamics into the ostensibly public space of the commercial office, where a Zimbabwean nationalism intertwines with neocolonialism and globalization in a reconfigured spatial regime.

Nervous Conditions takes place in the 1960s, when the white minority rules Rhodesia and the state maintains a neocolonial relationship to England; *The Book of Not* picks up where *Nervous Conditions* leaves off, as the guerilla war against the white rulers intensifies, eventually resulting in the end of apartheid and the declaration of an independent, democratic Zimbabwe in 1980. Neocolonialism, race, economic and cultural globalization, religion and notions of morality (tied to race and class), contending definitions of "woman," and various forms of patriarchy (Shona, Christian, popular, and "modern") all intermingle and often clash, not just influencing but often actually *constituting* the spaces that characters inhabit, which inform the characters' emotions, which in turn shape their subjectivities—not in a linear manner, but in an endless loop of reiteration, reinforcement, and sometimes, as evidenced in anger, conflict. The historical contradictions crammed into ideologically conditioned spaces find expression in the anger of the women caught within those contradictions and spaces.

In this chapter, I examine how such productions and regulations of the self through spaces yield what we might think of as large anger in *Nervous Conditions* and small anger in *The Book of Not*. Audiences find *Nervous Conditions* more satisfying than *The Book of Not* because of the outsized, dramatic nature of the first novel's scenes

of anger, particularly Nyasha's excoriations of patriarchy and colonialism; *Nervous Conditions* gives us satisfying scenes of revenge
and passages of ideological maturity. In contrast, *The Book of Not* is
about everyday, minor outrages that implicate larger systems of oppression, although the narrator rarely explicitly indicts these structures. These quotidian conflicts, however, are just as insightful about
anger emerging from the ideological conflicts embedded in spaces.[1]

THE SPACE(S) OF THE MISSION

Along with other scholars who argue for the importance of space in
considering cognition and narrative, David Herman contends that in
narrative domains, space is as crucial as time (*Story* 264).[2] Narratives
encode spatial relations among participants, actions, objects, and
places (*Story* 269), and in doing so, "spatial reference helps *constitute*
narrative domains" (*Story* 285). That is, space is not just backdrop,
setting, or peripheral atmosphere; it is integral to the narrative in a
variety of ways. Therefore, "narrative entails a process of cognitive
mapping that assigns referents not merely a temporal but a *spatio-
temporal* position in the storyworld" (*Story* 297). Postcolonial, ethnic,
and feminist texts in particular interrogate the ideological construction of racialized, gendered, and variously politicized spaces, such as
the colonial schoolroom, the plantation, and the domestic sphere.
Such spaces often function not only to regulate subjects but also to
create ideologically proper subjects.

Biman Basu astutely analyzes how *Nervous Conditions* "maps the
institutional spaces" that not only discipline but in fact create subjects through the body (8). Basu argues that "Decolonised space . . .
is a corporalized space in which the technologies of discipline pro-
liferate and attach themselves to the body" (11). Rather than controlling through a "transformation of consciousness," which implies
an already-existing subjectivity, "[d]isciplinary mechanisms" of institutional spaces "are aimed at bodies, and discipline is, we might
say, epidermalized. In the process, bodies are trained, bodily functions regulated, gestures are acquired, postures cultivated, styles
are adopted, and attitudes assumed" (11). In producing the governed
subjects, power thus "operates as a positivity": "[Power] is not limited negatively to objectification but positively to subjectification:
through technologies of self, it produces subjects" (10).[3] The successfully regulated subjects, those "Good Africans" (18), are chosen for an

advancement that is also a containment (18). In this "epidermaliza-
tion of discipline," "the body is caught in a continual process of encirclement, a process in which a 'technology of reform' impinges directly on the body" (19).

The mission, where Babamukuru is the headmaster of the school,
is an exemplary space of constitution-through-regulation of the body.
For Tambu, the mission as "intermediate space, marking a stage in
the process of discipline, is a space of seduction" (Basu 18). Tambu
sees her arrival at the mission as "the period of my reincarnation"
(Nervous 92). While, as Basu notes, she puts her transformation in
terms of consciousness—"I expected this era to be significantly profound and broadening in terms of adding wisdom to my nature"
(Nervous 92)—in fact the manifestations of her ideological condi-
tioning are as much, if not more so, in terms of the body and materiality. Now that she is "freed from the constraints of the necessary
and the squalid that defined and delimited our activity at home," she
proclaims,

> I was clean now, not only on special occasions but every day of the
> week. I was meeting, outside myself, many things that I had thought
> about ambiguously; things that I had always known existed in other
> worlds although the knowledge was vague; things that had made my
> mother wonder whether I was quite myself, or whether I was carrying
> some other presence in me. (Nervous 93)

In the regulatory space of the mission, Tambu learns that cleanliness
is tied to class and colonialism. She thinks in terms of space; she is
"meeting" ideas, experiences, and values that are "outside" her, alien
concepts from "other worlds." Space and temporality are interactive
axes in her ideological reformation; in becoming the proper colonial
female subject, the subject of the mission becomes retroactively more
herself than her previous self of the homestead. In desiring to be the
"good" colonized, fitting into the mission's model, her desire goes
backward in time and replaces her own "homestead" self with her
current self, making Tambu of the mission more real than Tambu
of the homestead. This trope of "possession" of her past homestead
body by her future mission self is also that of space; her future self
invades and replaces the flawed past self in the perceived boundaries
of Tambu's subjectivity. Moreover, Tambu's desire to go to the mission precedes her actual arrival there; her entire existence prior to

her brother's death is characterized by a longing to become the subject that her brother, Nhamo, is slated to be. Her brother's death and
her consequent taking in by Babamukuru constitutes, for Tambu, the
culmination of a dream. While she puts her explicit program of intellectual and moral improvement—what Basu calls "transcenden-
tal consciousness"—in terms of teleological time, the ideological dynamics are material, spatialized, and multidirectionally temporal.

But despite her desire to simply shed her old self, Tambu's process of education is a gradual and fitful one. Arriving at the mission, Tambu also says, "Babamukuru and Maiguru would now formally welcome me into their home; formally disinter me, my mind
and my body, from the village" (*Nervous* 85). The term "disinter" suggests that her "new" mission self is actually her freed, "disinterred,"
and true self. But immediately thereafter, she experiences confusion
about where to sit in her uncle and aunt's living room:

> It was a complex problem. Babamukuru was sitting in his armchair,
> the one that faced the fireplace, while Maiguru sat at one end of the
> sofa. There was room on the sofa between Maiguru and Babamu-
> kuru's chair, as well as an unoccupied armchair beside Babamukuru,
> but I could not take those seats since it would not do to sit so disre-
> spectfully close to my uncle. There was no alternative but to sit in
> the only other vacant seat in the room, an armchair across from both
> Baba and Maiguru which placed the three of us as far away from each
> other as was possible in that room. Having sat down in that chair I
> began to wonder whether it would have been more appropriate in this
> English place to sit closer to my uncle and aunt. (*Nervous* 86)

Tambu's agonizing indicates her instinctive sense of the cultural and
ideological dimensions of space, including considerations of distance
and relationality. She cannot sit too close to Babamukuru, but then
realizes that perhaps her assessment of proximity is incorrect, as the
mission is "an English place."

Her fitful negotiations also apply to bodily functions, such as men-
struation. Initially using cloth napkins that her mother gives her,
Tambu feels ashamed "washing those rags in Maiguru's white bathroom" and "making a mess in the toilet bowl before I flushed it away"
(*Nervous* 95). Nyasha instructs her on how to use tampons, which
although not for "nice girls" nevertheless trains the young colonial
woman to be clean and cosmopolitan. That is, despite the Christian

and bourgeois standards that she is imbibing, the control of women's bodies and related excreta, which are marked as materially and morally filthy, takes precedence. Tambu's training thus demonstrates how "the body is the prioritized site for the implantation, for the attachment of technologies of discipline," which occurs "almost imperceptibly with a surreptitious complicity" (Basu 20). In the instance of the tampons, even Nyasha is complicit. In such ideologically overdetermined spaces, both the mind and the body are regulated and disciplined. Yet because these spaces are also contradictory, the subjects (particularly the women) are often placed in untenable positions with conflicting goals, values, and roles.

NYASHA'S ANGER

In *Nervous Conditions*, the most explosive, disturbing, and unprecedented anger is that of Nyasha, directed against her father, in the bedroom, dining room, and bathroom. Each of these spaces is marked by certain codes and scripts that become violently disrupted by Nyasha's angry exposure of and resistance to the ideological systems. The most violent angry confrontation takes place in the bedroom, as Nyasha and her father struggle for control of her budding sexuality. After a dance, when Nyasha stays out a few minutes later than Tambu and Chido, learning dance steps from a white boy, her father rebukes her for failing to "behave like a young woman from a decent home" (113). Nyasha reassures her father, "'You know me,' she told him, but of course she was mistaken. 'You've taught me how I should behave. I don't worry about what people think so there's no need for you to'" (114). That is, she believes that she and her father share the same group norms of trust based on shared values, but she has woefully misread the situation. When her father tells her she is behaving like a whore, Nyasha responds, "'Now why . . . should I worry about what people say when my own father calls me a whore?'" (114), and her father strikes her:

> His whole weight was behind the blow he dealt Nyasha's face. "Never," he hissed. "Never," he repeated, striking her other cheek with the back of his hand, "speak to me like that."
> Nyasha fell on to the bed, her miniscule skirt riding up her bottom. Babamukuru stood over her, distending his nostrils to take in enough air.

"Today I am going to teach you a lesson," he told her. "How can you go about disgracing me? Me! Like that! No, you cannot do it. I am respected at this mission. I cannot have a daughter who behaves like a whore."

Nyasha was capable of pointing out that by his own definition that was exactly what he had, but she did not. "Don't hit me, Daddy," she said backing away from him. "I wasn't doing anything wrong. Don't hit me" . . .

"You must learn to be obedient," Babamukuru told Nyasha and struck her again.

"I told you not to hit me," said Nyasha, punching him in the eye.

Babamukuru bellowed and snorted that if Nyasha was going to behave like a man, then by his mother who was at rest in her grave he would fight her like one. They went down onto the floor, Babamukuru alternately punching Nyasha's head and banging it against the floor, screaming or trying to scream but only squeaking, because his throat had seized up with fury, that he would kill her with his bare hands; Nyasha, screaming and wriggling and doing what damage she could. (115)

Father and daughter's angers reveal contending ideological value systems. As Hershini Bhana points out, at the colonial mission with black and white children, Babamukuru's "reputation rests on his ability to both prevent and assuage white fears of 'inter-racial' sexual interactions" (21). The virulence of his response to her behavior arises not only from her disobedience but also from his perception—not entirely false—that any aberration, however minor, can threaten the entire edifice on which his privilege rests, or what Bhana describes as "his delicate negotiations around the over-determined field of black/ white relations, sexual and otherwise" (21). That is, he is not just disciplining Nyasha as an individual; he also maintains the colonial system in which he plays the role of a kind of middle manager of morality.

But his reaction is not limited to assuaging whites' fears of miscegenation; he also has imbibed and enacts Christian patriarchy. As anthropologist Carolyn Shaw notes, among the Shona, "fathers have little direct interaction with their daughters. Conventionally, sexual education of daughters is entrusted not to fathers or to mothers, but to aunts and to grandmothers" (10). We certainly see the difference between the moral surveillance of Babamukuru and Tambu's father (for which Tambu actually admires her uncle), and Babamukuru's family's awkward attempts to negotiate between the Shona beliefs they still hold to some extent and the Christianity of Babamukuru, their benefactor. Thus, Shaw writes that Babamukuru's "surveillance of Nyasha's sexuality derives in large part from the Christianity that he learned at the mission, but also is motivated by his need to protect and promote his position in the colonial system" (10).

Shaw also notes that some of the complex ideological dynamics of Babamukuru's control originates in the new spaces created by colonialism: "In the colonial-style residence where fathers and daughters live under the same roof, new modes of interaction came into being, but not without conflict from the traces of earlier patterns" (10). While at the homestead, sleeping arrangements are more spread out and flexible, at the mission, the bedroom becomes a strictly demarcated space of privacy, sexuality, the body, and femininity. When her uncle first comes charging into Tambu and Nyasha's bedroom, "so agitated that he did not knock but walked straight in," Tambu observes, "I was glad that I was under the covers in my pyjamas instead of still undressing" (112). The scene's overtones of incest and rape further perturb the space, with Nyasha's short skirt exposing her bottom when her father knocks her onto the bed, and then father and daughter rolling around on the floor, hitting and screaming. The fact that Babamukuru pursues his daughter into the bedroom, rather than calling her into the living room, the public space of domestic jurisprudence, indicates the extent of his anger. He is willing to violate the sanctified, separate space of strict sexual separation in order to prevent Nyasha, in violating racial-sexual rules, from irreparably damaging the boundaries and integrity of those very spaces.

For Babamukuru, Nyasha has clearly violated a set of rules that, in terms of colonialism/race, patriarchy, and Christianity, are hierarchical. But Nyasha's anger is also born out of a sense of betrayal of norms. Until her father hits her, Nyasha is still under the mistaken belief that her father's ideals of reason and humanism are real. Despite their clashes in the past, she demonstrates her still-naïve faith in reason by responding to his arguments with counterarguments. She tells him honestly, "I was only talking. And dancing" (113), and she reminds him that she has learned his values and should be trusted. Her anger is partly in realizing that the "group norm" of reason and fairness—which, whatever she may have said before, she demonstrates here that she believes she shares with her father—has been violated. As the novel continues, Nyasha's increasing aware-

ness that the structures and processes of power conflict with the pur-
ported values of the colonial world of the mission is what drives her
dramatic psychological decline. The irony of this episode is that actual sex is not really even a possibility; their conflict is not about
sex—or not only about sex—but rather about power.

Nyasha and Babamukuru's conflict also invades the space of the
dining room and the bathroom. The dining room is a symbol of class
privilege, both in the food consumed as well as in the very fact of its
existence; one must be rich and westernized to have a dining room
with a table and all its accoutrements. So, for instance, when Tambu
arrives at the mission, her first experience of a dinner, with its ritu-
als, prerequisite of cleanliness, abundance of food, fork and knife, and
family drama, is a confusing ordeal at which "many things . . . were
embarrassing" (82). Moreover, the dining room is a space of patriarchy (Babamukuru is served first) and sexual regulation (Babamukuru
confiscates his daughter's copy of *Lady Chatterley's Lover*). Nyasha
and Babamukuru's increasingly heated conflict about what and how
much Nyasha eats results in Nyasha becoming bulimic. In defying
her father and regurgitating her food, Nyasha upends the proper order—mentally and bodily—prescribed by these spaces of consump-
tion and evacuation.

Nyasha understands that their conflict about food is really about
morality; she tells Tambu, "It's more than that really, more than
just food. That's how it comes out, but really it's all the things about
boys and men and being decent and indecent and good and bad" (190).
But again, the problem is that Nyasha's conscious frame of reference
and what she believes should constitute shared values with her and
her father—reason, fairness, empathy—are belied by the force of the
power structure. She can see his point of view, so she thinks he ought
to see hers:

> Sometimes I look at things from his point of view, you know what I
> mean, traditions and expectations and authority, that sort of thing,
> and I can see what he means and I try to be considerate and patient
> and obedient, really I do. But then I start thinking that he ought to
> look at things from my point of view and be considerate and patient
> with me, so I start fighting back and off we go again. (190)

Her rage stems from the discrepancy between what he "ought" to
do—"look at things from [Nyasha's] point of view"—and his actual
behavior, which is not just licensed but necessitated by the ideologi-

cal systems in which they live. Nyasha's nervous breakdown is a result of this untenable position. Of all the fictional characters in all
the texts that I examine in *On Anger*, Nyasha perhaps best understands that her anger is systemic, historical, and ideological, but even
she cannot escape the hegemonic construction of anger as individual and pathological. Even as she rages against the histories and systems of capitalism, colonialism, and patriarchy, at moments she still
thinks of her father, "He's right, right to dislike me. It's not his fault,
it's me. But *I can't help it.* Really, *I can't.* He makes me so angry. I
can't shut up when he puts on his God act. *I'm just not made that
way*" (190, emphasis added). While on one hand, she recognizes that
it is her father's actions that cause her anger—"He makes me so angry"—on the other hand, she characterizes her anger as an innate pathology and/or personal failing.

Even her bulimia, the reasons for which she is not aware—"Don't
ask me why. I don't know" (190)—is a form of anger turned inwards,
taken out on the body that is the site of ideological struggle. Eating
disorders such as bulimia and anorexia are forms of attempting to exert control and/or punishment on oneself when the world seems out
of control, and its sufferers are usually high-achieving women who
believe they should be perfect. Here, while Nyasha is aware of the
structural oppressions, she is still trapped in those systems. As Basu
puts it, consciousness of a system is not enough; within this context
of an overdetermined mix of patriarchy, Christianity, colonialism,
and capitalism, Nyasha's body is still the site of ideological struggle, and her anger marks her as a pathological, immoral, disobedient,
flawed subject.[4] Basu writes, "Nyasha's resistance is directed not at
the individual agent ("it's not his fault"), but at a structure of relations" (14). For instance, while Nyasha is aware of her isolation as a
transnational intellectual, that consciousness alone is not sufficient.
Because she is implicated in discursive, material, political systems of
power, her situation cannot be truly remedied unless the patriarchal,
colonial/neocolonial, cultural imperialisms, and class hierarchies are
also undone. Despite Nyasha's consciousness, she is still trapped in
her body, constructed by the technologies of the body and the self
(Basu 10, 14). This is the "nervous condition" of the colonized, but
particularly the colonized woman, for whom the site of regulation is
intimately tied to space and the body.

As Lisa Eck writes, *Nervous Conditions* is "chronologically conflicted about the developmental assumptions imbedded in this im-

ported form—the European novel of education, or, more loosely, the novel of 'formation'" (580). Despite her beliefs, Tambu's development is not one of edification and improvement but rather one of ideological subject formation through the body, in ideologically overdetermined and multiply determinant spaces. Eck writes that "contrary to the linear logic of a routine biography," the novel shows how a palimpsest of times (Christian, precolonial, colonial, postcolonial) existed in an "unmapped, often uncertain present" (580). A number of historical contradictions not only inform but also constitute the spaces of the characters and variously inform and form their emotions. Nyasha's explosive anger and other emotions demonstrate conflicts between Shona, Christian, colonial, neocolonial, white Rhodesian, and revolutionary ideologies and systems. The conflicting systems create spaces and bodies that are likewise conflicted, even in their angers finding what Sartre called the "nervous condition" of the colonized.

LUCIA, MAIGURU, AND MAININI'S ANGERS

Just as Nyasha's anger is staged in overdetermined spaces, *Nervous Conditions* also explores the anger of Tambu's mother, Mainini, as well as of her aunts: Lucia, Mainini's sister; and Maiguru, Babamukuru's wife and Nyasha's mother. In their own particular ways, these women become angry at various systems and structures, although not necessarily with the same level of conscious political analysis as Nyasha. Instead, the adult narrator Tambu explicates the situations, sometimes reflecting on the implications of the different women's actions. While Lucia and Mainini were both raised poor, Lucia is "strong" and "bold" and has an "unfettered" "spirit," while Mainini is "dispirited" and sometimes listless (127). In contrast, Maiguru has been educated in England and is far richer (although not wealthy by colonizers' standards) than her husband's relatives. The adult narrator Tambu nevertheless argues that the women's only real way out of these various structures of patriarchy, colonialism, and class is by coming together and challenging and crossing borders in ways that those very spaces prohibit.

Lucia's outburst occurs when the family holds a *dare*, or a family trial, concerning the complicated situation that has arisen from Lucia becoming pregnant by Takesure, a cousin of Babamukuru; Lucia's claim that Tambu's father is the actual father; and by both Lucia and Takesure's refusals to leave the homestead. The *dare* consists "of the patriarchy—the three brothers, who were Babamukuru, my father and Babamunini Thomas, and their sister—and the male accused [Takesure]" (136). Excluded from the deliberations, the women revolt. The narrator tells us, "We, the women and children, were in the kitchen when the *dare* began. We all knew what was going on and my mother and the *maininis* [aunts] threatened to become quite violent in their opposition to the system" (137). The kitchen, one classic chronotope of domestic narratives,[5] is the space where the women collectively build and articulate their anger: "The mutterings and malcontent carried on, my mother and aunts fanning each other's tempers until Lucia, who enjoyed battle and liked to be ferocious at it, was seething with anger" (137). The women are enraged that Lucia is excluded when it is her fate being decided, and Lucia particularly is angered that "they are . . . telling lies about" her (137). Egged on by the other women (except Maiguru, as I will discuss below), Lucia strides into the *dare* and, grabbing Takesure firmly by one ear, berates him and boldly presents her side of the story to the patriarchy, much to the amusement of the entire family as well as the reader (143–144). The ridiculous descends into surreal when Babamukuru decides that the family's problems lie in Tambu's parents not being "married in church before God" (147), and thereupon arranges their wedding. Although more comic relief than high drama, Lucia and the women's anger stages a seeming revolt against the patriarchal system by taking the kitchen into the space of the *dare*.

But Lucia and the aunts' failure to recruit to their side the educated, upper-class, mission-dwelling Maiguru provides the adult narrator an opportunity to reflect on the events. Maiguru, although she does not say so in order to avoid further conflict, thinks "Lucia ought to suffer the consequences of her fecund appetites" and refuses to become involved (138). The other women are angered by Maiguru's refusal to join with them, but as the narrator tells us, the politics of these women are also hampered by a lack of vision beyond current boundaries:

What was needed in that kitchen was a combination of Maiguru's detachment and Lucia's direction. Everybody needed to broaden out a little, to stop and consider the alternatives, but the matter was too intimate. It stung too saltily, too sharply and agonizingly the sensitive images the women had of themselves, images that were really no more than reflections. But the women had been taught to recognise these reflections as self and it was frightening now to even begin to think that, the very facts which set them apart as a group, as women, as a certain kind of person, were only myths; frightening to acknowledge that generations of threat and assault and neglect had battered these myths into the extreme, dividing reality they faced, of the Maigurus or the Lucias. So instead of a broadening of both positions, instead of an encompassing expansion and a growth, the fear made it necessary to tighten up. Each retreated more resolutely into their roles, pretending while they did that actually they were advancing, had in fact initiated an offensive, when really, for each one of them, it was a last solitary, hopeless defence of the security of their illusions. (138)

Here, the division between individuality and collectivity is put into spatial and bodily terms. On one hand is the self, "retreat[ing]": the issue is "too intimate" and troubles "the images the women had of themselves," eliciting individual sensations: stinging, "salti[ness]," and sharpness. The women see their "reflections" as their selves; in Lacanian terms, a spatial error, mistaking a visual image for one's own self. Because it is "frightening" to acknowledge that the very "myths" that construct their identities—as well as their collectivity as women—are also what serve to control them, they "tighten up," "retreat," and put up a "solitary, hopeless defense." The forces of patriarchy, class, and colonialism become "extreme, dividing realit[ies]" between the moral, upper-class, educated Maiguru and the sexually active, poor, illiterate Lucia, physically and politically separating them. On the other hand, the narrator notes, what is needed is "broadening" and "encompassing expansion and a growth." But rather than risk losing the roles that, to again draw on Basu, lead to the women's positive subjective formation as well as their negative prohibition and control, they turn on one another and defend "their illusions" even more resolutely and systematically than they criticize the *dare*. The costs that Nyasha pays for her attempts to repudiate those roles and systems testifies to the power of those prohibitions against crossing ideological and literal spaces.

Maiguru's anger also draws attention to contradictions within spaces, and her anger actually leads her to leave—albeit temporarily—the space of the mission house. The expression of her anger may be satisfying for the reader in the short term, but it also fails to effect

any real change. Later in the novel, after Babamukuru has enabled
Lucia's education as well, Maiguru revolts. Her anger at Babamukuru
stems from conflict over the articulation of whose house the mission
actually is. When Maiguru objects to the harshness of Tambu's punishment for refusing to attend her parents' wedding, Babamukuru replies that as Tambu's father's brother, "I have the right to discipline
her. It is my duty" (172). Maiguru responds by venting all her accu-
mulated grievances, starting with "Yes, she is your brother's child . . .
but when it comes to taking my money so that you can feed her and
her father and your whole family . . . that's when they are my relatives too" (172). She also criticizes the "ridiculous wedding" to which
Babamukuru subjects Tambu's unwilling parents, ostensibly out of
Christian morality, but actually out of the desire to exercise power
while also avoiding being perceived by whites as condoning immoral-
ity. She asserts that while she also earns money to support the house-
hold, "I am tired of my house being a hotel for your family. I am tired
of being a housekeeper for them" (172). But she is most angry about
the indignity of being relegated to the sidelines in her own domestic
realm by Lucia: "And now even Lucia can walk in here and tell me
that the things she discusses with you, here in my home, are none of
my business" (172). The irony of Maiguru's anger at patriarchy being
directed at Lucia as much as at her husband is not lost on Nyasha.

Maiguru concludes, "I am sick of it. . . . Let me tell you, I have had
enough!" and the next morning, to the incredulity of all, she leaves
by bus. Tambu reflects "that there was something large and determined about Maiguru in the way that she made up her mind and,
making no fuss, carried out her plan" (173), and even Nyasha is im-
pressed. But ultimately Maiguru returns, "since her investment, in
the form of her husband and two children, was all at the mission"
(174). Even her choice of place to seek refuge, her brother's house, still
does not disturb patriarchy; as Nyasha puts it, "She always runs to
men . . . There's no hope" (175). Although Maiguru actually leaves
the space of the house, we see that it is not really the space itself
that creates her anger. Rather, the "norms" that she is supposed to
adhere to include the requirements of the liberal subject (educated,
modern, independently moral); patriarchies (of the colonizer and of
the colonized); class; nation; and Christianity. In other words, as Simone de Beauvoir wrote of women, Maiguru is in a contradictory position, supposed to be both agent and object, superior and servant, in a
variety of sometimes coinciding but more often conflicting systems.

The untenable contradictions of her position trigger her anger, but the lack of alternatives—unless she is willing to form alliances and change systems—leads her back to where she started. The bitterness and anger of Mainini, Tambu's mother, is neither as attractive as Nyasha's martyrdom nor as satisfying as Lucia and Maiguru's systemically minor but still noteworthy mutinies. Nevertheless, Mainini, a character who is generally not a favorite among readers and critics, is often correct in her implicit and emotional assessments of structures of power, partly because she inhabits the most abject space in the novel: the homestead with its latrine of contention. For instance, hearing about Nyasha's breakdown, she says, "It's the Englishness . . . It'll kill them all if they aren't careful" (202), and she warns her daughter, "The problem is the Englishness, so you just be careful!" (203). Given Tambu's thoughts and actions, Mainini's warnings are ineffectual and too late. Mainini's anger arises from her awareness of the systems in which she is ranked lowest and the physical spaces that make it impossible for her to suppress her abjection.

One of the places where Mainini's anger manifests is the latrine. Coming to visit the homestead, Tambu is disgusted by the state of the outhouse, particularly in contrast to the tightly controlled cleanliness of the mission. It had been built with Babamukuru's guidance and money "downwind from the huts," and Tambu used to clean it daily, but "now faeces and urine contaminated every surface, so that it was impossible to find a place to put your feet" and "glistening pale maggots burrowed fatly into the faeces" (123). Tambu chastises her mother, "Why don't you clean the toilet anymore?" Tambu is "annoyed with her for always reminding me, in the way that she was so thoroughly beaten and without self-respect, that escape was a burning necessity" (123). "The most disheartening thing," Tambu adds, is "that it did not have to look like that" (123). Tambu has successfully incorporated the colonial, bourgeois notion that dirtiness and slovenliness are not just issues of hygiene but moral failings, and that therefore her family is lazy, "beaten," "without self-respect," and therefore less than human. Her own goal, then, is to strive to become one of the elect, morally, financially, and hygienically.

Mainini, however, recognizes Tambu's incorporation into this alternative system, and she lashes out at Maiguru, the representative of privilege who is nevertheless also a mother and wife, closest to Mainini structurally. Mainini says to Tambu: "You think your mother is so stupid she won't see Maiguru has turned you against me with her money and her white ways? You think I am dirt now, me, your mother. Just the other day you told me that my toilet is dirty. 'It disgusts me,' that's what you said" (140). While Mainini attributes Tambu's ostensible transformation to Maiguru's "money," "white ways," and education, the truth is actually the other way around; we could say that money and education, as indicators of class, and the "white ways" of colonialism have formed both Maiguru and, in truth, Tambu, even before she left the homestead. But Mainini is correct that in this system, not only is Mainini's toilet dirty, she herself is considered "dirt." In contrast, she tells Tambu, "You want to eat the words that come out of [Maiguru's] mouth" (140). Mainini continues, "But me, I'm not educated, am I? I'm just poor and ignorant, so you want me to keep quiet, you say I mustn't talk. Ehe! I am poor and ignorant, that's me, but I have a mouth and it will keep on talking, it won't keep quiet" (140). Mainini senses that she is the "poor," "ignorant," female subaltern who should not speak, and while she does not come to structural and historical political analyses like Nyasha, she nevertheless revolts emotionally at her dehumanization. Mainini's anger emerges in relation to the space of the toilet, one of the most—if not *the* most—tightly regulated boundaries between public and private, clean and dirty, moral and immoral. Implicitly contrasted to the latrine are Maiguru's spotless bathrooms (the sites of Nyasha's secret bulimic vomiting), which stand as an alternative space of judgment. Mainini's explosive anger thus indicates the multiple ideologies and histories embedded in the space of the latrine.

Although the ending of *Nervous Conditions* is often read as optimistic, *The Book of Not* demonstrates that Tambu's immediate future is anything but enlightened. The Tambu character's experiences in both novels consist primarily of getting lost in moral and political mazes that she does not know how to map, and the adult narrator explicitly puts this in spatial terms:

> If I had been more independent in my thinking then, I could have thought the matter through to a conclusion. But in those days it was easy for me to leave tangled thoughts knotted, their loose ends hanging. I didn't want to explore the treacherous mazes that such thoughts led into. I didn't want to reach the end of those mazes, because there, I knew, I would find myself and I was afraid I would not recognize myself after having taken so many confusing directions. I was beginning to suspect that I was not the person I was expected to

be, and took it as evidence that somewhere I had taken a wrong turning. So to put myself back on the right path I took refuge in the image
of the grateful poor female relative. That made everything a lot easier. It mapped clearly the ways I could or could not go, and by keep-
ing within those boundaries I was able to avoid the mazes of self-
confrontation. (*Nervous* 116)

In other words, not only are actual spaces ideologically overdetermined, but the regulatory functions of those spaces shape how we
think about ourselves, and our narratives about ourselves, into spatial terms. Tambu fears "treacherous mazes" and "confusing directions," like the ones Nyasha has taken on, because the cost is so
great; Tambu prefers "the right path" that is "mapped clearly" and
"within boundaries." Thus, while *Nervous Conditions* is characterized by outsized anger that targets, more or less successfully, systems of power, explicated by either the adult narrator or Nyasha, *The
Book of Not* is much less dramatic and explicit, perhaps helping to
explain both the success of the first novel and the positive but lack-
luster reception to the second. The sequel's point of view stays primarily within the maze, without a bird's-eye view, as Tambu stum-
bles her way through it, all the while believing she is staying on "the
right path."

TAMBU'S ANGER

While Nyasha explicitly and Lucia, Maiguru, and Mainini implicitly
articulate the systemic causes of their rage in *Nervous Conditions*, in
The Book of Not, we only get indirectly, through the adult narrator's
ironic descriptions of the younger Tambu's thoughts and experiences,
the structural nature of a thousand small banalities; as Basu writes,
"The exercise of disciplinary power must be apprehended not [only]
at the level of the subject endowed with consciousness but [also] in
the space of the banal" (11). *The Book of Not* picks up where *Nervous Conditions* leaves off, with Tambu one of the few African students chosen to attend the Young Ladies' College of the Sacred Heart.
At the beginning of the novel, she sees herself as "a teenager, an in-
telligent one," "being transformed into a young woman with a future" (11). She is, as she puts it, "most interested in . . . myself and
what I would become" (11). But despite her self-involvement and plans
for individual advancement—dressed up as familial responsibility

and collective uplift—she cannot truly escape the colonial drama of which she is a part. Through the small outrages of the novel, in the spaces of the Sacred Heart convent, runs the image of the leg of Netsai, Tambu's sister, which was blown off by a land mine during the guerillas' trial and Babamukuru's beating for being a *tshombe*, or "sellout" (15). Netsai's activities make Tambu afraid of what the whites will say if they discover that her sister is a resistance fighter, of what the guerillas will do if they discover Tambu's investment in the whites, and of her own guilt and responsibility in relation to the anticolonial struggles. So rather than the narrator's explicit indictment of Tambu's conscious efforts to assimilate, the figure of Netsai's leg continually haunts the text.

What contributes to Tambu's confusion in *The Book of Not* is Nyasha's apparent lack of rage. On medication, Nyasha is still politically critical but displays more "resignation than she'd ever shown" (118). We do not see enough of Nyasha in this novel to truly understand what is happening; we would like to think that she is becoming more pragmatic and self-preserving without losing the political critiques that fueled her anger, but she is also described as "speaking with increasing enervation, the tamed flatness, even in strong emotion, of women whose genitals have been carved into and mutilated" (119). When Nyasha used to "fume and rage," it frightened Tambu, but it also gave her a foil against which to judge herself as more rational and balanced; she realizes, "It was comfortable for me to have someone else being angry for me, so that I did not need to become crazy myself from outrage" (119). Now that Nyasha is calmer, Tambu worries less about Nyasha's well-being and more about whether Nyasha has more *unhu*, the ideal of calm personhood, than herself (119). Because Tambu has no one to act as her emotional foil, she must fumblingly navigate the political spaces in which she finds herself. As shown in the episode of Lucia and the *dare*, anger can be communal and active; this potential may be part of the reason why Nyasha must be medicated and controlled. At the same time, as we also see from Nyasha's experiences, excessive anger or anger with no recourse can be harmful to the self. Tambu, deprived of an ally or an anger proxy, fears embodying excessive anger like Nyasha's former anger, of exceeding the strict physical, mental, and social bounds that she struggles to set for herself. As she did with the conceptual mazes in *Nervous Conditions*, Tambu muddles through the complex ideological topography of the convent's spaces, such as the dining hall, bathroom, and dormitory, and finally her mediocre rented room after finishing school.

At the convent, Tambu's nemesis is her classmate Ntombi, who is the same grade as Tambu but poorer and less placating towards the whites. Because Ntombi's similarity causes great anxiety in Tambu, Ntombi, rather than the whites or the ideological systems of power, becomes the most frequent target of Tambu's anger and "great indignation" (34). For instance, in the convent's dining hall, a subtle racial battle between Ntombi and a white student results in Tambu directing her anger and disdain at Ntombi. In the convent's dining hall— "sombre and imposing" with a "large mirror," over which reads a sign, "I saw them eat and I knew who they were" (36)—what and how one eats is part of the constitution of the proper subject. The African maids treat the African students differently than the white ones, indicating their disdain either out of identification with or hatred of the whites, and the kind of "tuck," or snacks from home, that one brings indicates one's class position. A white student, Bougainvillea, sparks this particular episode by praising the African girls' "fine hands"—"Look at those amazing fingers!" (37)—yet refrains from touching Ntombi. Ntombi strikes back by asking archly, "Can I have some Nesquik?" thereby putting Bougainvillea in a bind: if Ntombi touches the Nesquik chocolate powder, it will become defiled, yet if Bougainvillea refuses, "she could be blamed for being stingy, or even worse, a racist" (40). In this context, during the struggle against Rhodesian white rule and on the cusp of Zimbabwe's founding, explicit racism is seen as boorish by the liberal rich whites, yet the African students' touch is seen as dirty. Tambu briefly admires Ntombi's skill in thus having "outmaneuvered one of the white girls" (40), but the white girl deftly solves her dilemma "in masterly fashion" by herself dropping some Nesquik into Ntombi's milk, sidestepping the issue of touch. Rather than acknowledge the racist and class struggle in this small battle, Tambu indicts Ntombi: "What a mess that Ntombi was! . . . If she could not bring to table the tuck she wanted, why on earth did she have to go and embarrass everybody else by begging!" (43). As she did with Mainini, Tambu blames Ntombi: "I was convinced— Bougainvillea would treat the girl in a more dignified way if she put some self-respect into her query" (43).

Yet Tambu is aware at some level that blaming Ntombi is insufficient explanation for the situation. Tambu thinks, "I could not make up my mind what in this case constituted a proper sort of person-hood" (43). Uncertainty about what she should feel and think indi-cates her uncertainty about what kind of person she should be. More-over, in this space, in the middle of her struggle, Tambu suddenly thinks of Netsai: "Oh, Netsai! If it weren't for you, this very day I'd have my own carton of chocolate powder on the table! I could *offer* my roommate some, and humiliate her with generosity" (38). That is, Tambu exhibits a sense of the ideologically prescribed constructions of "personhood" in certain places and situations, and the text sug-gests that the colonial power structure and the anticolonial struggle permeate the politics of local, "small" spaces.

For instance, despite her attempts to do, think, and feel as she is told to, the very spaces that she inhabits—or is barred from occu-pying—constitute Tambu as a "biologically blasphemous person," in terms of gender and race, not only in relation to food but also, again, to bathrooms and waste (64). The African girls are not allowed to use the white students' bathrooms, but caught in an emergency far from her dorm's bathrooms, Tambu uses the forbidden toilet: "I was where I was not supposed to be. I was breaking the law, I castigated myself" (67). Having desecrated the "sanctified place" (66), Tambu is caught by one of the nuns, and *all* the African students are called into the headmistress's office and chastised, although in somewhat hypocriti-cal terms: "We don't want a situation where Rhodesian farmers come in here and insult you for using their daughter's bathrooms!" (73). Al-though Tambu is initially angry with the headmistress, she quickly shifts her anger to Ntombi, who, after a complex episode involv-ing a Marie biscuit and a white student, criticizes Tambu for caring more about the whites than the other African students. Tambu and Ntombi end up brawling again, and the specter of Netsai again ap-pears. In the middle of the fight, Tambu suddenly screams, "Do you know where my sister is? Do you know Netsai! She's my little sister! Do you know where she's gone to!" (78). Despite Tambu's attempts to become the ideologically model colonial subject, the sanctified space of the white-only toilet betrays the colonial, racist power structure underneath the rhetoric of charity and humanity. Tambu becomes angry at the headmistress, but she cannot sustain this anger without changing her entire conscious worldview, and thus shifts her anger to Ntombi as the embodied and explicit reminder of Tambu's blackness. Despite Tambu's attempts to avoid the truth, however, her angry altercation with Ntombi elicits the reemergence of the repressed, the violence undergirding the colonial apparatus, symbolized by Netsai. Moreover, in relation to toilets, Tambu now occupies the position of her mother, Mainini, whose structural abjection was encoded in the latrine. Despite Tambu's best efforts to be the "right sort" of African, and her adoption of the group norms, goals, and values of the white Rhodesians, she still runs into—to paraphrase Fanon—the fact of her own blackness. The conflict between her values and expectations—what the white culture tells her to accept—and the structure of white supremacy produces her anger. Like the narrator of *Woman Warrior*, she scapegoats an individual weaker than herself, Ntombi, reenacting the ideologies of colonizer/apartheid racism onto this racial other, who is also a double for Tambu herself. Tambu attributes to Ntombi not just individual malice but also racial malice, the entire weight of the colonial condition, which in turn leads to the figure of Netsai as a figure of anticolonial struggle.

Similarly, later in the novel, after Tambu has begun knitting for the white Rhodesian soldiers, Ntombi and Tambu clash in the space of the convent dorm, in the segregated room that the African students share. Ntombi finds Tambu's wool and knitting in their cupboard and excoriates Tambu for leaving out evidence of her support of the white Rhodesian government:

> "What if *vana sisi* [the sisters] who clean this room see this kind of thing in this room in this cupboard? . . . Which of us will still be speaking if the elder siblings decide some people here must stop being sell-outs! Oh, do you think any one of us will be excluded from it! By saying 'it isn't me'! Tell, me, *mhani*, do you think just saying that to someone is going to exclude you!" (137–138)

And again, apropos of nothing, in the middle of Ntombi's excoriation of Tambu, Tambu suddenly thinks of Netsai: "Looking at Ntombi— or even not looking at her—now it was so surprising I had not thought of it: the agony in the thin, thin air, the silence and the breathing, the slow, slow grace of the leg arcing in the air" (138). Ntombi, "enraged," storms at Tambu, who "no longer had the will to fight" (138). Here, Ntombi's anger indicates the extent to which the "private" space of the girls' dorm room is an arena of ideological conflict, regulated by the hygienic, racial, political, and religious rules of the nuns, yet also accessed by the African maids. Ntombi is angered that Tambu, by putting her collaborator knitting in the girls' shared cupboard, is endangering all of their lives: "What if they [vana mukoma] hear you talking, you know, about some of the things that some of the girls put in some of the cupboards in this room" (139–140). We learn later that Ntombi's family had been killed for collaborating with the colonizers (172). Having experienced the violence more closely than Tambu—who is haunted primarily by Netsai—Ntombi understands the stakes, that the colonizers as well as the guerillas who fight them are in fact "doctors of death" (172). That is, the violence of the anticolonial conflict suffuses the supposedly private spaces and renders every intimate action a political one as well.

By the same token, Tambu turns her anger at being robbed of the "best O-Level results" (113) toward Ntombi, and again their encounter takes place within the dorms. Tambu has the highest exams scores, but the nuns change the rules to give the award to a white student, Tracey Stevenson.[6] Ntombi comes to comfort Tambu and, implicitly, plead for solidarity, saying, "Tambu, you have to stop. Now. You have to stop it" (156). Helpless before the colonial system that she has invested so much in, Tambu lashes out at Ntombi; she "hissed" at Ntombi and remembers "my angry limbs upon her flesh" during past fights, "half in anticipation, half in shock" (156). While Tambu is "desperate with one half for peace," sensing that she is angry at a system that dehumanizes both girls, she also says with "fury" to Ntombi: "Don't talk to me!" (156). And when Ntombi gently proposes that they at least ask about the O-level award decision, Tambu raises the spectre not just of Netsai but also the entire anticolonial leadership: "Now, who are you? Bishop Muzorewa, Ndabaningi Sithole? Robert Mugabe, hey, or Herbert Chitepo?" (157). Tambu's anger belies the guilt she feels in her complicity with the colonial system; as Fanon puts it, the colonial drama is that while the colonized may try to repress their situation, everyday reality will force an unconscious, if not conscious, return of the repressed.

Tambu's repressed racial anger takes the form of doing poorly on her A-level exams, thus ruining her chance at further academic advancement. She rejects—albeit not consciously—the systems and spaces that she *wants* to occupy and belong to, but from which she is structurally barred at every turn. As Zimbabwe becomes independent of white rule, Tambu achieves "only a Bachelor of Social Science degree" and becomes a teacher (199). She feels her situation is beneath her; her "self esteem suffered another setback," because "my current position oppressed me as being much too low," and "even in this profession I was on the lower rung" (198–199). Tambu's rage at not being given the academic, social, and class advancement promised in her mission and convent years takes aim at the landlady of "the wretched room" she rents, which she describes thus:

> Mould shimmered blue, grey and green on this room's walls. On the ceiling dark whirlpools left over from last season's rain rushed round like vortices of sinister might until the murkiness sucked you in, tossed you around and drowned you. The gyp boards sagged and buckled at the marks, so that if drowning was a fancy to be shaken off, the ceiling had the last word, threatening at any minute to cave in and crush you. (199)

Tambu's room, far from the pristine cleanliness of Babamukuru's house or the convent, here is a malevolent force. While the rest of the nation celebrates, Tambu feels trapped, sucked in, drowned, crushed. The room "magnified [Tambu's] sense of failure and frustration," and her despair turns to anger at the landlady, who "had a home, a possession of her own. Insupportably, she had managed when I hadn't" (199). Tambu feels "passionately indignant" and "an impulse to perform drastic and damaging acts upon my landlady's body" (199). Since Ntombi is no longer around, the landlady becomes the object of Tambu's blame. On one hand, this space reflects more accurately Tambu's state of mind and even structural position; it is as crushed and limited as she feels herself to be. On the other hand, her continuing conscious commitment to some narrative of social and material advancement renders her angry. Her anger at her room and the body of her landlady speaks to the ideological conflicts forming this space and Tambu herself.

Despite her anger at her situation, Tambu cannot divest herself of the notion of anger as individual, pathological, and even immoral: "This perpetual rage was unbearable for me. I considered myself a moral person. In fact, as a moral woman I did not intend to harbour such uncharitable, above all, angry, emotions" (199–200). Whereas in *Nervous Conditions*, Nyasha embraces the systemic critiques that fuel anger and the adult narrator occasionally explains the political dynamics, in *The Book of Not*, we get, as the title suggests, Tambu's constant negation of and resistance to systemic critique despite the continual experiences of rage and anger—as well as fear and despair—produced by the gendered, colonial, and class apparatuses of power, in Tambu and in others. The I-narrator in *Book of Not* hews closely to Tambu the character, seldom explicating the situation. Rather, the text is more subtly ironic in its depiction of Tambu and exhibits occasional "slips," particularly the non sequitur references to Netsai, that indicate the ideological systems forming and informing Tambu's world.

The unrelentingly bleak end of *The Book of Not* signals the triumph of postcolonial, late-capitalist ideologies of the individual over the notion of anger as a cognitive analysis and ideological critique. The end of *The Book of Not* moves from the space of the convent, like the mission house still tied more directly to colonialism, to the city of Harare after Zimbabwean independence. In this new era, the rhetoric of the "new Zimbabwe" attempts to gloss over its colonial and bloody past in the rush toward finding a place in the new global marketplace.[7] In this new world, old colonial and racist legacies are swept under the rug, and the new logic of the market rules predominant. For instance, Tambu describes the market in Harare:

> From there [the university on Jason Moyo Avenue] to Robert Mugabe Avenue where the [Steers Advertising] agency was situated was two blocks, past fast food outlets populated by girls in too tight pants, and penny markets which matched imperfect foreign products to the local market perfectly and sold them for dozens of Zimbabwean dollars, past jewellery shops designed for someone else that glared at you in your office clothes forbiddingly. (212)

The streets have been renamed after anticolonial leaders Mugabe and Moyo, but they also become the space of commerce in which people are shaped and defined by commodities ("too tight" pants, foreign goods, jewelry) and class, in the context of unequal distribution of resources in a global marketplace (the imperfect foreign products are sold in Zimbabwe). As Tambu thinks bitterly of the rich Zimbabweans, "all wealth did . . . was make the person" (210).

The novel explores two places in Harare that show the dynamics of this new and not-new postliberation Zimbabwe: the Twiss Hostel, where Tambu moves after rejecting her dreary apartment, and the Steers, D'Arcy, and MacPedius Advertising Agency, where Tambu works as a copywriter (201). In both spaces, the narrator describes the ideological disciplining without overtly critiquing it. Neocolonial relations continue under ostensibly liberated and equal Zimbabwe, but racial and class hierarchies (mapped onto one another) continue. Tambu is aware that she has to navigate these spaces according to certain rules, but rather than resent them, she follows them whole-heartedly. Tambu is angered less by the strictures and more by other black people's interference—sometimes on purpose but more often just by the fact of also being black—with her desire to follow the rules and please whites. She is the perfect ideological subject, refusing to consciously feel anger except toward the prescribed recipients (other black Zimbabweans).

Rejecting her first apartment, Tambu moves into the Twiss Hostel, which comforts Tambu in its colonial vestiges as well as its proximity to the business district (203). Postindependence legal equality belies continuing structural—economic, racial, social—inequalities: "Even though the laws had been dismantled, the situation was very like school had been: there were only a few of us, the greater number of rooms being rented by white young women" (203). These hierarchies and histories are embedded in the spaces of the hostel. It is a "distinguished, clean, white-plastered building, built for an old colonial purpose which nobody who now lived there knew anything of, except that space and graciousness were essential" (201). Although the foyer is a space of "generous welcome" (202), above the entrance still remains "a sign which read 'right of admission reserved'" (203). This sign indicates that "whether before Independence or after it," "none but the most superior and exclusive" were admitted (203). For Tambu, "what a satisfaction it was to know one was now included!" (203).

The hostel's dining room, an ideological minefield that Tambu has to navigate carefully, harks back to the living room in Babamukuru's mission house. With "starched white tablecloths," the dining room has "heavy wooden tables for six, with napkins folded to attention beside the settings, very much like sentinels to ensure we did not eat too much, thus maintaining both our figures and the hostel fees within manageable proportions" (202). Shunned by and shunning the other few Africans, but not accepted by whites, Tambu thinks, "you stood in the entrance, surveying the options. For deciding where to sit was a dismal, discouraging business" (222):

The large room was almost empty, but we all knew the patterns. The white girls, who were in the majority, took the tables at the top and front of the room, away from the door and under the windows. This left a pair of tables, awkward as afterthoughts, as the hall filled up, unoccupied in the draughts of the entrance. Here the handful of us took our seats, beginning with chairs positioned as far from the door as possible. We were, practically to a person, young Zimbabweans who had no parental backing but who had acquired the means through some sort of tenacity, however dubious, to lodge at the respectable hostel. (222–223)

When Tambu enters, she says, "I stood working out where everybody might go so as to find the most stress-free position" (224).

Likewise, the Steers Ad Agency manifests the new Zimbabwe. Although both blacks and whites work there, the executives and upper-level workers are white. Dick Lawson, inept and prolix, is the senior copywriter who steals Tambu's work; her old nemesis from Sacred Heart, Tracey Stevenson, is the well-coiffed and modern young executive: "That was the new Tracey, in the new Zimbabwe, advertising executive for Afro-Shine, a local product by young entrepreneurs in baggy suits, and also Deputy Creative Director" (216). Afro-Shine, a product designed to make African hair "shine," represents the new logic of globalization: products are marketed to people of color by exploiting and subjugating other (or sometimes the same) people of color. It does not matter who the consumers are; what matters are profits and maintaining control of those profits. The company is built on the labor of the black Zimbabweans—Tambu, Belinda, Pedzi, Raphael—while the driven ad executive Tracey and the senior copy writer Dick Lawson collude with one another to keep the structure in place.

Moreover, in the workplace, as much as the private spaces of the mission and the convent, women's bodies are tightly controlled. Although Dick is "shaggy" and "his shoulders [are] permanently rounded" (232), the women of the workplace—Pedzi the receptionist, who is black, as well as Tracey the executive—are carefully made-up and controlled, from hair and nails to clothing, shoes, and body (213, 215). As with the dining room at Twiss Hostel, when Tambu steps onto the office floor, "all the other workers on the floor were white so that everything had to be thought out, the smallest greetings mapped and manoeuvred" (216). Like the other Zimbabweans, Tambu recognizes this situation, but she refuses to resent it; she plays along and refuses to get angry.

Tambu attempts to convince herself that both spaces are meritocracies: she has "earned" her way into Twiss Hostel, and her hard work at Steers will result in a promotion. But the novel shows that these doctrines of equality and meritocracy—pretty thin to begin with, as evinced by the skepticism of most of her fellow black Zimbabweans—belie the racist corporate reality. Dick Lawson takes credit for Tambu's advertising ideas for Afro-Shine, and the company colludes in his theft. Even when she is robbed and/or expelled from these spaces, she refuses to feel angry at the white elites and the raced, classed systems. Instead, she continues to direct her resentment toward the other Africans. She tells herself that "Bill, the Creative Director, had thought through all the aspects of the matter appropriately: what was good for Afro-Shine was good for the agency which I was a part of, thus what was good for Afro-Shine was good for everybody. This act that put Dick's name to my work was good for everybody" (237). She eventually quits the agency not out of anger toward Dick or the executives but in *shame*, not being able to bear humiliation in front of other Zimbabweans (243). Likewise, when Mrs. May (politely) evicts her from the hostel, Tambu thanks her "as warmly as I could" (246).

Tambu does exhibit fleeting moments of anger against Tracey (216) and Mrs. May (229), in both instances spurred by irritation, jealousy, and shame of other black women, including her coworkers Belinda and Pedzi, her hostel-mate Isabel, and her mother Mainini (who threatens to visit with Netsai). But despite the economic and social realities that continually confront her, Tambu can only express her emotions or even admit to feeling in certain strictly prescribed ways. Her astounding lack of anger against the blatant injustices in the spaces of the hostel and the ad agency speaks to the power of the ideological injunctions on cognition and emotion in these spaces. Through its depiction of Tambu's exclusion from both spaces despite her insistence on following these injunctions, the *novel* illustrates the inescapability of the reconfigured dynamics of the racial, class, and gender power structures in the new Zimbabwe.

TSITSI DANGAREMBGA'S NOVELS *Nervous Conditions* and *The Book of Not* eloquently excavate the layers of ideological conflicts embedded within spaces, which inform and shape the anger of the female characters. The women's angers are not simply expressions of individual affect or drives; rather, a number of social contradictions form them, their bodies, their spaces, and their feelings. *Nervous Conditions* supplies a more prominent I-narrator (the adult Tambu) who glosses the "large angers" of the characters, while *The Book of Not*'s narrator usually does not, leaving the reader to extract the threads tied together in its "small angers," and even the angers that spark momentarily and get extinguished. The novels suggest a few possibilities for crossing and revising those spaces of anger, but most pertinently for the theorizing of anger, they remind us that just as emotions take place in time, they also happen in spaces constituted and permeated by ideological forces.

CHAPTER 6

ESTRANGING RAGE:
NGUGI'S *DEVIL ON THE CROSS*
AND *WIZARD OF THE CROW*

Ngugi describes Devil on the Cross *as a novel loaded with—*
and surrounded by—the emotions of imprisonment; and yet few
readers and critics of the novel would characterize it as affective
in the familiar terms of the bourgeois novel; indeed, this work
is not emotive or sentimental in the same way as Ngugi's early
novels, nor does it contain the collective emotions generated by
his major plays. Are terms such as emotion and sentiment being
redefined here, or is the novel simply incapable of sustaining the
emotion behind it? Had Ngugi turned to ostreinane *(estrangement)*
because he now wanted "his audience to comprehend the action
intellectually," as Alamin Mazrui has argued, or was evacuating
emotions from Devil on the Cross *a way of repressing the*
subjective and—in Ngugi's lexicon—the bourgeois aspect of
the novel as a genre?
SIMON GIKANDI, *NGUGI WA THIONG'O*

IN HIS 2000 STUDY OF Ngugi wa Thiong'o's works, Simon Gikandi
notes an incongruity between Ngugi's description of the "strong emotions and deep personal feelings" involved in writing the novel *Devil
on the Cross*, and the lack of affect or sentiment in the novel itself.
In his memoir *Detained*, Ngugi describes painstakingly writing the
novel on toilet paper in prison, only to have the prison guards con-
fiscate the writings: "With this novel I had struggled with language,
with images, with prison, with bitter memories, with moments of despair, with all the mentally and emotionally adverse circumstances
in which one is forced to operate while in custody—and now it had
gone" (*Detained* 164; quoted in Gikandi, *Ngugi* 209). He also recounts his elation when the new warden returns the manuscript to
him; Ngugi only says aloud, "Thank you," but adds that the warden

"will probably never know the depth of emotion behind those two words" (*Detained* 165; quoted in Gikandi, *Ngugi* 209). But *Devil on the Cross* itself, Gikandi observes, is "not emotive or sentimental" like Ngugi's earlier realist novels and his plays; Gikandi asks how we should understand this change in affect (*Ngugi* 209).[1] My response to Gikandi's question is that rather than "evacuating" emotion, *Devil on the Cross* redefines, or rather, reimagines emotion, the relation between emotion and reason, and the collective, systemic nature of individually experienced emotions.

As I have been discussing throughout this book, we still tend to think of emotion as divorced from reason. For example, in considering why Ngugi turns to non-realist estrangement aesthetic techniques in *Devil on the Cross*, Gikandi quotes Alamin Mazrui in conjecturing that perhaps the change is because Ngugi wants "his audience to comprehend the action intellectually?" (*Ngugi* 209). But the full sentence from Alamin Mazrui and Lupenga Mphande's original essay reads: "In his early novels, Ngugi draws his audience into his descriptions emotionally; but now he wants his audience to comprehend the action intellectually *as well*" (171, emphasis added). The inclusion of "as well" is significant, marking the difference between thinking of reason as opposed to emotion, rather than reason as linked to emotion. Mazrui and Mphande discuss how, during the period when Ngugi embraces Fanonian Marxism, he also begins to employ Brechtian estrangement in order to depict the experiences of individuals as well as to explore and make explicit exploitative, dehumanizing systems of capitalism and neocolonialism.[2] In doing so, emotions, and the social forces that shape and are shaped by emotions, become no longer simply about an individual's atomistic experience; rather, emotions and reason are mutually determining and depend on a dialectical understanding of the individual and the collective, mutually forming through history.

In this chapter, I argue that both the perceptions of Ngugi as an angry, idealistic nativist and of his later novels as being less emotional than his earlier works rely on a shared error: a conception of emotion as individual and separate from reason, collectives, ideological systems, and history. I first discuss the construction of Ngugi the author as angry nativist, and how such readings, in separating the individual from the social and historical, remove the rational and cognitive grounds for political anger. Then I move to a discussion of emotions, particularly anger, in Ngugi's later novels *Devil on the Cross* and

Wizard of the Crow, which use Brechtian *Verfremdung,* or "estrangement," via orature and satire to reconceptualize emotion.[3] Ngugi's fictional and nonfictional writings, I argue, present emotion and reason as interlinked and linked to systemic analyses, and his later novels explore anger using aesthetically complex, estranging, hybrid literary techniques to highlight the dynamics of emotion and reason in late capitalism.

THE LANGUAGE QUESTION

In the wake of his "farewell to English" in 1986, Ngugi wa Thiong'o was and is still often characterized as a nativist who rejects any foreign impurities. Particularly during the poststructuralist heyday of the 1980s and '90s, Ngugi was seen as embracing simplistic binaries, such as native/foreign, pure/impure, and progressive/reactionary, which merely reified the existing terms of colonialism. Underlying many of these characterizations of Ngugi is an implicit notion of anger as a form of individual pathology and/or irrationality. When a supra-individual explanation is offered, the most common one involves Ngugi's European education and aesthetics and petit-bourgeois intellectual/artist class position. For instance, Anthony Arnove argues that Ngugi and Chinua Achebe, although often cast as disputants in a debate over the use of English, actually constitute two sides of the same bourgeois, idealist coin; they both centralize *culture* in their critiques of neocolonialism. James Ogude writes (somewhat contradictorily), "While in the earlier novels Ngugi expresses the possibilities of a syncretic culture, in the later novels he displays utter hostility towards anything deemed Western. In the postcolonial novels there is an increasing commitment to political, and more specifically Marxist ideals" (13). According to Nicholas Brown, Ngugi claims that "African experience can only be captured in African languages" (62). But such characterizations of Ngugi often rely on an underreading of the systemic and structural analyses that undergird Ngugi's arguments. For Ngugi's detractors, issues of language hinge on identity, culture, and the individual, whereas for Ngugi, identity, culture, and individuals are always inseparable from histories, capitalism, and colonial and neocolonial power structures.

For example, Christopher Wise is critical of what he characterizes as Ngugi's utopianism about language and idealization of the past. Wise writes: "By subverting the standard reception of the bourgeois novel of realism, and through abandoning the language of Kenya's colonizers, Ngugi felt that the final 'barriers' separating himself from the Gikuyu peasantry had been removed (*Decolonising* 45)" (135). According to Wise, all that Ngugi sees as lying between himself and the people is language. But the passage that Wise cites from Ngugi's *Decolonising the Mind*, which discusses Kamiriithu (Ngugi's collaborative popular theater experiment in 1970s, for which he was jailed), depicts a far more complicated situation and process. The original passage reads:

> Here the choice of language was crucial. There was now *no barrier between the content of their history and the linguistic medium of its expression.* Because the play was written *in a language they could understand* the people could participate in all the subsequent discussions on the script. They discussed its content, its language and even the form. The process, particularly for Ngugi wa Mirii, Kimani Gecau, and myself was one of continuous learning. . . . Learning our language, for the peasants were essentially the guardians of the language through years of use. And learning anew the elements of form of the African Theatre. (*Decolonising* 45, emphasis added)

Ngugi does not say that *he* has become united with the Kikuyu people; he says that the *language barrier* between the content and its medium, which in academic and literary circles is usually English, has been removed. Moreover, whereas English is generally the language of the elite (and moreover includes specialized intellectual and artistic terms), here the writers and artists are on the margins of the discursive field because they are not used to working in Gikuyu. Rather than speaking from a position of authority, at least in discussions of the play, they are struggling as much as the audience to figure out how to use the language and create new aesthetic forms. Contrary to the picture of perfect union that Wise paints, the situation Ngugi depicts is one of learning and of profound dis-ease and discomfort for the artists and intellectuals, a learning process brought about by a shift from the privileged mode of discourse (English language, academic terminology) that would actually be more "harmonious," or familiar, for the bourgeois writers and intellectuals.

Likewise, Wise claims that Ngugi idealizes his world before the advent of English language and education: "The imposition of English in his educational environment caused the pre-existing 'har-

mony' of his linguistic lifeworld to be shattered, chiefly through en-
acting a 'disassociation of sensibility' in his young mind" (136). But
whereas Wise casts this trauma in individual terms—"in *his* educational environment" and "of *his* linguistic lifeworld"—what Ngugi
actually discusses in *Decolonising the Mind* is the colonial educational apparatus and its use of language historically and systemically.
Ngugi does not say that the world—his own or the Gikuyu peoples'
or Africans'—before the advent of English is "harmonious"; what
he writes is, "Imposing a foreign language, and suppressing the native languages as spoken and written, were already breaking the har-
mony previously existing between the African child and the three aspects of language," i.e., "real world," spoken, and written (16). That
is, Ngugi is describing a *structural* relationship between a speaker
and different modes of a language, not his own individual worldview.
While elsewhere Ngugi does paint a happy picture of his childhood
before starting school (10–11), the break he discusses when he starts
school is one of structural disjunction: "The language of my education was no longer the language of my culture" (11). Ngugi here depicts the historical fact of the colonial educational apparatus, which
intentionally hierarchized the English language over Gikuyu and all
African languages precisely because these were the languages of the
colonized: "In Kenya, English became more than a language: it was
the language, and all the others had to bow before it in deference" (11,
original emphasis). Wise's response that all languages are alienated/
alienating misses Ngugi's point; *historically* speaking, English was
and is dominant, not by coincidence but by intentional design via
the colonial educational and bureaucratic state apparatuses, as well
as through continuing cultural imperialisms.

Against continual charges of nativism and failure "to rise above
the binary categories used in standard interpretations of domination" (Ogude 65), Ngugi maintains his arguments that language is
inextricably tied to power and knowledge. In a 2004 interview with
Angela Rodrigues, Ngugi emphasized the importance of understanding language within the hierarchy and structures of power: "The
language question should really be discussed in terms of power relations, and in terms of production and distribution of knowledge"
(Rodrigues 165).[4] As he argued in the 1970s, when Kenyan universities still had departments of English literature rather than African
literature, he says: "Something is wrong when you have an entire intellectual elite producing knowledge in a foreign language that is not

accessible to the ordinary men and women" (164). Rather than a simplistic or idealistic notion of language and culture, Ngugi views language as one consideration in complex configurations of power, history, and culture:

> Language itself is a material force and it holds many things together.
> But, of course, within a linguistic community there are the usual so-
> cial and political cleavages. It does not mean that if you speak En-
> glish, Portuguese, Italian, or Swahili, all political, social, gender, and
> class divisions suddenly vanish. There are class problems in the En-
> glish speaking world. But when in a colonial situation (and many
> countries in Asia and Africa are products of the colonial situation),
> the language of a people as a whole is marginalized—that is, that lan-
> guage is no longer the language of education, of administration, of
> cultural expression—that people's capacity to meaningfully partici-
> pate in economic, political, and cultural affairs is blotted out of the
> mainstream. This, of course, affects all classes in that society, but it
> affects even more so the socially marginalized. Take, for instance,
> a continent like Africa. The peasants and the workers, all men and
> women, are agents of social change. When you impoverish their lan-
> guage or do not let it be the language of knowledge production, you
> impoverish the capacity of that social group to meaningfully repre-
> sent themselves. *The language question cannot be divorced from the
> class question and from politics.* (Rodrigues 164, emphasis added)

Just as he sees languages as imbricated in class structures and politics, Ngugi's view of culture is similarly complex, "hybrid," and embedded in *history*. He says,

> I don't see that cultures must live in isolation. Every culture should
> borrow whatever is best and progressive in other cultures, including
> European ones. Progress comes through contact. The problem in the
> past was the advent of colonialism, since some cultures were domi-
> nated by others, which is not a fair exchange: domination and subju-
> gation induced psychic submission from the part of the dominated.
> (Rodrigues 163, emphasis added)

That is, as opposed to a binaristic or nativist view of language and
culture, Ngugi's claims about culture and his decision to write in Gikuyu are embedded in an understanding of the history and continu-

ing effects of colonial privileging of English and Western culture, and active suppression and denigration of Gikuyu and other languages and cultures of the colonized.

At the same time, while he advocates resistance to the continuing hegemony of English, he also understands that languages and cultures today are inextricably intertwined. When he is asked, "Do you think, then, that it is possible to use the knowledge you received from your European education in a different context?" Ngugi responds, "In fact, *you must do that.* There is nothing wrong with European languages" (Rodrigues 163, emphasis added), and indeed Ngugi has continued to translate his own novels into English. The problem is that, he continues, "generally speaking, European languages are taken as the only ones capable of producing knowledge" (Rodrigues 164). In other words, Ngugi does not wholly reject English because structurally speaking, he cannot; not only Western readers but also non-Gikuyu-speaking Kenyan and African readers would not have access to his texts. Rather, the problem is that European languages, particularly English, are seen as the *only* language in which knowledge can be produced. He therefore does not simply embrace language as an essential cultural trait, but as resistance to neocolonial systems of which the language issue is one of many forms.

So, far from claiming that "African experience can only be captured in African languages" (Brown 62), Ngugi's argument is that "the language of African literature cannot be discussed meaningfully outside the context of those *social forces* which have made it both an issue demanding our attention and a problem calling for a resolution" (Ngugi, *Decolonising* 4, emphasis added). This "resolution" lies not simply in embracing a more essential African language, but rather in exploring alternative modes of communication that can address a wider audience of people, i.e., peasants and workers, and, as Fanon wrote, address current political realities. Ngugi writes,

> But writing in our languages per se—although a necessary first step
> in the correct direction—will not itself bring about the renaissance
> in African cultures if that literature does not carry the content of our
> people's anti-imperialist struggles to liberate their productive forces
> from foreign control; the content of the need for unity among the
> workers and peasants of all the nationalities in their struggle to con-
> trol the wealth they produce and to free it from internal *and* external
> parasites. (*Decolonising* 29, emphasis added)

Although his arguments about culture and language have always been situated historically and structurally, continuing characterizations of Ngugi as a reactionary nativist isolate his claims from those histories and structures. In separating the language issue from the complex histories of colonialism, neocolonialism, and the information economy of late capitalism (in which English is a dominant currency), critics implicitly characterize Ngugi as angry without reason. Doing so does not just render his arguments pathological; it also denies that an argument, with *reasons*, exists at all. Ngugi's novels engage this relationship between emotion and reason—or emotion as cognition—even more sensitively by exploring the relationship between individual and collectives, both in history and as a means of analyzing human emotion.

MAKING STRANGE: ORATURE AND SATIRE

Fundamental to Ngugi's attempts to bridge the divide between individual/individualist and collective/systemic is the adoption in his later novels of orature and non-realist literary techniques (variously described as postmodern, satire, magical realism, and others). This shift happens in a number of interrelated but distinct ways. First, the *content* of the later novels shows the relationship between individual and collective(s) to be not static or divided but rather inextricable, mutually formative, and dialectical. While *Weep Not, Child*, more typically of a bourgeois novel, focuses on an individual's experience of colonial education and anticolonial struggle, both *Devil on the Cross* and *Wizard of the Crow* explicitly outline the grounds for not only cultural national solidarity but also feminist and international class solidarity. Second, as has been much discussed, Ngugi's use of Gikuyu and oral storytelling techniques in his later novels was an attempt to reach a wider audience in Kenya and Africa. Ngugi did not translate *Devil* and *Wizard* into English until several years after the Gikuyu versions had been published as well as performed publicly in Kenya. As Gikandi notes, *Devil* signals "Ngugi's rethinking of the place of the reader in the production of narrative" (*Ngugi* 210).

But a third shift also occurs in a way that interlinks ideology and aesthetics, emotion and reason. As Gikandi writes in the passage that began this chapter, the lack of emotion in Ngugi's later novels is his way "of repressing the subjective and . . . the bourgeois aspect of the novel as a genre" (*Ngugi* 209). That is, one way to think about the genre of the novel is as follows: if the rise of the novel coincides with the rise of capitalism and the bourgeoisie and the naturalization of liberal individualism, then the novel itself as a genre is politically flawed. Critics have characterized Ngugi's incorporation of orature into his later novels as an attempt to overcome this individualism, but there is still a great deal of critical unease about this melding; we are not yet sure how to think about it. Of *Devil on the Cross*, "a work that draws both on Gikuyu traditions and the European concept of the novel" (Gikandi, *Ngugi* 210), Gikandi notes,

> If literary critics now seem confused about the place of *Devil on the Cross* in Ngugi's *oeuvre* . . . it is simply because the genealogy of the novel is schizophrenic. It is a work that wants to maintain its generic identity as a novel in the European sense of the word while rejecting the central ideologies that have made this form what it is, including the assumption of an elite audience. (*Ngugi* 210)

Gikandi's characterization of *Devil* as "schizophrenic" is telling; the term implies a fragmented, incompatible juxtaposition of things that cannot fit together.[5]

But as Ngugi indicates above in his interviews, elements of culture and language do not have inherent political values; rather, it is their histories and uses that ideologically mark them, and these can change over time. This historicity of the ideology of aesthetic forms applies equally to the novel (realist, satire, or postmodern) as to oral traditions. As Mazrui and Mphande write,

> The ahistorical opposition between orality as African and writing as Western, and the undialectical relegation of orality to Africa's precolonial heritage have combined to make the oral literature of African intellectuals and academia frozen in time and virtually closed to organic growth. Contrary to its dynamic, growing, and creative character, oral literature is often regarded as a static heritage that can only be passed on "intact" from one generation to another. (161)

To echo Mazrui and Mphande again, as well as the Russian formalists, the relationship between aesthetic form and ideology is historical.[6] For example, as Gikandi writes, "commentators on the function of orality in the novel have called attention to the significance of songs or music in general" as evidence of Ngugi's incorporation of

Gikuyu and African oral traditions (*Ngugi* 213), such as the gicaandi performance, which is "a competitive, yet cooperative, riddle-like dialogue poem and poetic exchange" (Njogu 47). Yet, Gikandi continues, "what has not been emphasized enough are the multiple traditions of these songs," including Old Testament stories, Mau Mau songs, and urban "Congolese music" and pop songs (*Ngugi* 213). By the same token, Evan Mwangi points out that not only the narrator, introduced as "the Gicaandi player" at the beginning of *Devil on the Cross*, but also the *thieves* use oral storytelling techniques. As Mwangi notes, "the testimonies the thieves give are structured as oral performances, complete with proverbs, repetition, allegorical allusions, and song interludes that we would expect in a gicaandi performance" (36).[7] In other words, in depicting gicaandi performances from an array of ideological positions, Ngugi demonstrates the flexibility of cultural production.

In terms of emotion, Ngugi's incorporation of oral storytelling elements as well as satire shifts the affective dynamics of the text away from empathy for characters and toward the emotions produced by ideological and systemic analysis. In other words, Ngugi estranges feeling. Here it may be useful to revisit Brecht's notion of *Verfremdung* (estrangement) as a defamiliarizing, non-mimetic aesthetic technique. In "Theatre for Pleasure or Theatre for Instruction" (1957), Brecht writes:

The spectator was no longer in any way allowed to submit to an experience uncritically (and without practical consequences) by means of simple empathy with the characters in a play. The production took the subject matter and the incidents shown and put them through a process of [estrangement]: the [estrangement] that is necessary to all understanding. When something seems "the most obvious thing in the world" it means that any attempt to understand the world has been given up.

What is "natural" must have the force of what is startling. This is the only way to expose the laws of cause and effect. People's activity must simultaneously be so and be capable of being different . . .

The dramatic theatre's spectator says: Yes, I have felt like that too just like me—It's only natural—It'll never change—The sufferings of this man appall me, because they are inescapable—That's great art; it all seems the most obvious thing in the world—I weep when they weep, I laugh when they laugh.

The epic theatre's spectator says: I'd never have thought it—That's not the way—That's extraordinary, hardly believable—It's got to stop. The sufferings of this man appall me, because they are unnecessary. That's great art: nothing obvious in it—I laugh when they weep, I weep when they laugh. (71)

Estrangement involves "making strange" in terms of art and life, making us see things anew, and situating events in histories and systems. Brecht, arguing with Lukács about avant-garde art, contends that realism lies not just in form but rather in what version of reality the artwork reveals to us. In making us re-see an event in its historical and ideological contexts, the estranging work does make us feel but not necessarily *with* the characters. Brechtian estrangement therefore does not mean the *lack* of affect or emotion or even empathy; it means that our emotional responses do not necessarily mirror those of the characters, narrator, or implied author. Rather, estrangement here involves both rethinking and *re-feeling*. Naturalizing certain situations, experiences, values, ethics, and emotions suppresses their historical natures and implicitly works to sustain those processes by casting them as irrevocable.[8] The emotional acceptance of certain things suggests, "It'll never change." For instance, in the contest of thieves in *Devil on the Cross*, we may laugh at the contestants' antics, but we can also be angry about the real-world situation that the novel satirizes. In the next two sections, I explore some of the ways that *Devil on the Cross* and *Wizard of the Crow* use estrangement techniques, particularly oral storytelling and satire, to reconceptualize anger as systemic and political.

CAPITALISM AND CONTROL OF AFFECT

Devil on the Cross probes anger in both content and form. In some forms, anger—as felt, expressed, managed, and reacted to—helps maintain the status quo. The protagonist, Wariinga, recounting her own story using the pseudonym "Kareendi," describes how she will act after finding the "love of her life," Kamoongonye: "Because I am very lucky, and I have looked for and found a Kamoongonye, a young man with modern views, I, Kareendi, will never anger him or argue with him over any issue. If he shouts at me, I will remain silent. I will simply look down like the shy leopard or like a lamb cropping grass" (20). Here Wariinga sketches out a patriarchal system of feeling, in which women should not express anger, while a man's anger, expressed in shouting, is his right. In other words, the group norms of patriarchy dictate that men can exert their authority in displays of anger while women accept it silently. Much later in the novel, after Wariinga's politicization, she reconsiders this scenario in which women receive male anger. In considering what petit bourgeoisie or lower-/middle-class semi-professional women ("clerks, copy typists and secretaries") have given up in identifying with bourgeoisie, Wariinga includes "our humanity":

> Yes, because *Boss* Kihara and his kind work out their frustrations on us. When they quarrel with their wives at home, they bring their anger to the office; when something goes wrong with their business, they bring all their fury to the office. We are insulted, but we keep quiet because we are supposed to have hearts that are not easily moved to tears. (206)

In such discussions, the novel outlines how configurations of anger (who can be angry and how; appropriate responses) are gendered and classed; the boss's wives apparently do not have to accept their anger, while the secretaries and various working-class women do.

In contrast, Wariinga's political awakening begins through an experience of anger that she does not yet know how to articulate. When her lover John Kimwana (Kamoongonye in her story) abandons her, she initially experiences only "insistent self-doubt and crushing self-pity" (12) and is about to kill herself when a mysterious voice interrupts her and she has a vision of the Devil being crucified by a crowd of poor people. When she regains consciousness, she remembers her situation and becomes angry:

> For when I looked at the university buildings, and especially those of the Engineering Department, I remembered the dreams of my youth, when I was at school . . . and I recalled how later my dreams were trampled into the dust by the Rich Old Man from Ngorika. Then those memories fused with thoughts of John Kimwana, who abandoned me last night, knee-deep in the mire of my troubles, I suddenly felt my brain and heart burn with pain, and my anger seemed to suffocate me . . . (14)

Both the spaces of the (lost) university and the revisiting of past times, in the crisis of having lost everything that gives her social status, spark anger in her, arising out of a pseudo-conscious critical assessment of the situation and laying the groundwork for even further politicization. She is upset and angry, sensing that she has been injured and robbed, although she does not yet know the specific reasons why. Interestingly, both her heart and her brain "burn with pain," linking her emotions and thinking together, all within the context of her experiences within various institutions.

Later, her political and emotional views develop and become explicit in and through conversations with the politicized Muturi, a worker, and Wangari, a peasant, as well as Gatuiria, a young artist from a well-to-do family. Wariinga meets them—along with Mwireri wa Mukiraai, the nationalist capitalist, and Robin Mwaura, the driver—on a *matatu* (bus) en route from Nairobi to Ilmorog. The space of the bus allows a cross section of Kenyan society to be collected together; they review the status of the country—its history and current shape—in a variety of ideological ways, progressive and reactionary. After Gatuiria tells a story of patriarchy and the objectification and oppression of women in general, Wariinga starts to cry and says, "It is your story that has made me look back on my life in anger," because "I can see vividly where my own dreams fell to pieces" (137). Likewise, in *Wizard of the Crow*, the heroine Nyawira says, "Awareness of being wronged was the first step in political self-education" (431). Such instances reflect a conception of anger as arising out of a specific appraisal and political analysis.

But anger also works in unconventional ways through the texts' melding of oral storytelling and satire, particularly in the thieves' competition. At the center of *Devil on the Cross* is "A Devil-Sponsored Competition / To Choose Seven Experts in Theft and Robbery" (28, 68), at which Kenyan bourgeoisie compete to see who is the best thief. The spectators include First-World emissaries from the "International Organization of Thieves and Robbers (IOTR)" (87), a spoof of the IMF and World Bank, as well as other native bourgeoisie. Because "theft and robbery are the true foundation of modern progress and development" (80), the international observers are there to see that the competitors are effectively developing their skills of theft. As a relatively accurate portrayal of the exploitation and corruption perpetrated by international financiers and politicians as well as the native comprador class, the situation depicted by the competition should elicit anger. But whereas the content of Ngugi's indictment is scathing, the text does not produce emotions through empathy or identification with characters or the development of events.

Rather, the emotions are produced via the systemic analyses of the satire, in which humorous, grotesque, and fantastic elements overlay a serious ethical and ideological argument, in which anger functions in a variety of ways.

For example, anger first appears in the testimony of Kihaahu wa Gatheeca, a "tall, slim" man with "long legs, long arms, long fingers, a long neck and a long mouth" (108). He recounts how, when his "New Black Beauty Nursery School for Children of VIP Kenyans" failed, he successfully attracted rich Kenyans to his school by buying white mannequins to look like white students, hiring a white teacher, and advertising the school as mostly European and "Now Open to a Few Kenyans" (113). He also brags about sleeping with "other people's wives," "bourgeois women" (110); increasing his wealth by building "cheap houses for the poor" (115–116); and after gaining political and economic power, "send[ing] my thugs around to those who are obstinate" in critiquing the government and ruling classes (117). But, distracted by his own mention of the "obstinate" protestors, he launches into an apparently tangential but telling rant:

> I don't believe in this democracy nonsense. In the morning the topic is democracy. In the evening the topic is democracy. Is democracy food and drink? If I could get hold of those kids at the university, together with their pygmy-sized teachers . . . I would load them on to an aeroplane and request them to take their communist nonsense to China or the Soviet Union. (117)

After the rant, he apologizes: "Raging anger with that lot temporarily distracted me from the business in hand" (118). He concludes with his proposal to increase "the whole country's hunger and thirst, because the degree to which there's a property famine determines exactly the level to which the price of houses will rise and hence the level to which profits will climb" (118). In the content of this episode, Kihaahu becomes angry at the threats to the system that ensure him ever greater wealth and power. The form, however, invites laughter because it is satiric, and the object of the satire is less Kihaahu as an individual than the systems that form him and that he supports. That is, we—and Wariinga—do not become angry at Kihaahu the character so much as the system that is the target of the novel's satiric critique.

Then, following his speech, Kihaahu is met not with applause but

with silence and then anger from the crowd of thieves, primarily because he has disgracefully exploited his own class but also because
he was too obvious in the oppression of the masses. One competitor,
Ithe wa Mbooi, says to him, "To rob and to cheat the poor is *all right.*
Where else would our wealth come from?" But he castigates Kihaahu
for "bragging about deceiving people of your class. . . . If we start rob-
bing, thieving and cheating one another, how will our unity as a class
take roots?" (120–121). Another competitor, Gitutu wa Gataanguru,
argues that Kihaahu's plans "to build sparrow's nests as houses" is
too obvious, and that Kihaahu "wants the workers to become so angry that the scales will fall from their eyes, and they will rise up
against us with swords and clubs and guns" (120). Of course, Gitutu
himself wants to "sell soil in tiny dishes, and trap air so we can sell
it in tins or through meters" (120). Yet another contestant, Fathod
Marura wa Kimeengemeenge, puts it most bluntly: "How dare he
come here and boast about how he fucks other people's wives" (122).
Following these outbursts, "the cave now became a beehive of angry
noise. Much of the anger was directed at Kihaahu wa Gatheeca" (122).
Here again, the anger is satiric. The distance between Kihaahu's arrogant assumption that he will be praised for enriching himself and the
audience's outrage at his offenses against his own class creates humor. But beneath the ironic humor lies a serious indictment of both
the selfishness of the bourgeoisie as well as the dynamics of a capitalist system in which self-enrichment is the only goal. The reference to the workers' potential anger attests to how important it is to
the wealthy to avoid any reinterpretation of systems and institutions
("the scales will fall from their eyes") that might lead to collective
anger ("they will rise up against us"). Kihaahu's greedy overreaching
could lead to the workers' reappraisal of their best interests, and the
thieves certainly recognize that such a situation would hamper their
own interests.

When Kihaahu responds angrily to his critics, tensions esca-
late to the point where everyone jumps up and pulls out guns (124).
This pseudo-slapstick show of anger and threat of violence notwith-
standing, the master of ceremonies calms down the combatants by
reminding them what is really at stake. The disputants' displays of
anger and violence—the violence between them showing what truly
underlies their ruthless competition for profit—may also ultimately
hurt all of them by also connoting a lack of civilization and "stability" needed for the market and international investments. The mas-

ter of ceremonies reminds the contestants and combatants that emissaries from rich nations, such as the U.S., Great Britain, and Japan, are in attendance and watching their every interaction:

> Do you want to strip each other naked in front of our foreign guests? What do you imagine they think of us now, after witnessing this chaos and a threatened shoot-out in broad daylight? Our actions may make them lose faith in us and rethink their position. They must be wondering: Can these people really look after the products of our theft and robbery in their country? Are they really capable of looking after our finance houses and stores and all the industries underwritten by these? (125)

His words stop everyone cold, because despite the other systems that may be threatened (patriarchal possession of their wives, competition for the greatest profits), they realize that their ultimate collective profit lies in impressing and placating the international investors and bankers. This reassurance of international markets relies, more than anything else, on *the control of affect*, particularly of the kinds of emotions coded as violent, non-white, unstable, and "savage." This control of emotions, sometimes manifested as the absence of emotions, is key to the capitalist marketplace that produces profit.

Ngugi here depicts a "structure of feeling" that is indeed widespread and yet for which we have no good terms. In late capitalism, the danger of anger and emotions in general lies not so much in that they are separated from reason, but rather because anger and emotions, particularly when associated with brown and non-Western peoples, threaten the "political stability" that is necessary for unimpeded neoliberalization and capitalist development. A display of emotions is not merely an indication of an individual's temperament or experiences; it is the index of an entire people and geopolitical region's ability to earn profits. And anger is the most volatile emotion, and therefore most antithetical to capitalism.

GOD, THE DEVIL, AND QUEUES

In exploring a situation where emotion itself is seen as antithetical to the smooth operation of the market, Ngugi uses unusual metaphors for systems and structures: religion in *Devil on the Cross* and queues in *Wizard of the Crow*. In *Devil*, religion becomes an analogy for systemic analysis: How does the system work, and what do we find acceptable and unacceptable? Or, to put it in the terms of cognitive psychology, religion becomes a way to think about how we define our group norms for justice and humanity. For instance, Muturi, the worker, says,

> I believe that God and Satan are images of our actions in our brains as we struggle with nature in general, and with human nature in particular, in our search for something to eat, to wear and to shelter behind to keep out the sun, the cold and the wind. The nature of God is the image of the good we do here on Earth. The nature of Satan is the image of the evil we do here on earth. The question is this: *what are evil actions, and what are good actions*? (57, emphasis added)

Mwaura, the *matatu* driver, small-time entrepreneur, and one-time leader of the "Devil's Angels," whose "task is to liquidate those who prevent the work of God from being done on Earth" (252), embodies an amoral or an-ethical stance. For Mwaura, there are no "group norms," or consistent ones, on which he would be able to base an appraisal that might lead to anger. In conversation with Muturi about "whose side" Mwaura is on, God or the Devil's, Mwaura replies,

> I'm equally at home on either side. Didn't you say just now that I was someone who cooks two pots simultaneously? You were quite right. . . . Can't you see, then, that each is capable of improving or ruining your fortunes on this Earth? Just as you find candidates vying with each other as they tout for votes during elections, so we businessmen play off God and the Devil against each other. We don't like to anger either of them. We pray to both. (48)

In being incapable of anger or of angering, Mwaura thus embodies the perfect capitalist. Or as he puts it, "Business is my temple, and money is my God" (56).

In *Wizard of the Crow*, Ngugi expands upon this reconceptualization of emotions more explicitly. The novel begins speculating on the possible reasons for the mysterious disease of the Ruler, a despot of a fictional African country, Aburiria, modeled on Kenya. The first of the rumored reasons is anger that while in the U.S., the Global News Network refused to interview him on the air. His anger literally wells up inside him:

The illness, so claimed the first [theory], was born of anger that once welled up inside him; and he was so conscious of the danger that it posed to his well-being that he tried all he could to rid himself of it by belching after every meal, sometimes counting from one to ten, and other times chanting *ka ke ki ko ku* aloud. . . . Just as offensive gasses of the constipated need to be expelled, thus easing the burden on the tummy, anger in a person also needs a way out to ease the burden on the heart. This Ruler's anger, however, would not go away, and it continued simmering inside till it consumed his heart. (3)

We later learn that the Ruler is not only angered by the Global News Network, but moreover—and worse—by the Global Bank's refusal to support his Marching to Heaven project (a building that reaches heaven, modeled on the Tower of Babel). In rage, he literally puffs up and floats to the ceiling:

> The Ruler was quite candid with the doctor. He explained that when he read the news from the Global Bank, he had become so angry that his body started to expand even more. He had called his special advisor to have somebody to talk to in the hope that this would ease the anger within. While waiting for Tajirika, he had read some more newspapers, only to feel his anger mount until it almost choked him, and that was when he felt himself lifted uncontrollably. He could not tell exactly when it started, but it was definitely when he was already in the air that his tummy began to ache. (652)

The Ruler's anger here works on a number of levels. His own anger, like that of the thieves in *Devil on the Cross*, is shown to be born of his arrogance, greed, and lust for power. But also, the figure of the Ruler puffed up with rage parodies the Aristotelian *and* psychoanalytic notions of emotions as emerging from within, capable of being bottled up and/or repressed, and needing to be "released." The rumors and the Ruler himself rely on the notion that anger comes from some internal physical ailment; that is, even if anger can be triggered by an external event, it is a personal illness, and its cure lies in some emotional equivalent of flatulence.

So when the narrator asks, "Could anger, however deeply felt, cause a mystery illness that defied all logic and medical expertise?" (4), the question is both satiric and serious. The cause of the Ruler's illness is his own greed within a particular ideological and economic world system, and the novel satirizes his puffed-up sense of his own importance by having him literally swell up. Furthermore, Ngugi also depicts a *conception* of anger that is internal or individual, pathological, and delinked from systemic understandings. Indeed, it is the Ruler's inability to divorce himself from anger, and an investment in emotions in general, that ultimately costs him his power. A special envoy, "sent by Washington and by the capitals of the leading industrial democracies" (578), tells the Ruler to step down in favor of his minister Machokali because "he reasons more than he emotes, and we in the West can certainly do business with him" (583). Even though he has Machokali killed, the Ruler himself is eventually supplanted, with quick approval from the international business community, by Tajirika.

Tajirika is an opportunistic businessman whose total lack of morals and, relatedly, absence of emotional investment in anything other than his own advancement make him the perfect replacement. Initially, Tajirika seems like anything but a likely candidate to rule the country. He is a bootlicking toady; even compared to the Ruler's other scheming ministers, Tajirika is a "dithering crook" (751). Early in the novel, he suffers from "white-ache," an ailment that causes him to seize up and be unable to say anything but the word *"If!"* The problem, Kamiti/the Wizard of the Crow tells him, is that Tajirika wants to be white. Thus, Kamiti advises, Tajirika needs to start thinking like a white person: "A certain African sage says that whites are driven by logic and blacks by emotion. Think with white logic, not black emotion" (183). Tajirika, like Mwaura in *Devil*, thus relinquishes emotion for the amoral reasoning that undergirds the capitalist system, in which the only goal and "group norm" is profit. In other words, the terms of emotion have shifted from emotions as innate or moral to emotion and reason as purely in service of the market.

Tajirika is also an appropriate person to become ruler of Aburiria, in the eyes of the international market, because he is the originator of the queues that come to plague the country, or as Nyawira calls them, "queues without an end" (141). These queuing lines are manifestations of the systems that are so entrenched and ubiquitous that they seem to have no origin and are simply accepted as natural. When Tajirika is made chairman of the Marching to Heaven Building Committee, people immediately clamor to bribe him for favors. Their office overrun, Nyawira (his secretary, who is later revealed to be a revolutionary leader) makes a sign reading, "MAKE A QUEUE:

NO SERVICE FOR THOSE NOT IN THE QUEUE" (103), and an immense line of businessmen and politicians start to line up to see Tajirika (who by now has been felled by the white-ache). Later, when Nyawira needs help and puts up a sign saying that a job is available ("TEMPA JOBS: APPLY IN PERSON" [138]), another line of poor people forms. We are told:

> Imagine her surprise when she raised her eyes and found two long lines of people in the yard outside her office!
> One was made up of people in custom suits, standing stiffly and solemnly as if at a fashion parade. . . . The second line . . . was composed of people in patched-up clothes and worn-out suits in all colors of the rainbow, a stunning contrast to the array of black and gray in the queue of the rich. (138)

Eventually queues form everywhere in the country. The authorities sometimes see the queues as politically threatening and sometimes as beneficial, but the people start to accept them as a natural part of life:

> For a time it was as if everybody in Eldares was possessed. If a person happened to be window shopping, he would suddenly find that a queue had formed behind him. People did not even bother to ask what the queue was about; they simply assumed that there was good reason for it and wanted their share of whatever was being dispersed. . . . Sometimes a person would start a queue without being aware that he had done so, go home, and on the following day join the same queue, still ignorant that he had been its innocent first cause. Lines simply assumed lives of their own. (159)

Queues in *Wizard of the Crow* allegorize the systems in which people find themselves, from bureaucracies to global trade networks to lines for buses, and which we take for granted and accept as inevitable. Ngugi's stories of the queues illustrate how these systems have material histories, with a variety of ideological valences, and that these structures and processes shape human behavior as much as the pathologies, emotions, or tummy aches of any given individual.

Tajirika, as the unwitting originator of the queues and a person with no loyalty, thus serves as a better instrument of rule by the global capitalist system than the temperamental Ruler. Although he is not consistent in his views, the Ruler's condemnation and repudiation of the queues indicates his inability to think non-emotionally, amorally, and in terms of the capitalist system. In fact, upon being chastised by the envoy for failing to maintain order, the Ruler replies:

> Queuing, as an expression of order, organization, and discipline, was a very Western idea, and they should be mindful that they were now in Aburiria, Africa, where people are guided more by emotion than by reason, and therefore to scramble for things is "what comes easily" to Aburirians. (578)

The Ruler's investment, inconsistent and opportunistic as it may be, in nativism and emotion over reason is less appealing to the international financiers and politicians than Tajirika's commitment to the system. As Tajirika tells the Ruler (shortly before taking power),

> the Global Bank and the Global Ministry of Finance are clearly looking to privatize countries, nations, and states. They argue that the modern world was created by private capital. . . . The world will no longer be composed of the outmoded twentieth-century divisions of East, West, and the directionless Third. The world will become one corporate globe divided into the incorporating and the incorporated. We should volunteer Aburiria to be the first to be wholly managed by private capital, to become the first voluntary corporate colony, a corpolony, the first in the new global order. With the privatization of Aburiria, and with the NGOs relieving us of social services, the country becomes your real estate. (746)

In other words, the international financiers' and politicians' investment in reason over emotion wins out over the Ruler's privileging of emotion because the economic system dictates politics (e.g., stability needed for markets) and emotion (what kind of person should provide that stability). Tajirika, even before he realizes that he is going to replace the Ruler, instinctively knows that the ruling logic is that of capitalism, and the affects demanded by the global capitalists are the ones that will win out.

Thus, far from evacuating emotion in *Wizard of the Crow*, Ngugi makes an examination of emotions within structures (queues, global corporations) central to his satire. The form of the novel may not invite empathic emotions, but emotions, particularly anger, are at the center of the novel's critique of the all-pervasive rapacity of global capitalism. Although divisions between dangerous racial anger and "white logic" are still operative, the logic of the system is headed away from East/West or First-/Third-World divides and toward "one corporate globe divided into the incorporating and the incorporated," the exploiters and the exploited. Part of this corporate privatization includes the full shunting of volatile, political emotions such as anger into the realm of the individual private sphere; one cannot have orderly queues if people are angry, and certainly not if they are angry *together*. The characterizations of Ngugi as angry, which often have the effect of attenuating the force of his political critiques, is part of this process. At the same time, the novels' depictions of farcical anger (Kihaahu's and the Ruler's angers) also indicate that anger is not an inherent indication of progressive political analysis. The estranging of anger by Ngugi in *Devil on the Cross* and *Wizard of the Crow* shows that this most intimate of feelings arises from historical, systemic, and ideological (progressive and reactionary) factors, while also retaining potential political value.

SIMON GIKANDI WRITES THAT Ngugi's political convictions and experience of political repression led him to "a renewed investment in the instrumental function of the art object" that would constitute a "way out of the prisonhouse of postcolonialism" (*Ngugi* 208). This project involved Ngugi's transforming the role of the audience in the production of a narrative, including its language and space of distribution and reception, and reimagining "postcolonial space" beyond disenchantment and toward international solidarity against capitalism (*Ngugi* 210). I end this chapter by suggesting that the vehemence with which Ngugi has been cast as angry nativist has precisely to do with what Gikandi notes is Ngugi's relatively successful bridging between art and life, the unmet goal of the historical avant-garde,[9] by if not joining, then bringing closer together the personal and collective in language, form, and content. That is, it is Ngugi's better union of the public/private, individual/collective, art/world divisions that motivates the vehemence and insistence of his detractors, whose conceptions still rely on emotion as individual and even pathological. Ngugi has said, "People tend to avoid issues of domination and submission" (Rodrigues 165). His novels' explorations of the ways that people participate in systems that subjugate others in order to enrich themselves and the roles that the politics of emotion plays in this process, as well as his refusal to stay within existing boundaries of art, culture, and politics, have led some to dismiss him as simply "angry," narrowly defined. But as with texts by Maxine Hong Kingston and Tsitsi Dangarembga, Ngugi's later novels demonstrate that conceptions of anger are as embedded in systems of suppression and discipline as we are.

CHAPTER 7

"THIS GAME IS RIGGED":
THE WIRE AND AGENCY ATTRIBUTION

This game is rigged, man. We like the little bitches on a chessboard.

BODIE, *THE WIRE*

THE EIGHTH EPISODE OF THE FIRST SEASON of HBO's series *The Wire*, "Lessons," provides a brief but striking example of the inter-actions of cognition, emotion, and context. Sarah, a young girl under the care of Wallace, a sixteen-year-old low-level drug dealer in the Barksdale drug organization, comes to ask him for help with her math homework. Wallace quickly and easily reads the problem aloud for her.[1] He shrugs at its simplicity and says, "Just do it in your head." She thinks and responds, "Seven, right?" Wallace shakes his head, so she guesses again, "Eight?" Exasperated, Wallace reframes the problem for her: "Damn, Sarah, look. Close your eyes. You're working the ground stash, twenty [vials total]. . . . Two tweaks [drug addicts] come up to you and ask for two each, another one cops three. Then Bodie hands you off ten more. But some white guy rolls up in a car, waves you down and pays for eight. How many vials you got left?" Sarah answers almost immediately, "Fifteen." Wallace responds, exasperated, "How the fuck you able to keep the count right [but] you not able to do the book problem then?" Sarah responds, "Count be wrong, they fuck you up."[2]

This brief episode illustrates how cognition in its most obvious guise—learning—is not a purely individual, atomized process, but rather interactant with context and emotions. The mental processes involved in basic math are, for Sarah, inseparable from her context and the emotions, which are in part induced by her (accurate) cognitive assessment of that context (the repercussions of getting the "count" wrong). This episode reflects the dynamics of how emotion works in the entire series. While many characters are angry—both cops and criminals—and while individual persons may become the temporary "face" of the problem, the real sources of anger are the systems in which they all live. And because cognition and emotion are shaped by economic and social structures, our understanding of emotion and cognition needs to take into account these systems. *The Wire* demonstrates the importance of thinking of emotion and cognition as not strictly individual or even collective but also as institutional, inter-subjective, and ideological processes.

Most police procedurals and cop shows satisfy the protagonists' and audience's desire to locate one or a few culprits on whom viewers can blame injustice, violence, and other violations of communal standards.[3] In doing so, these shows fulfill the desire for agency attribution, in a kind of catharsis of blame and punishment. But in fulfilling this desire, they reinforce narrow, individualist categories, forms, and structures of anger and blame. In other words, the single culprit of many police shows promotes the idea that there is one agent to blame for social problems. In contrast not only to other television shows but also to some scholarly conceptions of anger, *The Wire* demonstrates that characters' anger often does not result from the illegitimate actions of a single malevolent dispositional entity; the form and content of the series often works to erode and complicate that vision of a discrete dispositional agent. Characters repeatedly experience anger, first nominally against a person or persons, but then repeatedly and increasingly against structures in which no one individual is shown to be the agent of harm—or rather, in which no one person is shown to be the sole cause of harm, although many people are more or less complicit in perpetuating the structures that cause real harm in people's lives. Moreover, the viewer experiences anger and frustration; some of the debate about the implications of the show has hinged on whether *The Wire* actually advocates "hope and change" or cynicism and despair. I argue that the difference between a productive anger and a despairing cynicism rests on whether or not one thinks in terms of individual human agents, or in terms of complex relations between structures and ideological apparatuses that create us even as we are continually re-creating and reinventing them. My reading of *The Wire* suggests that an individualistic notion of human agency—

and emotion—rather than a dialectical understanding of the relationship between human beings and the conditions of their existence is what differentiates despairing responses from productive anger.

So in contrast to cognitive psychology, cultural productions such as *The Wire* that analyze systems (that is, individuals dialectically related to systems—shaped by and shaping those systems) trouble the concepts of agency attribution and coping potential, basic concepts of the appraisal theory of emotion that, while useful in describing some of our tendencies, may also reinforce an individualistic view of the causes of and solutions to anger. Too often, the shape of solutions to problems is rooted in our culturally conditioned cognitive processes of anger, in which we assume that an agent will be to blame for harm to us and/or blockage of a goal. In some ways, we still lack adequate models to comprehend anger and frustration as produced by *systems*, such as capitalism, in which we are complicit. That is, while certain agents are more culpable than others, i.e., those agents with more power and wealth, much anger today is produced by systemic logics from which we cannot voluntaristically remove ourselves. Despair arises when our solutions are still as individualistic as our conceptions of our anger; some things, such as poverty being the leading killer of children around the world and one in four children in the U.S. (the richest nation) living under the federal poverty line, *should* make us *collectively* angry about systems that produce such atrocities.[4]

CAUSE AND EFFECT

Is HBO's critically acclaimed television series *The Wire* ultimately defeatist? This question may seem odd, given that the show attempts to bring to light the very social problems that middle America wants to ignore: crime, poverty, educational failures, corruption, bureaucratization, rationalization. As David Simon, the show's cocreator and one of the writers, puts it, the show seeks to show "the other America." But this question, particularly in terms of anger, merits some consideration. In March 2008, Simon and Ed Burns, the show's other creator, and George Pelecanos, detective novelist and another one of the show's writers, contributed to *Time* magazine an essay testifying to their sense of urgency produced by the show, but their solution was hardly adequate. Deluged by concerned viewers' questions ("What can we do?"), the writers characterized their previous "arguments about economic priorities or drug policy" as "lame" and "duck[ing] the question" (Burns, Simon, and Pelecanos). The solution they offer, however, is jury nullification by always voting to acquit, regardless of the evidence. This voluntarist action—an individual action rather than collective, ongoing effort—speaks to the critique of the show raised by John Atlas and Peter Dreier later that same year.

In the summer 2008 issue of *Dissent*, Atlas, a lawyer and activist, and Dreier, an academic, argue that *The Wire* "reinforced white middle-class stereotypes of inner-city life," providing a partial picture in showing only individual actions and completely leaving out the history of actual collective action in Baltimore. Worst of all, they say, the show's "unrelentingly bleak portrayal" worsens a sense of despair and hopelessness among its viewers. They argue that, on *The Wire*, the only "heroes" are "individual renegades and gadflies," such as McNulty, Omar, and Cutty Wise. As they put it, "these do-gooders don't seek to empower people as a collective force. They try to help individuals, one at a time, rather than try to reform the institutions that fail to address their needs" (82). Atlas and Dreier seem to miss that that is part of the show's point; individual efforts are insufficient without systemic change. Marsha Kinder writes, "Since no single individual can solve all of the systemic problems raised in the series, we soon realize that it's the relations that count" (54). Nevertheless, Atlas and Dreier's main point stands: the show does not really portray any collective efforts to change the system. Atlas and Dreier point to the success of grassroots community organizations in Baltimore to pass the nation's first "living wage" ordinance in 1994 (79–80), to fight cutbacks in teachers and resources in schools (80–81), and other collective actions. In failing to include stories about successes in community organization, they write, "Simon's portrayal of Baltimore buttresses the myth that the poor, especially the black poor in the city's ghettos, are drug dealers or users, eternally helpless victims, unable to engage in collective self-help and dependent on government largesse, or crime, to survive" (81). In its unrelenting bleakness, the show "reinforces the notion that the status quo cannot be changed" (81–82). Thus, they argue, "we are left with a view of Baltimore's poor as people sentenced for life to an unchanging prison of social pathology" (82).

Sociologists Ammol Chaddha, the renowned William Julius Wilson, and Sudhir Venkatesh (the author of a study in which actual gang members watched and responded to *The Wire*) respond to Atlas and Dreier's critique by arguing that the show is groundbreaking and rare in showing the extent and reach of the problem. While grassroots organizing is important, Chaddha, Wilson, and Venkatesh argue, we should not at the same time underestimate the strength and entrenchment of institutional forces: "We should be wary . . . of overly optimistic portrayals that present the active involvement of community groups as sufficient counterweights to entrenched structural forces" (83). The fate of ACORN (Association of Community Organizers for Reform Now), one of Atlas and Dreier's examples of a Baltimore community organization that had achieved some concrete goals in the 1990s and 2000s, speaks to the point about the extreme power disparity in clashes between community organizations and political and/ or financial institutions. Among ACORN's achievements that Atlas and Dreier discuss includes the campaign to convince the city of Baltimore to sue Wells Fargo Bank in 2008 for "targeting risky sub-prime loans in the city's black neighborhoods" (Atlas and Dreier 81). But the lawsuit was thrown out of court in 2010 by a judge who blamed foreclosures not on predatory lending practices, but rather on "extensive unemployment, lack of educational opportunity and choice, irresponsible parenting, disrespect for the law, widespread drug use, and violence," as he wrote in an opinion accompanying his ruling (quoted in Bishop). The case against predatory lending by some of the largest financial institutions continues,[5] but in the meantime, ACORN itself came under devastating right-wing attack, particularly targeting the Baltimore office. ACORN has seen its federal funding withdrawn and been crippled as a national organization, as documented by John Atlas in his 2010 book *Seeds of Change*.

With such powerful structural forces arrayed against social change, and when two-thirds of Americans blame the poor for their poverty,[6] Chaddha, Wilson, and Venkatesh argue that *The Wire* is more than ever an important educational tool (84–85). While Atlas and Dreier are correct that *The Wire* does not account for successful grassroots community organizations, and that this omission risks creating the perception that there is no hope, they do not give the show enough credit for presenting a uniquely complex and challenging analysis of the situation. Not only does the show analyze the structural forces that exacerbate racialized economic disparities in the U.S., but in some ways the show also indicates how the very models of cognition that we have, particularly for understanding anger, in fact exacerbate the problems and prevent solution or even full comprehension of the situation.

Part of the way that the show captures the interlinkedness of institutions, people, and practices that may be difficult or impossible to map visibly (in terms of space and place), despite the relatively linear nature of the television viewing format (that is, you can only watch one scene at a time), is through the exploitation of techniques unique to serial television. While *The Wire* has been called "Dickensian" for its scope and number of characters, Sean O'Sullivan characterizes the serial television form as a kind of poetry-like genre that, while "broken on purpose," creates unity through techniques such as anaphora, or repetition of poetic elements, and caesura, or the disruption of a line that highlights some element of it. For example, O'Sullivan identifies opening credit sequences and the "cold opening" structures as forms of anaphora, which create "a progressive structure while reminding us of each preceding iteration" ("Broken" 65). Similarly, gaps between scenes and episodes can be likened to caesuras. While other genres (including the novel) also make use of gaps and repetitions, I take O'Sullivan's point that serial television can be a more broken form than a film or a novel. *The Wire* in particular refuses to bridge the gaps; viewers find the show challenging because it usually does not explain explicitly what is happening. In other words, it refuses to do the kind of bridging that is necessary for viewers who come into the show mid-series or mid-season. Unlike the explicit explanations, interpretations, and summaries that abound on crime shows like *Law & Order* and *CSI*, viewers of *The Wire* must often make connections and draw conclusions themselves (sometimes with the help of outside sources).

The serial format in this case underscores the show's content, which focuses on the interrelations between things and people often not understood to be connected. The show explores how, while anger is often thought of as punctual, or as isolated in time/space, the actual causes, expressions, and repercussions of anger are as historically and socially situated and dispersed as those of any other cultural production. Through formal and thematic connections, the series progressively shows how the apparently homogenous/discrete/flat surface of malevolent agents constantly breaks through into depth, into webs and structures and interconnections beyond that one individual's actions. Blame and responsibility still fall partly on the person as moral agent, but comprehension of the motivations, determinants, and repercussions of each person's actions becomes complicated and non-individual. Coping potential is sometimes absent, resulting in depression and/or despair; at other times, characters' beliefs that they *ought* to be able to effect change themselves is what increases their frustration. In fact, anger often derives from that very inability to effect change in the system—despite your belief (as bourgeois individual, as police officer, as teacher, as middle-class, etc.) that you should be able to.

Take for example the very first episode of the show, titled "The Target." In the first several scenes, the classical rebel insider-outsider Detective Jimmy McNulty, the show's ostensible protagonist, seems to be pitted against the inefficacy, ignorance, and indifference of the police force. Certain television conventions invite us to identify with McNulty, such as the alternation of establishing shots of McNulty—showing us where he is situated and/or what he is doing—with what he sees. The episode starts with McNulty attending a murder trial that is undermined by drug kingpins Avon Barksdale and his lieutenant Stringer Bell, who intimidate one of the prosecution's two witnesses into silence (and murder the other one). McNulty tells the judge, an old friend, that the police are not pursuing Barksdale's organization because the various interlinked bureaucracies of the police and government (city, state, and federal) are only interested in numbers—arrests of low-level street dealers, the clearance of current year's homicide cases, etc.—rather than in systematic, in-depth police work. While himself experiencing a kind of low-level disgust/frustration, McNulty more often provokes the pointed ire of others, including other police detectives and his superior officers, particularly when he "rocks the boat," or disrupts social hierarchies. By speaking to the judge, he has gone outside the chain of command and angered his superior officers; by refusing to perform simplistic buy-busts that will only result in the arrest of low-level drug dealers (as opposed to systematic police work), he enrages Lt. Daniels, the commander of the special detail started to investigate Barksdale's drug organization. "Chain of command, detective," Daniels tells McNulty. In response, we hear what will become McNulty's anaphoric refrain throughout the series: "What the fuck did I do?"

But unlike many other police procedurals, *The Wire* shows us an increasing de-centering of McNulty's point of view, and a proliferation of viewpoints or, in narratological terms, focalizers. As early as the second episode, we see that Lt. Daniels himself is caught in a game in which there is no way to win. In terms of appraisal, Daniels is in an intellectual, ethical, and emotional quandary because he is torn between two conflicting goals: to advance his career and to be a principled and just being. If he follows his superiors' orders to simply let the special unit die out in order to advance his career (i.e., one kind of goal attainment), he sacrifices an ostensibly larger goal of being just—either way, he loses. His wife tells him, "The game is rigged, but you cannot lose if you do not play," but Daniels doubts that this individual extraction is possible. We also see the viewpoints and experiences of other characters, including Kima Greggs, the mixed-race African/Korean American lesbian police detective; D'Angelo Barksdale, nephew and midlevel manager for drug kingpin Avon Barksdale; drug addict and fan favorite Bubbles; and robin-hood hero Omar. Throughout the five seasons, juxtaposed and interlinked, are not only characters and events, but also repeated practices that—while they may or may not serve the plot or character development—also serve to tie the characters to intangible and invisible yet very real bureaucracies. For example, both Kima Greggs and McNulty are shown struggling with typing up reports for superiors on outdated typewriters.

Via such practices repeated throughout the series, we learn more about the paralleled structures of the police force and the highly organized Barksdale drug clan. As several critics have noted, the show parallels the two organizations to explore how they are part of the same system, working within a capitalist-bureaucratic state. In this way, the first two seasons both invoke and undermine the usual cop show formula of good guys versus bad guys. Part of the excitement of seasons 1 and 2 is watching the police work together under the leadership of Detective Lester Freamon, the savvy older veteran, as they try to crack the Barksdale drug empire. But although Avon Barksdale and Stringer Bell as the ringleaders/kingpins are the objects/targets of the investigation and the police's ire, we are continually shown how their criminal enterprise is connected to a crumbling urban economy, the loss of stable (as opposed to transitory) jobs and the weakening of unions, globalization (including and especially of the drug market), real estate and high finance, city politics, etc.—in other words, as Simon has discussed repeatedly in interviews, the vast social changes wrought by late capitalism. The challenge to viewing *The Wire* is that some of these connections are not explicit; the connections between the old and the new happen through recurrent characters, scenes, references—the "gaps" or betweens.

So when Avon Barksdale is convicted and imprisoned and Stringer Bell is killed, there is and there isn't change. The traditional mafia-style drug industry represented by Barksdale and Bell is gradually supplanted by one run by the ruthless Marlo Stanfield. Much like Tajirika in Ngugi's *Wizard of the Crow*, Stanfield's lack of affect perfectly embodies the new depersonalized, decentralized market logic of the drug trade, or the "McDonaldization" of the streets. In many ways, Barksdale and Bell reflect a Fordist capitalist model that is outmoded, and that results in the "downsizing" of their followers as well. For example, Bell's attempts to become a legitimate businessman according to what he learns in college economics courses demonstrate that he is following group norms that do not apply equally to everyone; when he tries to access those business and political circles as a "legitimate" businessman, he is shown to be out of his depth in dishonesty and graft. In other words, while Bell is certainly not a pawn, like low-level street dealers such as the teenage Bodie, Wallace, or Namond, he is far from the most powerful piece on the board, and certainly not one of the players. By exposing the larger, corrupt, and intertwined logics and systems of finance and politics, the show demonstrates how agency attribution and blame are insufficient to account for the anger and frustration of both the police and the criminals. Season 4, in particular, zeroes in on angry urban black youth (such as Bodie and Namond) and demonstrates the methodological insufficiency of even the best scholarly efforts to explain and intervene in such problems.

ANGRY URBAN YOUTH: "AT-RISK" YOUTH

Despite a recent movement in adolescent psychology toward "multi-factor" approaches, research on youth, poverty, and anger is still relatively narrow for disciplinary and methodological reasons, focusing on a few causal factors. Thus, as the investigators themselves often note, the studies will have limited explanatory power. One recent article serves as a case in point: a 2011 study in *School Psychology Quarterly* "empirically derived a multiple risk factors model of the development of aggression among middle school students in urban, low-income neighborhoods" (Kim et al. 215). Kim et al.'s approach is "multi-factor" compared to previous studies, which have been too narrow. They write,

> A model of the development of adolescent aggression should reflect the transactional processes of a variety of proximal and distal contexts. However, few empirical studies integrate multiple factors at multiple levels, especially for early adolescents from disadvantaged neighborhoods. To fill this gap, the present study developed and tested a multiple risk factor model of the development of aggression among ethnically diverse middle school students living in urban, low-income neighborhoods. (226).

Kim et al. focus on the problem of aggression, defined as "intentional behavior that may cause physical or psychological harm to others" in schools. They also call for more attention to how "multiple contextual factors simultaneously influence the development of aggression in early adolescence" (215–216), because previous explorations have focused on "only a few risk factors in the child or proximal contexts" (216). One exception to these narrower studies is Deater-Deckard, Dodge, Bates, and Pettit (1998), "who developed and tested a multiple risk factor model of externalizing problems in middle childhood," using "20 risk factors from four domains: characteristics of the child, sociocultural factors of the family, parenting experiences, and peer relationships" (216). Yet, Kim et al. note, even Deater-Deckard et al.'s model was limited in not including larger social contexts (e.g., the communities) and social institutions (e.g., churches) (216). In other words, even the most multifaceted previous studies of "urban, low-income" youth still have significant lacunae in their scope of consideration. In addition, Kim et al. note that a great gap still exists between the research and the actual prevention programs in schools. Despite the "school-based programs" proposed and implemented by researchers, "unfortunately, the majority of these programs have produced nonsignificant or limited effects on reducing aggression" (215).

To remedy this situation—admittedly partially and gradually—Kim et al. adopt what they term an "ecological perspective" that "emphasizes the influences of various contexts on human development" (217). Their four "domains of risk factors" include (1) the "individual domain"; (2) the "family domain"; (3) the "community domain"; and (4) the "media domain" (217). These four domains were assessed individually and as "covariants," and their subjects were "early adolescents attending eight middle schools from an urban school district in the southwest" with a large Latino population (218). To measure these variables, the researchers used questionnaires about life conditions and behaviors. For instance, they measured aggression using "the Aggression Scale," "an 11-item self-rating of aggressive behaviors for early adolescents" in which subjects are "asked to indicate how many times they engaged in a particular behavior during the seven days prior to the survey" (218). The "individual risk" measures included gender, ethnicity, and school grades. "Family risk" was measured with one question: "The parents or guardians you live with most of the time are: mother and father, mother and stepfather, father and stepmother, only mother, only father, grandparents, or other adults" (219), but because the answers were coded binarily ("0—both biological parents, and the remainder of the responses were coded as 1 = other family living" (219), the questions really only had two possible responses. The researchers also asked about community risks (nine kinds of violence students may or may not have seen during the past year) and media risk (the number of hours per day a subject watches TV and plays video games).[7]

The researchers recognize the many limitations to their study; for instance, they collected data through self-reporting, which is not entirely reliable and limits the respondents to the scope of the questionnaire, and several of their participants, "especially high-risk individuals," dropped out over the course of the investigation. Moreover, future studies could include many more variables, "such as peer aggression, school norms about aggression, and bonding to school" (227) and examine longer periods of time. But from a cultural studies standpoint, the problems with such research go beyond the number of factors included in algorithms or the limitations of self-reported studies. The separation of family and "media" and community into separate spheres is not actually tenable, as family members—as individuals and as a collective structure—are shaped by the ideologies, models, and, unofficially, prohibitions and enforcements from "culture," whether in communities or in the media. Moreover, the history of the shaping of communities is inextricable from the shaping of and by the media, which is itself a vastly differentiated thing. For instance, a well-fed, middle-class, middle-aged, white woman playing "Angry Birds" and a poor youth of color playing "Grand Theft Auto" are not equivalent in the contexts and effects of the individual playing the game, and certainly not in the public perception of them (the former is seen as harmless and fun, while the latter is seen as a threat to society). The bifurcation of families into two-biological-parents versus everything-else is also problematic; is it preferable to have abusive or neglectful biological parents over, say, a loving, supportive single parent or gay parents? In other words, all the considerations of ideology, ethics, rhetoric, class, social construction, and culture are necessary to complete a picture of adolescent aggression—that is, any one adolescent's apparent aggression. To understand the entire social phenomenon requires even more moving parts.

This study is just one recent example of the scores of research projects that, though they question the limitations of previous studies, are still themselves limited by the methodological boundaries of their discipline.[8] I do not mean here to dismiss entirely developmental and adolescent psychology; rather, my purpose is to acknowledge that this academic field is a particular historical product, with ideological and methodological limitations that may prevent it from fully capturing the actual multitude of possible causal factors. Every discipline has methodological limitations, which is why critical interdisciplinarity is more important than ever. Here, the intervention need not even come from outside psychology; the studies cited above limit themselves to "aggression" in youth, but as discussed briefly in Chapter 1, conversation about aggression and its relationship to anger is wide and varied. Usually, anger is defined as the felt emotion while aggression is one of the possible expressions, often dependent on a measure of coping potential (a sense that one can affect, however limitedly, the situation) and the cultural construction of appropriate expressions of anger (e.g., masculine aggression). Cognitive psychology's dissection of the elements of anger can help parse the underlying emotions producing the aggressive behavior. But more than that, cultural productions such as The Wire, even more than historiography and cultural theory (which are usually limited by having to make one point at a time in a linear, logical argument), can capture the actual variety and multiplicity of overdeterminations—never the same in any two individual cases—that shape and are shaped by "at-risk" urban youth. In following particular characters, The Wire can show the multiple, interdeterminant local and global factors shaping any single individual: economic, political, education, community, and other institutional structures; the family and friend relationships within, shaped by, and shaping those institutions; the individual's predilections and inclinations; and the ethical, rhetorical, and power complexities of a single conversation. Even if they are fictional, and even if *all* factors cannot be accounted for, this picture is still wider and deeper than that of any single disciplinary study.

"NO CORNER LEFT BEHIND"

Season 4 in particular highlights the undertheorized yet all-too-prevalent phenomenon of the rage of inner-city, poor black youth. This season explores the links between the failures of the urban school system (focusing on four eighth-grade boys) and the all-too-successful late-capitalist logic of Marlo Stanfield's new drug empire. Here, the young men who are angry have reasons to be angry; as opposed to say, *Law & Order*, *The Wire* gives us fuller sketches of characters like Bodie, a roughly seventeen-year-old "angry" drug dealer who rises through the ranks, only to discover—like Daniels—that group norms/duty do not apply equally to everyone; thirteen-year-old Namond Brice, whose father Wee-Bey is the Barksdale enforcer in jail for life; and Raymond Carver, a police detective who is a bungling thug in the first season but by season 4 has grown to become wiser and more sensitive, and hence more frustrated and angry.

The development of Preston "Bodie" Broadus, played by the excellent J. D. Williams (also of *Oz*), testifies to the close relationship between emotion, cognition, and context. Bodie is initially presented as someone who has just always been angry; as early as season 1, his grandmother says that when she took him in when he was four years old, "even then, I knew he was angry" ("Refugees"). But we see Bodie develop from a low-level drug dealer to a midlevel lieutenant, only to be downsized when another organization takes over the streets/market. One of the most poignant moments of the series takes place in the last episode of season 4, when Bodie makes an angry—and futile—stand against Stanfield's drug organization. Bodie's anger—he says, "This is my corner. I ain't running"—is ostensibly directed at an individual, but really the local drug trade system and, more generally, the logic of the marketplace are the objects of his rage. This scene could be seen as just a turf war of individual, pathologized black male rage—street violence is more often than not portrayed that way (hence the "warrior gene" hypothesis). Here, however, Bodie's fate is shown to be a product of the implacable logic of market consolidation and undermining of both small businesses and the presumably be-

nevolent management style typical of an older Fordist model (i.e., un-
skilled labor + loyalty = retirement & pensions). These changes are
undergirded by a force that is more *direct* (violence) than the world
of business usually allows itself to appear, although the latter's uti-
lization of enforced scarcity and competition is no less forceful and
implacable.

Indeed, Bodie's words shortly before his death resonate with the
words of the out-of-work union dockworkers in season 2:

> I been out there since I was thirteen. I ain't never fucked up a count,
> never stole off a package, never did some shit that I wasn't told to
> do. I been straight up. But what come back? Hmmm? You'd think
> if I get jammed up on some shit they'd be like, "A'ight, yeah. Bodie
> been there. Bodie hang tough" . . . They want me to stand with them,
> right? But where the fuck they at when they supposed to be standing
> by us? I mean, when shit goes bad and there's hell to pay, where they
> at? This game is rigged, man. We like the little bitches on a chess-
> board. ("Final Grades")

The line "This game is rigged" echoes Marla Daniel's advice to her
husband in season 1, an anaphoric refrain that emphasizes Simon's
point that the socioeconomic changes connect and affect everyone
across social groups. Another anaphora is Bodie's reference to chess
pawns, which also links us back to season 1, when D'Angelo teaches
chess to Bodie and Wallace, another low-level drug dealer whom
Bodie will eventually help kill ("doing as he's told"). Each of these refrains structurally tie different elements of the show together, while
also associating and paralleling the systems in which the characters
are enmeshed.

By the end of season 4, all three—Wallace, D'Angelo, and Bodie—
are dead, pawns in a game that, while they can see the board and
the other pieces, and can understand the rules, they know that they
do not have control over. More than anything else, this sense of being in a game that is rigged, in which your individual choices and
actions do not matter, is what produces the frustration and rage not
only of the characters but also of viewers of the show. That is, even
what we perceive as our goals (as conceived with appraisal theory of
emotion) is circumscribed by bureaucratic and capitalist institutions
that go beyond individuals. While agents have more or less power and
responsibility (e.g., Marlo Stanfield versus Bodie), we cannot com-

pletely understand their anger without understanding the structures that produce such situations and processes, and we also cannot completely eradicate or assuage that anger unless we change those structures.

A younger character who might at first glance look like a "typical" angry or aggressive adolescent is Namond Brice, one of the four middle-school protagonists introduced in the outstanding fourth season of the show, which focuses on education. Out of the four friends—the others being Michael, Randy, and Dukie—Namond is the most cocky and aggressive in school and on the streets. At Tilghman Middle School, where they are in the eighth grade, Namond's uncooperative and belligerent behavior gets him chosen for an experimental and, during its brief period of existence, successful school program to prevent criminal behavior while kids are still young. David Parenti, a University of Maryland sociologist, enlists the help of Howard "Bunny" Colvin, the former police major, to lead this program. In one of the earliest meetings of the special class, Namond is so disruptive and belligerent that Colvin takes him into another room to talk to him in private. Despite Colvin's best efforts, Namond responds with a series of "Fuck you!"s. Turning to a colleague (a sociology graduate student), Colvin observes, "This is gonna be harder than we thought" ("Unto Others").

But what *The Wire* shows us over the course of the season is that Namond and his apparent anger and aggression are products of multiple personal, social, and institutional factors that are shown to be mutually interacting and forming. We learn, for example, about Namond's family environment, but here "family" means more than factors such as family structure, size, and even income. The series explores how Namond's particular situation, including his mother and father, is produced by—and helps constitute and produce—not only the community but also the local economy, which is tied to various kinds of larger economic and political systems as well as to various forms of media and consumer culture. Likewise, the school itself, the site of intervention for many studies of adolescents (since schools are the best way to gain access to large groups of students), is scrutinized as variously imbricated in political, economic, social-cultural systems and processes.

As critics have noted, Namond is the most "middle-class" of the four boys. He wears designer clothes, he has money to buy ice cream treats for himself and his friends, and he and his mother live in a nicely decorated house with flat-screen televisions and video games. This relative wealth comes from the "success" of his father, Roland "Wee-Bey" Brice, in the Barksdale drug organization. For Namond, his parents, the Barksdales and their (former) employees, Namond's friends, and even to some extent the police (they recognize that Brice is a high-ranking lieutenant), success is defined as advancement in the Barksdale hierarchy, which is ironically more of a meritocracy than the police force or the newspaper (the subject of season 5). Wee-Bey advances not only through his physical and mental strength, but also through his loyalty; he is serving a life sentence in prison, having admitted to a dozen or so murders (not all of which he committed) in order to shield the Barksdales. As a result, the Barksdale family supports Namond and his mother De'Londa in relative wealth. Ironically, however, it is the privilege afforded to Namond by this financial security that renders him too "soft," insufficiently tough and masculine, to succeed on the streets. Rather, what the middle-class support has brought him, in the forms of adequate nutrition and rest, intellectual stimulation in the form of media, and "a room of his own," is an intellectual curiosity, particularly in debate and rhetoric, as well as a sense of entitlement, at least on the streets. Despite characterizing Namond's "work ethic" as "late-to-work, early-to-play," Bodie hires Namond as one of his "corner boys," saying, "Young'uns don't got a scrap of work ethic nowadays. If it wasn't for his pops, I wouldn't even bother" ("Boys of Summer"). The way that Namond's comfort informs his intellectual and social development contrasts sharply with the situations of Michael or Dukie, who live in extreme poverty and constant fear and uncertainty because their primary caretakers are drug addicts. Nevertheless, Namond and certainly all the "troublemakers" in Colvin and Parenti's experimental school program also perceive themselves as outsiders from "mainstream"—i.e., middle-class, suburban, white—society. Colvin takes Namond and two other students from the special class, Zenobia and Darnell, to a fancy restaurant, where they are mortified by their lack of cultural capital.

De'Londa Brice, whom viewers love to hate, wholeheartedly accepts and espouses the selfishness and greed of consumer culture and embraces the gender roles of mainstream patriarchy. When Namond and his mother are cut off from the Barksdale payroll, Namond's mother tells him that he must "step up" and "be man" ("Margin of Error"). Namond also feels pressure to "be a man," narrowly defined as aggression and cockiness, from his various social circles. Even among the four friends, Namond wants to be as "tough" as Michael (who is driven to his perceived toughness by agonizing circumstances of his own), and often resorts to demonstrating this toughness by bullying the hapless Dukie. Indeed, the show suggests that even relatively successful school-based intervention programs cannot help students such as Michael, who is seething with rage at his untenable situation (his drug-addicted mother has welcomed back into their home Michael's stepfather, who sexually abused him as a child). In school Michael demonstrates none of the apparent traits of aggression and anger that Namond does; in the relative safety of the school, as Colvin later notes, "corner boys" can practice their swagger by putting one over on the system. In contrast, Michael is forced into the drug trade and shows "real" toughness on the streets because his circumstances require it. In other words, the indicators that the fictional Parenti and real-life scholars use to identify angry urban youth in the schools, such as they did with Namond, would fail not only to explain Michael's situation and the overdetermined, multiple historical forces shaping him, but even to take note of him as a "problem." He is not disruptive like Namond and not as obviously destitute as Dukie.

Most powerfully, the show explores the larger, multiple, and interlinked systems in which the school itself operates, by juxtaposing thematically and formally the institutional bureaucracies of the school and the police. The first episode of season 4 is a beautiful example of pointed comparisons of the flawed logic of the bureaucracies driving both inner-city schools and police forces, as well as the extreme shortage of support for these institutions and the pressures they are under. For instance, viewers are introduced to Edward Tilghman Middle School via a conversation between Principal Claudell Withers and Assistant Principal Marcia Donnelly. The school finds itself beginning the school year "short two in math and four in science," as Donnelly puts it. Some teachers have not returned for the new school year, either because the job is too difficult or, because of their competence, they have been recruited by other school systems and/or the school administration. In other words, the grunts on the ground suffer brutal conditions, while the climbers get ahead into administration (of whatever institution). Into this conversation walks Roland "Prez" Pryzbylewski, a former police officer, starting his teaching career at Edward Tilghman Middle School. Although he does not have official system identification yet (and will not even have his teaching certificate until the following year), the school is so desperate for teachers that, as Donnelly jokes, they "buzz him in before he changes his mind."[9]

In the same episode, we see Daniels, who is now a major and district commander of the Western district, discussing police duty assignments with his second-in-command, Lt. Dennis Mello. Daniels tries to recruit McNulty, who has been reduced to car patrol (and chooses to stay there for personal reasons), to return to more extensive duties. Daniels tells McNulty, "McNulty, I'm short two men in Ops, and my follow-up squad couldn't make a case to save its life." As with teachers, experienced detectives, already in short supply, either wear out (like McNulty) or move up into administration, and those who are left are overwhelmed. New recruits tend to be, as Donnelly puts it, "lambs to the slaughter." When Withers and Donnelly discuss scheduling teachers to oversee the cafeteria, Donnelly says, "You see that's gonna leave Ernest alone for second period, and he can't handle it alone." Immediately following Withers and Donnelly's exchange, the scene cuts to a parallel conversation between Daniels and Mello, discussing police duty assignments:

> MELLO: That leaves Tullman, as I see 'em, for the 12th. You think he can handle the whole shift?
> DANIELS: Now which one's Tullman, again?
> MELLO: Goofy redhead, kind of looks like Opie from Mayberry. But less fierce. ("Boys of Summer")

Both institutions are also driven by statistics and numbers to meet arbitrary requirements of achievement and success. For instance, we see a boring, meaningless meeting for teachers at the beginning of the school year, which provides no guidance or support for the actual needs of students and teachers. A speaker explains that "the only tool that they will need" to reach students is I.A.L.A.C., an acronym for "I am lovable and capable." Such irrelevant and absurd activities are juxtaposed with similarly useless activities for the police; the show parallels scenes from the teachers' meeting with an equally meaningless and jargon-filled police meeting about "soft targets" of terrorism ("Boys of Summer"). The parallel between the two meetings underscores not only the bureaucratic goals that have eclipsed meaningful approaches to preventing crime and teaching (linked activities), but also a shared emphasis on control and criminality. Moreover, as the show emphasizes again and again, the same economic, political, and cultural conditions that create crime as well as the police state also shape the public school system and the students who learn how to "game" that system. Both teachers and police officers learn how to "juke the stats"—police officers with manipulated crime statistics and teachers with test scores.[10]

The most egregious example of the flawed logic of the bureaucratic systems is the parallel fate of Colvin's experiments. Just as his experimental, admittedly flawed Hamsterdam drug-legalization project of season 3 resulted in his demotion and dismissal from the police force, the experimental youthful offender program—despite the real progress it makes with some students—is abruptly halted not due to actual concerns about funding but to anxiety about meeting test goals and bureaucratic requirements. What really counts is meeting the narrowly defined measures of the school system; Principal Withers and Assistant Principal Donnelly refer to the Board of Education as "Puzzle Palace" ("Alliances"), and another teacher observes that the Baltimore City Public Schools system is "all about the leave-no-child-behind stuff getting spoon-fed" ("Corner Boys"). When Prez asks, "What do they learn?" an experienced teacher advises him to find some middle ground between the state and his conscience. Another experienced teacher tells him, "First year isn't about the kids. It's about you surviving" ("Corner Boys"). As Prez observes, in the school system as in the police system, it's all about "juking the stats," or narrowly focusing on meeting the numbers of a few indicators, rather than understanding the entire situation systemically. For Colvin and Parenti as well as the other teachers, the police, the media, and government (and increasingly, universities), the quantitative has won out over the qualitative.

In an admittedly complex situation with an almost infinite number of factors, a relatively arbitrary set of a limited number of factors is measured in order to assess learning, as well as aggression, "family structure," and other variables. There is a conflict between, on one hand, the narrow assessment models of some disciplines and bureaucracies and, on the other hand, the actual multifaceted nature of the "social problem" of angry urban youth. The show thematizes this conflict in several ways. The character of Ms. Duquette, a doctoral candidate in psychology who helps lead the experimental class

("Unto Others") and then later protests its closing, represents what people in sociology and education could do if they were not as handicapped by narrow assessment measures as the police and the teachers are. When the students start making progress, she tells Colvin and Parenti, "We're in unchartered territory here" ("Unto Others"). *The Wire* thus critiques the narrow institutional thinking that fails to make connections and draw parallels between systems.

For instance, when Colvin describes the youth as using the school as "training for the streets. The building's the system, we the cops," Namond responds indignantly:

Yeah, like y'all say—don't lie, don't bunk, don't cheat, don't steal, or whatever. But what about y'all, huh? What, the government? What's it—Enron? Ha! Steroids, yeah. Liquor business. Booze is the real killer out there. And cigarettes—oh, shit. [To Ms. Duquette:] Hey, you got some smokes in there?

[Ms. Duquette responds:] "I'm trying to quit." [The students laugh at her and she smiles.] . . .

We do the same thing as y'all, except when we do it, it's like, "Oh my God, these kids is animals." Like it's the end of the world coming. Man, that's bullshit, all right? 'Cause it's like—what is—hypocrite—hypocritical. ("Boys of Summer")

This scene works on many levels. It is character development, because Namond is partly showboating and disingenuous, and as we will see, he is better with his brain and mouth than his fists. But it also relays the show's scathing indictment of the hypocrisy of "legal" capitalist society, which brands urban youth as "aggressive," dangerous, or "at-risk," even though drug kingpins like Stringer Bell cannot even come close to the graft, corruption, and wrongdoing found on Wall Street, in city hall, and in Washington, DC. As another student, Zenobia, adds, "I mean, yeah we got our thing, but this is just part of the big thing." School test scores and arrest statistics are not necessarily inherently dangerous, just as measuring quantities is not inherently problematic (and is sometimes necessary). But the show points out repeatedly that these narrowly quantitative approaches do not enable and sometimes actively prevent links to structural parallels (e.g., illegal drugs versus tobacco and alcohol; petty theft versus white collar crimes) or to the examination of ideological cultural and moral assumptions that hide and undergird hypocrisy (e.g., theft by Wall Street is clever; theft by the poor constitutes them as a social menace).

This anger against structures, rather than individuals, culminates in *The Wire* when Ellis Carver, a police detective, has a fit of anger at the end of season 4. This one scene in the last episode of the fourth season, in which Ellis Carver cannot save thirteen-year-old Randy from a boys' home, captures the multiple emotions—frustration, anger, despair, guilt—produced by overdetermined and invisible bureaucratic, economic, political, and social structures. When Carver and the police inadvertently leak that Randy gave the police some information, Randy is labeled a "snitch," ostracized, and beaten; his foster mother's home is firebombed and she is seriously injured. Wanting to keep Randy from having to return to the group boys' home—which Randy knows from his previous experiences is a place of brutality and hardship—Det. Carver tries to negotiate with a social services agent. Unable to get Randy into a foster family, Carver offers to take in Randy himself. A nameless, expressionless Department of Social Services agent tells Carver that there is nothing he can do to help Randy. Tellingly, Carver offers an individual solution to this individual case—he himself will take in Randy—but again the individual solution, just like the individual frustration and anger, cannot change the institutions that create this situation. Both Carver and Randy lose out to the logic of state bureaucracy, poverty, and the streets—imbricated yet very real systems. When Carver returns to his car, he vents his frustration against the multiple systems that created this situation—the DSS, the police, the economy and culture of the streets, including models of masculinity, capitalism, and racism—by angrily pounding on his steering wheel.

The Wire illustrates emotion and anger as linked to cognition in systemic and multivalent ways, in importantly complementary ways to the psychological research. In the show, we repeatedly see persons directing anger toward others perceived (explicitly or implicitly) to be illegitimately and/or intentionally obstructing a goal. The terms of illegitimacy are based on group norms, whether that "group" is the police force, the labor union, the gang, the school system, or other, more amorphous norms of ethics or justice. But *The Wire* explores how this narrative of anger—individual versus individual—informs the experience and expression of anger; in other words, the narrative(s) play a significant role in creating and reproducing emotions. One of the strongest narratives, particularly for the middle-class officials of the police, the government, the school, and the newspaper, as well as the working-class members of the labor union, is that of "coping potential," or the notion that one ought to be able to change a situation. The contradiction between this constitutive narrative—constitutive of the emotion as well as of the subject—and the institutional, historical, collective forces that actually structure the situation produces not only frustration but also explosive anger.

The expression of this anger is also culturally mediated. *The Wire* demonstrates how some forms of anger—even and particularly in the most demonized "angry black youth"—can be a manifestation of what bell hooks describes as presence, "the assertion of subjectivity that colonizers do not want to see" (12). Against the anger of Namond and Bodie, Marlo Stanfield's coldness and lack of emotion particularly suit him well to enter the worlds of business and politics that the more intellectual but also more naïve Stringer Bell—that is, naïve in believing that what he learned in business classes applies equally to everyone—cannot seem to navigate. At the same time, Bodie and Namond's anger in and of itself does not lead to solutions; the series, while tracing where their anger comes from, does not romanticize it. In fact, Bodie's anger ultimately does not make any difference for him. What is different for Namond is that someone else—Bunny Colvin—who does understand the larger context, is willing to help Namond recognize that context and try to change it. In other words, the character Colvin and the show overall illustrate how anger is in part an individual experience and cognitive process, but is also—in terms of causality and remedy—even more importantly a product of historical, social, and ideologically constructed contexts. The characters' goals are just as historically, socially, and ideologically constructed as are the collective (not in the good sense) institutions, bureaucracies, and systems that block them.

The Wire demonstrates that anger, as we tend to think of it and feel it, is both too individualistic (and insufficiently systemic) and, ironically, not *human* enough. That is, agency attribution (defined as an external agent causing harm to the self) as a constitutive part of anger is itself part of what renders modern anger impotent. The notions of a single factor, single agent, and single response are inadequate to explain the sources and effects of racial and class anger. At the same time, the show explores how the characters' anger is produced by systems that render the individual human being worthless.

As Simon has said of *The Wire*, "It's the triumph of capitalism over human value" (O'Rourke).

So when we talk about emotions in texts, the issue is not simply what the characters feel and think, or what emotions readers or viewers experience, or what formal strategies the texts use to elicit these emotions. It is all of these things, plus the ideological and material struggles of which these narratives are a part. While a film like *Crash* is shaped by and promotes an individualist notion of anger that endorses the liberal multiculturalism of late capitalism, the television series *The Wire*—along with the texts I discussed by Kingston, Dangarembga, and Ngugi—offers alternative models of anger as intersubjective, collective, institutional, historical, and ideological. Against the regulation, pathologizing, and isolation of the feeler of—particularly racial—anger, such texts suggest that not only racial anger but also anger in general, in its various guises, is embedded within structures and processes that need to be unraveled in order to understand the nature and implication of that anger. The key then is to harness what activists call "cold anger," or "outrage against injustice" at systemic and structural levels, and turn it into collective action against those systems (Atlas and Dreier 82).

ANGER AND OUTRAGE

The worst attitude is indifference. "There's nothing I can do;
I get by"—adopting this mindset will deprive you of one of the
fundamental qualities of being human: outrage. Our capacity for
protest is indispensable, as is our freedom to engage.
STÉPHANE HESSEL, *INDIGNEZ-VOUS!*

I STARTED THIS BOOK BEFORE the Arab Spring, the European anti-austerity protests, and the Occupy Wall Street movement. Since then, however, people around the world have transformed their frustration at capitalism, political repression, and explicit or implicit rule by the wealthy, or the 1 percent, into political and moral outrage. This shift was sparked by the global economic recession, the material result of the increasing concentration of wealth in the hands of the very few over the past several decades. Although the problems had existed previously (Muammar Gaddafi had been in power for forty-two years, and U.S. median middle-class wages had been falling for decades), the catalyst into outrage was sparked by massive unemployment and economic stress, *as well as* developing collective articulations of group norms, such as democracy, human rights, equal opportunity, and a living wage. This continuing articulation of the norms being violated played an important role in making people angry because it provided them with focus (agency attribution, coping potential, group norms). This shift helped us move from the cynicism and complacency of the 1990s to widespread political mobilizations. Furthermore, it reminds us that anger—like all emotion and cognition—is not only culturally and historically situated, but also materially and ideologically determined.

In these transitions, we can also see more clearly the distinc-

tion between frustration and outrage. Frustration is the sense of being balked from goals without a clear agent to blame. The goals in
question may be individual or collective (or both). The subject may
be aware of how to achieve the goal but prevented from doing so, *or*
the subject may not even be aware of how to achieve that goal, a situation we see particularly with bureaucracy (e.g., *The Wire's* Carver
Ellis and the child welfare agencies). Moral outrage, however, is based
on a perception that a group norm has been violated, whether or not
one as an *individual* benefits; or rather, moral outrage unites individual and collective goals, so that individual goals and hopes are concomitant with collective goals.

Stéphane Hessel's 2010 *Indignez-vous!*, translated into English as
Time for Outrage, has been sweeping across Europe for the very reason that it reminds us of the definition and role of moral outrage. In
cognitive psychological terms, because our goals have seemed so dis-
torted and limited, the external agents unclear, and our coping potential so limited, we have been in danger of losing our basic human faculty of outrage. Hessel writes,

> It is true, the reasons to get angry may seem less clear today, and the
> world may seem more complex. Who is in charge; who are the deci-
> sion makers? It's not always easy to discern. We're not dealing with
> a small elite anymore, whose action we can clearly identify. We are
> dealing with a vast, interdependent world that is interconnected in
> unprecedented ways. But there are unbearable things all around us.
> You have to look for them; search carefully. Open your eyes and you
> will see. (11)

Hessel exhorts young people to look around them and engage, rather
than giving in to indifference, "the worst attitude." Such passivity, he
argues, stunts a basic human capacity to engage with the world.

Seen in light of Hessel's insights and the examinations of *On Anger*, appraisal theory is problematic not necessarily because it is incorrect in identifying the mechanics of anger, but because its focus
is individual—or rather, it limits itself to the description of the individualistic conceptions of goals and emotions that we tend to live by.
This model, however, does not account for a different kind of anger,
an outrage based on ethics, compassion, and justice. Outrage is, technically speaking, a form of anger, but the texts examined in this book
repeatedly point to two elements that distinguish political, ethical

outrage from the cognitive psychological definitions of anger. First, it is systemic and collective. While appraisal and other theories in cognitive psychology rely on *implicit* collectivities—the group decides which actions are legitimate and which are not—appraisal theory in particular is still based on individual agents, actions, desires, and goals. Second, it is *principled*. That is, rather than being based on individual desires and goals, or even communal ones, outrage is based in collective notions of justice, ethics, and rights.

For instance, Hessel describes the 1944 Declaration of Policy by the National Council of the French Resistance, which put forth "a set of values and principles upon which to ground our nation's modern democracy once it was freed from occupation" (2). The things they listed were not extravagant, yet in 2011 we still remain woefully far from achieving these goals, such as freedom of the press (including a media not controlled by wealthy and/or media conglomerates and/or driven by profit) (4); equal opportunities for education (4); food, clothing, and shelter for everyone; and "a true democracy, both economic and social . . . which implies the eradication of the economic and financial feudalism ruling our economy" (3). In Hessel's words, "Today, more than ever, we need these principles and values" (2). Hessel also identifies the increasing wealth gap along racialized lines as one of the most pressing outrages:

> The grievous injuries inflicted on people deprived of the essential requirements for a decent life, not only in the third world—in Africa, Asia, Haiti, and elsewhere—but in the suburbs of our largest Western cities, where seclusion and poverty breeds hatred and revolt. The widening gap between the very poor and the very rich is made all the more insulting by the access the poor now have to the internet and other forms of mass communication that highlight these inequalities. (12)

To remedy the systemic and ubiquitous—but often decentralized—violations of human rights and to achieve the goals of democracy, freedom, and equity, we need not anger fueled by a sense of individual harm or desires, but rather *outrage* produced from collectively articulated and agreed-upon principles and values.

Outrage, moreover, is tied to action. But rather than directing blame or punishment toward a single agent, principled outrage should be directed toward collective, ethical action. Of the anger in the wake of the Murdoch news empire's phone-hacking scandal, Priyamvada Gopal writes,

> Real indignation is born not of hatred but of empathy and solidarity with others. It seeks to move beyond the particulars of one's self and community to something more universally human. Our shared anger at Murdoch drew on a humane sense that the sufferings of other people matter and the further exploitation of the already vulnerable is not to be tolerated.

Or, as Viet Thanh Nguyen succinctly puts it, "There are some things we should be angry about."

Hessel reminds us, moreover, that this outrage does not need to produce violence:

> The messages of Gandhi, Martin Luther King, Jr., and Nelson Mandela remain relevant even in a world where ideological confrontations and invasive totalitarianism have been overcome. They are messages of hope, of faith in a society's ability to overcome conflict through mutual understanding and watchful patience. To achieve this, we must rely on our belief in human rights, the violation of which—whoever the perpetrators may be—must provoke our indignation. We must never surrender these rights. (25)

Just a quick look at the objects and causes of outrage, on the left and right, reminds us that principles and values determine what we consider outrages. These are the battles that must be fought on the ground of culture and ideas; cognitive psychology as it currently exists does not and cannot necessarily account for this aspect. Therefore, the stories that we tell about the world, ourselves, and our values are among the most important things we can study in order to understand anger as a complex combination of cognition, biology, ideology, history, and ethics.

NOTES

INTRODUCTION

1. Here I refer specifically to the Marxist tradition of cultural studies in the Frankfurt and Birmingham schools, but for most of this book I use the term "cultural studies" to encompass a wide variety of approaches to studying literature and culture. I discuss this issue further in Chapter 2.

2. For just a few discussions of such issues, see Frederick Luis Aldama, *Postethnic* and *Why the Humanities Matter*, especially Chapter 10; Kimberly Chabot-Davis; Rey Chow; Madhu Dubey; and Sue J. Kim.

3. In some ways, this book complements Anne Cheng's project of engaging psychology, although here I address cognitive psychology instead of psychoanalysis. Both Cheng and I take individual emotions seriously while also not limiting our understanding of emotions to individuals. Anne Cheng writes that racial melancholia, "far from denoting a condition of surrender, embodies a web of negotiation that expresses agency as well as abjection" (17). In terms of anger, we might alter this statement as follows: far from denoting a condition of victory—or indeed, any simple singular thing—anger embodies a web of negotiations of cognitive, ideological, structural, and historical factors that may express agency as well as abjection. In this book I focus on racial anger, but I would contend that this complex dynamic of anger, which may include agency as well as abjection depending on historical contexts, is generally true. A more sustained engagement between psychoanalysis, with its investment in the unconscious, and cognitive psychology, with its emphasis on conscious and semi-conscious mental processes, remains to be done. I find both fields useful, although in this book I deal primarily with cognitive psychology.

4. For more on racial formations, see Omi and Winant, as well as Haney López.

5. As Trotsky writes in "The ABC of Materialist Dialectics," "The fundamental flaw of vulgar thought lies in the fact that it wishes to content itself with motionless imprints of a reality which consists of eternal motion. Dialectical thinking gives to concepts, by means of closer approximations, corrections, concretisation, a richness of content and flexibility; I would even say 'a succulence' which to a certain extent brings them closer to living phenomena. Not capitalism in general, but a given capitalism at a given stage of development. Not a workers' state in general, but a given workers' state in a backward country in an imperialist encirclement, etc." We could add, not anger in general, but anger in and about raced, gendered, and classed bodies at a given historical moment, demonstrating certain common cognitive capabilities that are, in part, a product of these racial, gendered, and classed social formations.

6. Here "cognitive studies" encompasses developments in neuroscience, psychology, and philosophy, while "cultural studies" is shorthand for approaches that focus on cultural productions of all kinds (no longer just literature and art, but also speech, city planning, etc.) and emphasize the social construction of identities and meaning. The terms "science" and "humanities" are not quite ac-

curate because many cognitivists (and much of many of the cognitive studies on emotion I refer to in Chapter 1) are located in the social sciences, and many cultural studies critics straddle the humanities and social sciences. The distinction is not so much about disciplines as about basic principles and orientation.

7. See also work by Timothy Brennan, Priyamvada Gopal, Biodun Jeyifo, Neil Lazarus, Manning Marable, David Palumbo-Liu, E. San Juan, and Ellen Meiksin Wood.

CHAPTER 1

1. For overviews and assessments of the work of James and Lange, see Antonio Damasio's "William James and the Modern Neurobiology of Emotion" in Evans and Cruse, *Emotion, Evolution, and Rationality* 3–13; Power and Dagleish 30–33; Ortony, Clore, and Collins 4–5; K. Young 81; Brennan 4; and Lyons.

2. See also Miller; Power and Dagleish 33–37; and Lyons 34–35.

3. See Dagleish and Power, particularly Chapters 1 and 2; Power and Dagleish 48–54; Ortony, Clore, and Collins 5–6; and the *International Handbook of Anger* (Potegal, Stemmler, and Spielberger).

4. Just the relatively short opening section, titled "Are There Basic Emotions?" in *The Nature of Emotion: Fundamental Questions*, edited by Paul Ekman and Richard J. Davidson, demonstrates the range of views on the question. Basically, it depends on what one means by "basic" and "emotions." James Averill argues that "there appears to be no compelling reason to postulate basic emotions, regardless of the criteria used" (*Nature of Emotion* 14), while Paul Ekman contends that there are no "nonbasic emotions," because he uses "basic" to refer to the evolutionary nature of emotions (19). Jaak Panksepp maintains that basic emotions "aris[e] from coherent brain operating systems that have a considerable number of shared neural characteristics" (23), in contrast to physiological reflexes that do not engage higher cognitive functions at the moment they are triggered (e.g., hunger, startle); in other words, brain sciences are key to identifying basic emotions. In contrast, Richard A. Shweder denies that we can identify basic emotions yet, because emotions are "interpretive schemes" and "we do not yet know whether all peoples of the world emotionalize their feelings to the same extent, or whether they emotionalize their feelings with the same 'emotion' schemes when they do" (33). For more information on debates about the number of "basic" or universal emotions, see Ahmed 5–12; Power and Dagleish; de Souza; Hogan, *Cognitive Science*; Evans and Cruse; Ekman; Clore and Ortony; Johnson-Laird and Oatley; Oatley and Johnson-Laird; Ortony, Clore, and Collins 25–29; and Ekman (Chapter 3) in Dagleish and Power.

5. My discussion emphasizes cognitive psychologists' approach to emotion. Although there is a growing body of work on neurology and the brain, I do not deal with that material, not in small part due to disciplinary limitations. Further surveys of cognitive as well as evolutionary and neurological accounts of emotion can be found in Keltner and Lerner, who note that "the experience of anger involving high levels of agency has been associated with activation in the left-frontal regions of the cortex" and "the amygdala is involved in primary evaluative appraisals" (321). Carol Tavris vigorously argues that anger is not more bio-

logical or genetic than social. More interdisciplinary work is certainly something that is needed in the future.

6. Dagleish and Power go on to note, however, that anger is not always active and sadness not passive (6).

7. Most psychologists differentiate between the emotion of anger and a range of possible expressions. While aggression is most commonly associated with anger, it is usually distinguished from the cognitive, affective, and somatic processes that go into the emotion of anger per se. According to Cox and Harrison, while the "behavioral dimension of anger" is usually identified as aggression, or attempting to harm others, "the cognitive dimension of anger" most often refers to cognitive appraisals (372). Tavris differentiates the emotion of anger from a range of possible expressions—from hostility to aggression to an angry cry— which are gendered and culturally specific (200–209).

8. See Oatley and Johnson-Laird; and Ortony, Clore, and Collins, Chapter 3.

9. I discuss further Berkowitz and Harmon-Jones's critique of appraisal theory in the next section.

10. Power and Dagleish outline a slightly different spectrum. Citing the work of Ulric Neisser, author of the seminal 1967 text *Cognitive Psychology*, they say that cognitive psychologists range in their views of cognition from "constructivism," "in which the individual perceives the world based in part on existing mental representations of the world," to "realism," in which mental representations are judged against reality, both social and physical. Neisser, they note, ultimately espoused a "constructive realism," in which "the individual is seen to be struggling towards mental representations that bear semblance to reality" (9). Neisser's work is important because, they conclude, "if cognitive approaches can be placed on a continuum from constructivism to realism, approaches to emotions and their disorders might best be placed at the mid-point between the two" (9). This model of cognition, rather than focusing on the input-output process implied by appraisal—information goes in, an appraisal analysis comes out—is one way of modeling the world.

11. See also Hopkins.

12. See also Averill, *Anger and Aggression*, and "Studies on Anger and Aggression."

13. Thus, Frijda continues, anger constitutes a stage in the grieving process: "Anger helps to maintain the illusion that the lost object is still to be found, that the situation of misery can still be modified" (430). Real grieving, he continues, takes place only after the protest of anger is worked through.

14. By the same token, Berkowitz and Harmon-Jones challenge Frijda and others' distinction between mood and emotion. They write, "It is often held that emotions, unlike moods, are about something in particular; they have a more definite cause, more specific target, or both" (123). But they argue that this distinction fails to account for the various factors that actually constitute both moods and emotion: "If people can vary the extent to which they have a clear conception of the cause of their affective arousal, where do we place the cutting point on this continuum, putting mood on one side and emotion on the other?" (123). For example, as I will discuss further in the next chapter, before the various theories of feminism, an "appraisal" may not have been possible because a possible goal of

gender equality—or simply being treated like a human being—may not have been possible. Rather, a general "mood" of frustration, anger, bitterness, sadness, or depression, depending on the particular person and context, may have prevailed. In this sense, political analyses, such as Satya Mohanty's postpositivist realism, are akin to appraisal theory, but the question remains: what about the "excess" of emotions that don't fit into such straightforward analyses?

15. Likewise, Lazarus argues that physiological arousal is not equivalent to producing *emotion*: "Emotion, for example, is not just physiological arousal, though such arousal is one of the traditional defining attributes. Arousal can be produced by exercising vigorously or entering a hot or cold room . . . [Arousal] will produce an emotion only if we appraise the encounter (e.g., the physical and social conditions and the bodily state it produces) as having a bearing on our well-being, as when, for example, it presents some physical danger or brings blissful relief from discomfort" ("On the Primacy" 124).

16. The culture- and context-dependent nature of emotions has led some, like Russell and Fehr, to repudiate the entire notion of a categorical definition of anger that entails a checklist of characteristics and/or a common set of features. Instead, they espouse a "fuzzy," context-specific definition of anger, in which there are different scripts for different situations. On one hand, they note, are the "classical" definitions of anger, in which "the varieties of anger fail to form a true class-inclusion hierarchy as envisioned in both classical and prototype accounts" (186). But in reality, they argue, "boundaries between categories are fuzzy, with members of one category blending into members of neighboring categories" (187); instead, they argue for "context-sensitive scripts within a fuzzy hierarchy," in which "the word *anger* takes on a specific meaning in a specific context. Within limits, any user can create meaning by specifying how he or she is using the word" (203).

17. See also Frijda, Manstead, and Bem; Forgas; and most of the books in the Cambridge University Press series Studies in Emotion and Social Interaction, second series.

18. See "Inner Workings," Regan, and Vedantam; see also further discussions of and challenges to the ethical effects of empathy in Keen.

19. For further work on gender differences and "display rules" of emotion, see Fischer; Sadeh et al.; Hess, Adams, and Kleck; Hall and Matsumoto; Simpson and Stroh; Fischer et al.; and Davis.

20. See also Hart for a longer list of works related to cognitive approaches to literature and culture. For a sampling of the cautionary reactions to the interface of cognitive studies and literary studies—on both sides of the disciplinary divide—see Jackson, Mellard, and Atkinson and Delamont.

21. Hogan's example of a schema: "Being organic is more central to our conception of a human than is having two arms—a person with one arm would count as human, but a statue with two arms would not" (57); his example of a prototype is that most people would think of "human" as "having two arms, two legs, and so forth" (58). The variations, however—gendered or racial, for example—demonstrate how history and culture are necessary to understand any of these cognitive processes.

22. Hogan goes on to argue that prototypical narratives, such as the romantic and heroic tragicomedies, arise from prototypes of emotions (*Mind* 88–98).

23. Herman argues that storyworlds are a kind of "mental model" or "discourse model." Mental models, according to Johnson-Laird, are "theoretical constructs designed to make sense of inferences, both explicit and implicit" (quoted in *Story* 18). This model, Herman argues, is a better way to conceptualize *how* we think than "the formal rules of a 'mental logic,'" like a computer, which are overly rigid. Mental models are a way to think about how individuals conceptualize storyworlds beyond the realm of language: "Mental models can be characterized in general terms as nonlinguistic representations of the situation(s) described by a sentence or a set of sentences, that is, a discourse" (*Story* 18). Herman relates mental models and storyworlds to "discourse models" in linguistics, described as "emergent, dynamic interpretive frames that interlocutors collaboratively construct in order to make sense of an ongoing stretch of talk" (19). Rather than "the conduit metaphor," or the notion of language as simplistic means of direct communication, in the discourse model, "sentences are like blueprints, planned artifacts whose design is tailored to the goal of enabling an interlocutor to reconstruct the sets of discourse entities after which the blueprints are patterned" (19). But unlike the notion of language as a vessel or conduit, "the blueprint analogy predicts that wholly successful interpretation of linguistic designs will be rare—given the complexity of processes involved in planning, executing, and making sense of the blueprints" (19).

CHAPTER 2

1. For examples of such studies, see Brescoll and Uhlmann; Carter, Pieterse, and Smith; Izard; Parkinson, Roper, and Simons; Phelps; and Stimmel et al.

2. See also Monga and Rodriguez. In contrast, Goodwin, Jasper, and Polletta's collection *Passionate Politics* (2001) seeks to return the analyses of "emotions as culturally or socially constructed" to the sociological studies of social movements, as does Hoggett and Thompson's *Politics and the Emotions: The Affective Turn in Contemporary Political Studies* (2012).

3. Feminist literary critics, including Brenda Silver, Jane Marcus, Carolyn Heilbrun, Kathleen Helal, and Lili Hsieh, have particularly examined the discourses of anger in and around the work of Virginia Woolf.

4. Woodward draws on feminist work on anger to think about how we talk about emotions and older people: "In a way the reverse is true with the old: being wise, which entails being without anger, is held up as an ideal" ("Against Wisdom" 206).

5. Tavris convincingly argues that men and women in the U.S. today do not feel or express anger more or less often than the other gender, and women generally feel their anger is as legitimate as men's. What differs are the contexts in which they express anger (men are more likely to express anger in public than women, but both are likely to suppress anger at the workplace); some of the forms of expression (both men and women will yell and become violent, but women are more prone to the angry cry); and the *perceptions* and *consequences* of anger:

"What insulting words and the stereotype of sex differences reflect . . . is not a real difference between men and women in the likelihood of feeling or expressing anger, but a *status* difference" (215).

6. I discuss some possible ways to think about time/history, narrative, and anger in Chapter 4.

7. Postpositivist realists such as Satya Mohanty and Paula Moya follow Jaggar in their attempts to account for emotions as knowledge by linking to this kind of political appraisal. But postpositivist realism focuses too much on identity, thereby risking enforcing liberal humanist, individualist, and discursive notions of power. Barbara Foley and Robert Young argue that postpositivist realism actually shares with the postmodernism that it critiques an emphasis on identities and heterogeneity, which fit so neatly with liberal individualism, and the suppression of capitalism as the cause of systemic inequality.

8. The dynamics of anger in *Aiiieeeee!* (and even more so in *The Big Aiiieeeee!*) are a fascinating study themselves; the editors are angriest at the likes of Maxine Hong Kingston and David Henry Hwang. I hope to pursue anger in Asian American literature in a later project.

9. Just a few of the works that deal with black rage include Audre Lorde's "The Uses of Anger" (*Women's Studies Quarterly* 1981), republished in *Sister/Outsider* (1984); William Grier and Price M. Cobbs's *Black Rage* (1992); Cornel West's *Race Matters* (1993); bell hooks's *Killing Rage* (1995); Paul Harris's *Black Rage Confronts the Law* (1999); Rosevelt Noble's *Black Rage in the American Prison System* (2006); and Leonard Nathaniel Moore's *Black Rage in New Orleans* (2010).

10. But, again, anger is historical; despite the continuity and/or exacerbation of stark racial inequalities, Ellis Cose follows up his 1995 *Rage of the Privileged Class* with a new book, *The End of Anger: A New Generation's Take on Race and Rage*, which maintains that a significant attitudinal shift toward optimism has taken place among both young African Americans and whites. Cornel West differentiates anger, which is "a bitterness that devours your soul," from "righteous indignation," which is "morally" and "ethically driven" (A. Taylor 9).

11. In other words, capitalism as a system is not machines or martians but a relationship among persons, based upon specific notions of value, which Marx explains in *Capital*, vol. 1.

12. See also Clough and Halley as well as Gregg and Seigworth.

13. Rather, Sedgwick writes, "perhaps attending to the textures and effects of particular bits of language, as I try to do in many of these essays, requires a step to the side of antiessentialism, a relative lightening of the epistemological demand on essential truth" (6).

14. For instance, she contrasts the "paranoid" approach (or the search for truth) and the "reparative" (a more contingent project of making better), advocating for the latter at this moment in time. As Muñoz writes, "Sedgwick wishes to consider how certain strong theories of the social, theories that can be codified as prescriptive and totalizing, might not be as advantageous at this particular moment as weak theories that do not position themselves in the same masterful, totalizing fashion" ("Feeling Brown, Feeling Down" 682).

15. Although Williams would disagree with—and indeed writes *Marxism and Literature* in part to critique—the tendency in literary theory to privilege ab-

sence, fissures, the unconscious, incommensurability, etc.: "Yet the actual alternative to the received and produced fixed forms is not silence: not the absence, the unconscious, which bourgeois culture has mythicized" (131).

16. Ngai writes that structures of feeling "cannot be equated with what we ordinarily think of as emotional qualities, since the former are defined as formations that are still in process and barely semanticized, while the latter have distinct histories and come heavily saturated with cultural meanings and value" (360, note 28). Rather than focusing on affect or emotions, Williams is "strategically mobilizing an entire register of felt phenomena in order to expand the existing domain and methods of social critique" (360, note 28).

17. That is, while his emphasis is on "meanings and values as they are actively lived and felt," nevertheless "the relations between these [lived meanings and values] and formal or systematic beliefs are in practice variable (including historically variable), over a range from formal assent with private dissent to the more nuanced interaction between selected and interpreted beliefs and acted and justified experiences" (Williams 132).

18. In Williams's example of a structure of feeling related to an emergent social formation, he contrasts the early Victorian conception of poverty and illegitimacy as "social failure or deviation" with the later concept of "exposure and isolation as a *general condition*," of which "poverty, debt, or illegitimacy" are instances. The "semantic figures of Dickens, of Emily Brontë, and others" capture this "structure of feeling," but an explicit ideology, an explanatory fixed form, does not come until *after* the literature. Concomitantly, the articulation of "structure of feeling" into "ideology" involves "a reduced tension," because the contradiction between lived experience and "social explanation" have, presumably, been resolved and "the intensity of experienced fear and shame now dispersed and generalized" (134).

19. I use the term "classed" here as shorthand to refer to issues of economic structure, but class is and is not different from the other indicators of identity. On one hand, there are markers of class that mark persons as different, e.g., "poor white trash" as a racial, classist epithet that marks certain whites as Other (see Brooks Bouson; see also Bourdieu, etc.). On the other hand, Immanuel Wallerstein and others argue that class is not so much a marker of personal identity as an indicator of a capitalist system. Furthermore (need more hands!), one could argue that gender and race are also not markers of identity so much as indicators of location in social structures, e.g., "Asian American" only has meaning within the racial formations of the U.S. In this case, class would then be parallel with the other terms; they are all indicators of systems and processes of power.

CHAPTER 3

1. See also Chang and Chan, Howard and Dei, and the *Symposium* on *Crash* in a 2007 special issue of *College English*.

2. For more information about the different models and modes of "multiculturalism," see Sivanandan, C. Taylor, the Chicago Cultural Studies Group, and, in education, May and Sleeter.

3. Rather, as E. San Juan argues, whiteness is subsumed into an "orthodox

conception of the dominant culture as simply comprising lifestyles that one can pick and wear anytime one pleases" (*Racial Formations* 106).

4. Liberal multiculturalism is in many ways *the* ideology of late capitalism. E. San Juan writes, "neo-liberal multiculturalism idealizes individualist pluralism as the ideology of the 'free market' and its competitive utilitarian ethos" (*Racism* 9-10). David Theo Goldberg concurs, "It was but a short step from privatizing property to privatizing race, removing conception and categorization in racial terms from the public to the private realm" (337). See also Harvey and Žižek.

5. With the possible exception of the African American police detective played by Don Cheadle. The black man plays a particularly vexed role in the liberal multicultural imaginary.

6. Wikipedia perfectly sums up the film's liberal viewpoint: "The film differs from many other films about racism in its rather impartial approach to the issue. Rather than separating the characters into victims and offenders, victims of racism are often shown to be racist themselves in different contexts and situations. Also, racist remarks and actions are often shown to stem from ignorance and misconception rather than a malicious personality" ("Crash." *Wikipedia.* The Wikipedia Foundation, Inc. 10 June 2012. Web. 1 July 2012).

7. For analysis of this image, see Hsu 132-133.

8. A 2011 Pew Research Center study found that, in the U.S., "the median wealth of white households is 20 times that of black households and 18 times that of Hispanic households" (Kochhar, Fry, and Taylor). On average, full-time working women earn 77 percent of what a full-time working man does (American Association of University Women). According to the U.S. Department of Labor, in 2012, black women's weekly earnings were less than 70 percent of weekly earning by white men (United States).

9. In 2010, Shirley Sherrod was fired from the USDA after a conservative blogger selectively excerpted a speech she'd given to make it appear that she'd denied help to white farmers (she did not). After viewing the full speech and the records, the USDA and other organizations that had initially condemned her remarks later apologized to Sherrod. Yet, although the USDA has admitted to systemic discrimination against black, Native American, Latino, and women farmers—and agreed to pay over two million dollars in restitution—"nobody has been fired for proven discrimination," says Jerry Pennick, director of the Federation of Southern Cooperatives Land Assistance Fund (Thompson). See Etter, Findell, Thompson, and the USDA's website on "Settle and Claims Processes," and also *Pigford vs. Glickman* and *Brewington vs. Glickman.*

10. In contrast to, for example, films such as *Indiana Jones and the Temple of Doom,* in which the music, stylization, and play with genre conventions obviously cue us to feel and think certain things about the characters.

11. Viewers who openly identify with Ryan will be very few in number in the likely audience for this film. But if we suppose a viewer who identifies and agrees with Ryan, oddly enough this viewer's reaction may hold within it the seeds of its own demise. Someone who has experienced what he/she believes to be reverse racism or who accepts a collective narrative about reverse racism will agree with Ryan and share his anger in relation to the viewer's situation, goals, society, etc. Interestingly, however, in empathizing with Ryan, such a viewer has

moved beyond his/her individual interests and participates in a collective narrative. Structurally speaking, the simple phenomenon of empathizing with the emotions of a fictional character for both collective and individual reasons denaturalizes the "innateness" of ideology or emotions. While I do not want to make too much of this point, I do believe it is significant. On one hand, this denaturalization itself would most likely not be an effective political tool in convincing people that structural racism still exists. On the other hand, the fact that human beings share the cognitive ability to participate in the emotions of others and to have their own emotions informed by collectives suddenly puts us in a world where we share common bases and tools and can, ostensibly, identify, analyze, assess, and debate these emotions. In a sense, we can take this viewer's anger seriously as real (physiologically, phenomenologically, existentially, neurologically, etc.), while also providing potential grounds upon which to assess it. We can ask questions such as: What are the implied goals of the angry individual (appraisal), and how do that individual's goals relate to the community's goals? If such emotions are in part tied to individual and collective memories of perceived reverse racism, can we assess the factual validity of those memories?

12. Along these lines, I would argue that the district attorney played by Brendan Fraser is one of the most realistic characters in the film.

13. It's interesting to note that Paul Haggis wrote the film after being carjacked at gunpoint and the events of 9/11. It is typical of a liberal multicultural view that explanations for such events would be cast in terms of race and ethnicity instead of economics, politics, ideology, history, and/or institutions.

14. The script and a later conversation between Anthony and the chop shop dealer indicate the prisoners as "Cambodian," but we never get any actual confirmation of this designation, which is part of the erasure of their subjectivity and history.

15. See Saito.

CHAPTER 4

1. For discussions of these developments in Asian American studies, see Shelley Wong and Lee.

2. For further reading on this debate, see King-Kok Cheung, David Leiwei Li, Shirley Geok-lin Lim, Sheryl Myland, Yuan Shu, Sau-ling Wong, and Kingston herself in "Cultural Misreadings."

3. For explication of the first argument, see Lowe; for explication of the second, see Schueller and S. Smith, 150–173.

4. Particularly for discursive psychology, which does not assume that minds preexist discourse, narratives play a crucial role in the very constitution of minds; as Herman writes, "Storytelling practices . . . themselves help constitute the minds engaged in the production and interpretation of narrative discourse" ("Storytelling" 314). Likewise, in moral philosophy, Martha Nussbaum argues that because emotions have "a complicated cognitive structure that is in part narrative in form, involving a story of our relation to cherished objects that extends over time" (2), literature and other art forms should have a place in moral philosophy.

5. For a further discussion of "cultural narratives," see Phelan, *Living* 8–9.

6. See Yalom.

7. Smith and Watson's point about the supra-individuality of texts can apply, I would argue, to writers from other backgrounds and in other contexts as well.

8. For further discussions of the relationship between author and text, see Lanser and Kim, "Narrator."

9. Cheng reads the narrator's repetition of the violence she has experienced as producing a self based on hypochondria: "For Kingston's narrator, the act of assuming the position of authority simultaneously projects a sick self outside and installs it within, in a coincidence of desire and denigration—literally, a malady of otherness" (78).

10. In her psychoanalytic reading, Anne Cheng writes about this sadness as a form of racial melancholia, the subject grieving for a loss of his/her own (racial) self, while also finding productive force in that grieving. She writes that racial melancholia is "a structural identificatory formation predicated on—while being an active negotiation of—the loss of self as legitimacy" (20).

11. I would like to thank Jennifer Wilks, the respondent for my 2008 Narrative conference panel, for many insightful comments and useful suggestions, particularly on the implications of the silent girl's alternative paths of resistance.

12. Forter critiques current models of trauma studies for failing to provide ways to account for collective, "everyday" traumas that occur over time, such as racism and patriarchy. Most models of contemporary trauma studies often render trauma the result of ahistorical/antihistorical conditions of being-in-language; rather, Forter explores analytical models that help us to understand trauma as *social* and *historical*.

13. Yen Le Espiritu's text *Asian American Panethnicity* outlines some of the contradictions in inhabiting and mobilizing a panethnic political grouping like "Asian American."

14. For a more in-depth discussion of the implications of empathy, see Keen.

15. I once had a conversation with a writer who had studied with Maxine Hong Kingston at UC Berkeley. This person, informing me that Kingston regularly taught Charles Dickens's *David Copperfield*, expressed surprise and puzzlement that this was one of Kingston's preferred texts. In turn, I was puzzled; I could not figure out why this person should be puzzled by Kingston's use of *David Copperfield*, since both authors write texts that are character-focused, panoramic, roving, funny, and insightful. (Moreover, Kingston and Dickens are two of my favorite writers, so in my mind they naturally go together.) I was so busy puzzling that I neglected to ask the person to clarify, but the obvious and somewhat depressing answer would be that Dickens and Kingston have been categorized into separateness.

CHAPTER 5

1. Although I do not have time to delve too deeply into the issue here, the relationship between non-Western cultures and psychology is interesting to note. Although Herman talks about "emotionologies," which are "the collective emo-

tional standards of a culture" ("Storytelling" 322), and Tavris discusses different cultures' approaches to anger, in a postcolonial, globalized world it is not so
easy to demarcate boundaries between cultural ideas. For instance, recent research by Kimberly Richards et al. on mental health counseling in Zimbabwe
draws on both Western and African sources, ranging from the Central Intelligence Agency to Fanon. They argue that counseling in Zimbabwe predates colonialism, "exist[ing] among the indigenous cultures" (Richards et al. 105), a tradition that "continues to be reflected in modern Zimbabwe, particularly in the
rural areas" (Richards et al. 102). White Rhodesians excluded others from the profession of psychology, which in the colonial period sought "to undermine the humanity of people of color in Southern Africa" (Richards et al. 103). In calling for
more counseling programs, the researchers write that "the racism and brutality of colonialism still haunts Zimbabwe" (Richards et al. 105). In another 2005
study, Richards, Pillay, Mazodze, and Govere find that the legacy of colonialism
still has a large impact on identity construction for both whites and blacks in
South Africa and Zimbabwe. They find that despite the negative psychological
impact of colonialism and racism, the subjects were also energized by active resistance to racism and oppression. Thus, the researchers argue that counselors
"can also actively work as an advocate against human oppression in the community" (47). Swami, Mada, and Tovée's study of Zimbabwean women in Zimbabwe
and Britain finds that a greater level of exposure to Western media—in both Britain *and* Zimbabwe—resulted in the women having a greater dissatisfaction with
their bodies. See also Abas and Langhuag et al. Such studies, which are still relatively few in number, attest to the inextricable imbrication of native and colonial
cultures, and they also speak to heartening directions in psychology that draw on
the postcolonial studies. At the same time, as I discuss in Chapters 1 and 2, psychology is just one methodological approach, and novels such as those by Dangarembga (who studied psychology before becoming a writer and filmmaker) can
also yield crucial, slightly different insights into the dynamics of emotions, subjectivity, and ideology.

    2. In cognitive psychology, Olesya Blazhenkova and Maria Kozhevnikov ar-
gue that the traditional verbal-visual cognitive model must incorporate space
into a "three-dimensional cognitive style" (639). In narrative theory, Susan Stanford Friedman likewise argues that space should be as integral as temporality; in
writing of *The God of Small Things*, Friedman writes, "Spaces—particularly bor-
der spaces—generate and shape the story of caste and gender division as they unfold in the palimpsestic sequence of colonial, postcolonial, and postmodern time"
(197). Such turns reflect a larger intellectual move toward the ideological construction and function of space, particularly urban spaces, influenced by the work
of Henri Lefebvre, Michel de Certeau, Edward Soja, and David Harvey.

    3. Drawing on Basu's work, Christopher Okonkwo focuses on how the novel
demonstrates that "its female characters' plight is codified in various domestic
and public spatial structures, ideologies, and experiences that differently impede
the women's lives under (post)colonization, which itself is an unfinished tale of
history and identity—a work in process, in progress, in motion" (54).

    4. I do not go as far as Basu, however, in rejecting consciousness and subjec-

tivity as possibilities and even perhaps necessities. Basu argues that "the category of a transcendent consciousness and . . . liberated subjectivity" offer particularly appealing yet dangerous "possibilities of resolution offered at the level of transcendent categories" to conflicted postcolonial intellectuals, who "inhabit a Western intellectual structure, all the while questioning and ejecting the very structure they inhabit" (7). He contends, "If power is apprehended not *negatively* as repression, prohibition, or objectification but *positively* as producing subjects, the narrator's rhetoric of consciousness signals this subjectification and serves to elide the materiality of her contradictory position" (21). But Basu also argues that "[c]onsciousness of these processes, moreover, is not effective as a means of resistance" (10). While I agree with Basu about the importance of understanding power as "positive" in producing subjects and modes of thought (e.g., consciousness), I would argue that we should not jettison the notion of power as *also* negative, or repressive and objectifying. I would further argue that even if we understand *some* modes of consciousness and "transcendent subjectivity" as ideologically problematic, the novel also provides grounds for an alternative, progressive consciousness in the critical, ironic distance between the adult narrator and the younger Tambu narrator.

5. The principle chronotope of some European domestic novels would probably be the drawing room, whereas the kitchen may be the place of more working-class and/or ethnic or postcolonial narratives.

6. Tracey had been "angry at not having the best results," but her anger at the violation of the "group norm" of white privilege turns out to have been unnecessary (151).

7. Neither the white nor the black Zimbabweans can even speak of the war for freedom from apartheid. At a Steers office party, when Dick Lawson drunkenly stutters about his wartime experience, it is only a coworker from Mozambique who can refer to "the war," the "liberation struggle," *Chimurenga* (Shona for liberation struggle), or *hondo* (Shona for battle or war) (240).

CHAPTER 6

1. Other critics have also noted the shift in emotional tone of Ngugi's novels. Steven Tobias characterizes Ngugi's later works *Devil on the Cross* and *Matigari* as "more characteristically postmodern," "more ironic," and cynical (166).

2. Mazrui and Mphende do, however, write, "In this transformation, Ngugi's central intention is to present ideas, and not just to entertain" (171). While I agree that Ngugi wants to present the systemic analyses more overtly in the later novels, his earlier novels certainly are not merely "to entertain." The early novels of course present ideas as well, but in ways more individualistic in content and accessible in form than his later novels.

3. I follow Peter Brooker in using the term "estrangement" to translate Brecht's *Verfremdung*, because the usual translation of "alienation" is not quite accurate, particularly since it also refers to Marx's notion of alienation of individuals from their labor and one another. The purpose of estrangement is, as Brooker puts it, rather to "de-alienate" or work against the alienation under capitalism by

"making strange" or defamiliarizing situations, events, and experiences that literary realism, in hiding its artifice, naturalizes. But rather than inherently naturalizing, aesthetic realism produces ideologically quietist effects in contexts in which it is the dominant and thus unmarked and invisible aesthetic form.

4. Ngugi echoes the conclusions of a 2011 International Conference on Decolonising Our Universities in Pelang, Malaysia, which stated, "We agreed that for far too long have we lived under the Eurocentric assumption—drilled into our heads by educational systems inherited from colonial regimes—that our local knowledges, our ancient and contemporary scholars, our cultural practices, our indigenous intellectual traditions, our stories, our histories and our languages portray hopeless, defeated visions no longer fit to guide our universities—therefore, better given up entirely" ("Another World").

5. Although Gikandi does actually argue that Ngugi's later works, particularly *Matigari*, are successful reinventions of the African novel through the use oral traditions (*Ngugi* 210).

6. Realist literature does not call on the reader simply to feel or to be entertained without any thought; while perhaps not explicit, there is always some kind of cognition and processing that goes along with reading or viewing texts, whatever its form. That is, realism also presents emotions *and* ideas. The ideological characteristics of a style rely *both* on its features (e.g., literary realism does try to approximate a linear narrative, while modernism does not) *as well as* its relationship to the conventions and expectations of an audience at a given historical moment. The issue is that in this historical moment, tracing back to the nineteenth century, the dominant aesthetic form has been realism, so its effects and processes go "unmarked" or unnoticed, whereas estrangement techniques draw our attention. Yet just because we are used to these processes does not mean that they do not exist, and, in fact, they become illuminated by nonrealist aesthetic techniques. The effect of an aesthetic form is always historical. For example, while I understand feminist reconsiderations of "romance" and "sentimental" genres and agree that, as popular genres, they call for more critical attention, tearjerker films of the kind shown on Lifetime usually have the opposite of their intended emotional effect on me; they alienate, bore, and sometimes anger me. My "gut" reaction is most likely because I am the product of literary critical tendencies of the late twentieth century that aesthetically and ideologically privilege modernism and postmodernism.

7. I would not, however, go so far as Mwangi in concluding that "the thieves . . . out-compete the narrator" (39), because of the irony. As David Cook and Michael Okenimpke argue, irony in the earlier novels is pointed out by an omniscient narrator, whereas in *Devil*, the narrator is less authoritative. The characters, in fact, do most of the analyzing, and the narrated events are satiric.

8. The most obvious contemporary example of such ideological naturalizing in aesthetic realism is the "romantic comedy," in which it is assumed that young, good-looking, upper-/middle-class boys and girls will find and fall in love with each other. For millions of young women in particular, this script remains unchanged.

9. For more on the history of the avant-garde and the attempt to bridge the di-

vide between art and life, see Andreas Huyssen's *After the Great Divide* (1986); Peter Bürger's *Theory of the Avant-Garde* (1984); and Renato Poggioli's *Theory of the Avant-Garde* (1968).

CHAPTER 7

1. "A bus traveling on Central Avenue begins its route by picking up eight passengers. At the next stop, it picks up four more, and then an additional two at the third stop while discharging one. The next-to-the-last stop, three passengers get off the bus, and another two get on. How many passengers are still on the bus when the last stop is reached?" ("Lessons").

2. Wallace and the children under his care are squatting in an abandoned building with no running water or electricity; Wallace forces the children to go to school, because if they are truant they will be sent to "foster care," i.e., sucked into an overwhelmed, problematic system that will separate them (a fate that is explored in greater detail in season 4). Wallace, who has fallen into a deep depression following his involvement in a brutal murder, has started taking drugs and sleeping all the time, and despite his efforts to leave the streets, eventually he will be shot by one of his friends. On the door of the building they live in appears an ironic sign: "IF ANIMAL TRAPPED CALL 396-6286." There is no number to call, however, if children are trapped inside such buildings and systems.

3. See Gibb and Sabin.

4. See Minujin and Nandy.

5. For instance, the Obama administration filed a federal lawsuit against Wells Fargo and other mortgage companies in September 2011 (Leonard).

6. In fact, since this 2008 issue of *Dissent*, and despite the general economic recession, the middle class has come to blame the poor in even greater numbers. A 2009 Pew Research Center Study found that almost ¾ (72 percent) of respondents agreed with the statement that "poor people have become too dependent on government assistance programs" (Lubrano). In 2007, 69 percent of respondents agreed with that statement. As Elijah Anderson, a Yale sociologist, puts it, "People ignore the structural issues—jobs leaving, industry becoming more mechanized. . . . Then they point to the poor and ask, 'Why aren't you making it?'" (quoted in Lubrano).

7. Kim et al.'s conclusions are that—not surprisingly—aggression increases in middle school but that not all expected factors—low grades, video game playing—increase aggression. In other words, their "ecological" approach finds that while communal and media influences play a relatively minor role, the family context plays the largest role.

8. See also Stevenson (1997); Graham and Hudley (1994); Shahinfar, Kupersmidt, and Matza (2001); Whaley (2003); Black and Hausman (2008); Hall, Cassidy, and Stevenson (2008); McMahon (2009); Bellair and McNulty (2010).

9. Even the physical resources—the building, the classrooms, the furniture, etc.—are as dilapidated as the police forces. The secretary buzzes Prez in, but through the old black-and-white security camera (resonating with the security and surveillance cameras woven through the show), we see him futilely attempting to open the locked door. The secretary buzzes open the door and instructs

him how to open it, but Prez cannot access the ancient, dilapidated door, insisting, "It's locked." The secretary goes downstairs to open the door herself, shaking her head and remarking, "Not a goddamn thing up in here works like it should" ("Boys of Summer").

10. A hopeful sign, however small, is that in both meetings the teachers and police officers revolt; one teacher points out the insufficiency of meaningless slogans when students are disruptive and aggressive in the classroom (and dealing with a constellation of possible difficulties outside of the classroom), and the police point out that sections of Baltimore are as poverty-stricken and violent as areas of Baghdad (a reference to the show's running critique of the "war on drugs" as such a failure as the "war on terror," as well as the latter literally drawing resources away from the former).

Abas, Melanie A., and Jeremy C. Broadhead. "Depression and Anxiety Among Women in an Urban Setting in Zimbabwe." *Psychological Medicine* 27 (1997): 59–71.

Abbot, H. Porter, ed. "On the Origin of Fictions: Interdisciplinary Perspectives." Special issue of *SubStance: A Review of Theory and Literary Criticism* 30.1–2 (2001).

Abernathy, Alexis D. "Managing Racial Anger: A Critical Skill in Cultural Competence." *Journal of Multicultural Counseling and Development* 23.2 (April 1995): 96–102.

Ahlquist, Roberta, and Marie Milner. "The Lessons We Learn From *Crash*." *Undoing Whiteness in the Classroom: Critical Educultural Teaching Approaches for Social Justice Activism*. Ed. Virginia Lea and Erma Jean Sims. New York: Peter Lang, 2008. 101–118.

Ahmed, Sara. *The Cultural Politics of Emotion*. New York: Routledge, 2004.

———. *The Promise of Happiness*. Durham: Duke UP, 2010.

Alber, Jan, et al. "Unnatural Narratives, Unnatural Narratology: Beyond Mimetic Models." *Narrative* 18.2 (May 2010): 113–136.

Aldama, Frederick Luis. *Postethnic Narrative Criticism: Magicorealism in Oscar "Zeta" Acosta, Ana Castillo, Julie Dash, Hanif Kureishi, and Salman Rushdie*. Austin: U of Texas P, 2003.

———. *Why the Humanities Matter: A Commonsense Approach*. Austin: U of Texas P, 2008.

———, ed. *Toward a Cognitive Theory of Narrative Acts*. Austin: U of Texas P, 2010.

American Association of University Women. *The Simple Truth about the Gender Pay Gap*. Washington, DC: American Association of University Women, 2012.

"Another World Is Desirable." *MultiWorldIndia.org*. Citizens International, 29 June 2011. Web. 15 June 2012.

Appadurai, Arjun. *Fear of Small Numbers: An Essay on the Geography of Anger*. Durham: Duke UP, 2006.

Arnett, J. "The Neglected 95%: Why American Psychology Needs to Become Less American." *American Psychologist* 63.7 (2008): 602–614.

Arnove, Anthony. "Pierre Bourdieu, the Sociology of Intellectuals, and the Language of African Literature." *NOVEL: A Forum on Fiction* 26.3 (Spring 1993): 278–296.

Atkinson, Paul, and Sara Delamont. "Rescuing Narrative from Qualitative Research." *Narrative Inquiry* 61.1 (2006): 164–172.

Atlas, John, and Peter Dreier. "Is *The Wire* Too Cynical?" *Dissent* (Summer 2008): 79–82.

———. "John Atlas and Peter Dreier Respond." *Dissent* (Summer 2008): 86–88.

Averill, J. R. *Anger and Aggression: An Essay on Emotion*. New York: Springer-Verlag, 1982.

———. "Studies on Anger and Aggression: Implications for Theories of Emotion." *American Psychologist* 38.11 (1983): 1145–1160.

Basu, Biman. "Trapped and Troping: Allegories of the Transnational Intellectual in Tsitsi Dangarembga's *Nervous Conditions*." *Ariel* 28.3 (July 1997): 7–24.

Bellair, Paul E., and Thomas L. McNulty. "Cognitive Skills, Adolescent Violence, and the Moderating Role of Neighborhood Disadvantage." *JQ: Justice Quarterly* 27.4 (2010): 538–559.

Berkowitz, Leonard. *Aggression: A Social Psychological Analysis*. New York: McGraw-Hill, 1962.

———. "On the Formation and Regulation of Anger and Aggression: A Cognitive Neoassociationistic Analysis." *American Psychologist* 45.4 (1990): 494–503.

Berkowitz, Leonard, and Eddie Harmon-Jones. "Toward an Understanding of the Determinants of Anger." *Emotion* 4.2 (June 2004): 107–130.

Berlant, Lauren. "Affect Is the New Trauma." *Minnesota Review* 71/72 (Winter/ Spring 2009): 131–136.

———. "The Subject of True Feeling: Pain, Privacy and Politics." *Feminist Consequences*. Eds. Elisabeth Bronfen and Misha Kavka. New York: Columbia UP, 2000. 126–160.

Berlant, Lauren, ed. *Compassion: The Culture and Politics of an Emotion*. New York: Routledge, 2004.

Bhana, Hershini. "The Political Economy of Food: Hunger in Tsitsi Dangarembga's *Nervous Conditions*." *Proteus* 17.1 (Spring 2000): 18–24.

Bishop, Tricia. "City's Wells Fargo Lawsuit Dismissed." *BaltimoreSun.com*. *Baltimore Sun*, 7 Jan. 2010. Web. 1 July 2011.

Black, Sally, and Alice Hausman. "Adolescents' Views of Guns in a High-Violence Community." *Journal of Adolescent Research* 23.5 (2008): 592–610.

Blazhenkova, Olesya, and Maria Kozhevnikov. "The New Object-Spatial-Verbal Cognitive Style Model: Theory and Measurement." *Applied Cognitive Psychology* 23 (2009): 638–663.

Bordwell, David. "A Case for Cognitivism." *Iris* 9 (Spring 1989): 11–41.

Bouson, J. Brooks. "'You Nothing but Trash': White Trash Shame in Dorothy Allison's *Bastard Out of Carolina*." *Southern Literary Journal* 34.1 (2001): 101–123.

Brecht, Bertolt. *Brecht on Theatre: The Development of an Aesthetic*. Ed. and trans. John Willett. New York: Palgrave, 1964.

Brennan, Teresa. *The Transmission of Affect*. Ithaca: Cornell UP, 2004.

Brescoll, Victoria L., and Eric Luis Uhlmann. "Can an Angry Woman Get Ahead?" *Psychological Science* 19.3 (2008): 268–275.

Brooker, Peter. "Key Words in Brecht's Theory and Practice of Theatre." *The Cambridge Companion to Brecht*. Eds. Peter Thomson and Glendyr Sacks. Cambridge, Eng.: Cambridge UP, 1994. 185–200.

Brown, Nicholas. "Revolution and Recidivism: The Problem of Kenyan History in the Plays of Ngugi wa Thiong'o." *Research in African Literatures* 30.4 (Winter 1999): 56–73.

Burns, Ed, David Simon, and George Pelecanos. "*The Wire*'s War on the Drug War." *Time.com*. *Time*, 5 March 2008. Web. 2 July 2011.

Buss, Arnold H. "Anger, Frustration, and Aversiveness." *Emotion* 4.2 (June 2004): 131–132.

"Can Genes and Brain Abnormalities Create Killers?" *Talk of the Nation*. National Public Radio. 6 July 2010. Radio.

Cantalupo, Charles, ed. *Ngugi wa Thiong'o: Texts and Contexts*. Trenton, NJ: Africa World Press, 1995.

———, ed. *The World of Ngugi wa Thiong'o*. Trenton, NJ: Africa World Press, 1995.

Carter, Robert T., Alex Pieterse, and Sidney Smith III. "Racial Identity Status Profiles and Expressions of Anger in Black Americans: An Exploratory Study." *Journal of Multicultural Counseling & Development* 36.2 (2008): 101–112.

Chabot-Davis, Kimberly. "'Postmodern Blackness': Toni Morrison's *Beloved* and the End of History." *Twentieth Century Literature* 44.2 (Summer 1998): 242–260.

Chaddha, Anmol, William Julius Wilson, and Sudhir A. Venkatesh. "In Defense of *The Wire*." *Dissent* (Summer 2008): 83–86.

Chang, Jeffrey, and Sylvia Chan. "Can White Hollywood Get Race Right?" *AlterNet.org*. AlterNet, 19 July 2005. Web. 17 March 2009.

Cheng, Anne Anlin. *The Melancholy of Race: Psychoanalysis, Assimilation, and Hidden Grief*. Oxford: Oxford UP, 2001.

Cheung, King-Kok. *Articulate Silences*. Ithaca: Cornell UP, 1993.

Chicago Cultural Studies Group. "Critical Multiculturalism." *Critical Inquiry* 18.3 (1992): 530–555.

Chin, Frank, et al., eds. *Aiiieeeee!: An Anthology of Asian-American Writers*. Washington, DC: Howard UP, 1974.

Chow, Rey. "The Interruption of Referentiality: Poststructuralism and the Conundrum of Critical Multiculturalism." *The South Atlantic Quarterly* 101.1 (2002): 171–186.

Clore, Gerald L., and David B. Centerbar. "Analyzing Anger: How to Make People Mad." *Emotion* 4.2 (June 2004): 139–144.

———, and Andrew Ortony. "Cognition in Emotion: Always, Sometimes, or Never?" *The Cognitive Neuroscience of Emotion*. Eds. Richard D. Lane and Lynn Nadel. Oxford, Eng.: Oxford UP, 2002. 24–61.

Clough, Patricia Ticineto, and Jean Halley, eds. *The Affective Turn: Theorizing the Social*. Durham: Duke UP, 2007.

Colbert, Stephen. *The Colbert Report*. Comedy Central. Television. 17 Oct. 2005.

Collins, Patricia Hill. *Black Sexual Politics: African-Americans, Gender, and the New Racism*. New York: Routledge, 2004.

Colson, Robert. "Arresting Time, Resisting Arrest: Narrative Time and the African Dictator in Ngugi wa Thiong'o's *Wizard of the Crow*." *Research in African Literatures* 42.1 (Spring 2011): 133–153.

Cook, David, and Michael Okenimpke. *Ngugi wa Thiong'o: An Exploration of His Writings*. 2nd ed. Oxford, Eng.: Heinemann, 1997.

Cose, Ellis. *The End of Anger: A New Generation's Take on Race and Rage*. New York: HarperCollins, 2011.

———. *The Rage of a Privileged Class*. New York: HarperCollins, 1995.

———. "Revisiting 'The Rage of the Privileged Class.'" *Newsweek*. Newsweek/Daily Beast, 24 Jan. 2009. Web. 10 June 2011.

Cox, David E., and David W. Harrison. "Models of Anger: Contributions from

Psychology, Neuropsychology and the Cognitive Behavioral Perspective."
Brain Structure Function 212 (2008): 371–385.

Crash. Dir. Paul Haggis. Screenplay by Paul Haggis and Bobby Moresco. Lion's Gate, 1995.

Dagleish, Tim, and Mick Power, eds. *Handbook of Cognition and Emotion.* West Sussex, Eng.: John Wiley & Sons, 1999.

Dangarembga, Tsitsi. *The Book of Not.* Boulder: Lynne Rienner, 2006.

———. *Nervous Conditions.* 1988. Boulder: Lynne Rienner, 2004.

Davis, Teresa L. "Gender Differences in Masking Negative Emotions: Ability or Motivation?" *Development Psychology* 31.4 (July 1995): 660–667.

de Sousa, Ronald. *The Rationality of Emotion.* Cambridge: MIT Press, 1987.

Dollard, John, et al. *Frustration and Aggression.* New Haven, CT: Yale University Press, 1939.

Downey, Greg. "We Agree It's WEIRD, But Is It WEIRD Enough?" *Neuroanthropology.net.* N.p., 10 July 2010. Web. 10 June 2011.

Dubey, Madhu. *Signs and Cities: Black Literary Postmodernism.* Chicago: U of Chicago P, 2003.

Ebert, Roger. Rev. of *Crash,* dir. Paul Haggis. *RogerEbert.com. Chicago Sun-Times,* 5 May 2005. Web. 3 March 2009.

Eck, Lisa. "Thinking Globally, Teaching Locally: The 'Nervous Conditions' of Cross-Cultural Literacy." *College English* 70.6 (July 2008): 578–598.

Ekman, Paul. "Facial Expression and Emotion." *American Psychologist* 48 (1993): 384–392.

Ekman, Paul, and Richard J. Davidson, eds. *The Nature of Emotion: Fundamental Questions.* Oxford: Oxford UP, 1994.

Elliot, Anthony, and Charles Lemert. *The New Individualism: The Emotional Costs of Globalization.* New York: Routledge, 2006.

Epatko, Larisa. "'Indignez-Vous!' Stéphane Hessel's Guide to Outrage." *PBS Newshour.* Public Broadcasting Service. 6 Oct. 2011. Web. 5 Nov. 2011.

Espiritu, Yen Le. *Asian American Panethnicity: Bridging Institutions and Identities.* Philadelphia: Temple UP, 1993.

Etter, Lauren. "Black Farmers, USDA Agree to $1.25 Billion Settlement." *Wall Street Journal,* 18 Feb. 2010. Web. 2 June 2012.

Evans, Dylan. *The Emotions.* New York: Oxford UP, 2001.

Evans, Dylan, and Pierre Cruse, eds. *Emotion, Evolution, and Rationality.* Oxford: Oxford UP, 2004.

Findell, Elizabeth. "Hispanic Farmers Seek Compensation for USDA's Discriminatory Lending." *The Monitor* Online. AIM Media Texas, 21 June 2011. Web. 2 June 2012.

Fischer, Agneta, ed. *Gender and Emotion: Social Psychological Perspectives.* Cambridge, Eng.: Cambridge UP, 2000.

Fischer, Agneta, et al. "Gender and Culture Differences in Emotion." *Emotion* 4.1 (Mar. 2004): 87–94.

Foley, Barbara. Rev. of *Reclaiming Identity: Realist Theory and the Predicament of Postmodernism.* Eds. Paula L. M. Moya and Michael Hames-Garcia. *Cultural Logic* 4.2 (Spring 2001). Web. 30 Sept. 2011.

Forgas, Joseph P. *Feeling and Thinking: The Role of Affect in Social Cognition.* Cambridge, Eng.: Cambridge UP, 2000.

Forter, Greg. "Freud, Faulkner, Caruth: Trauma and the Politics of Literary Form." *Narrative* 15.3 (Oct. 2007): 259–285.

Frank, Adam. "Some Avenues for Feeling." Review essay. *Criticism* 46.3 (Summer 2004): 511–524.

Friedman, Susan Stanford. "Spatial Poetics and *The God of Small Things*." *A Companion to Narrative Theory*. Eds. James Phelan and Peter J. Rabinowitz. Malden: Blackwell, 2005. 192–204.

Frijda, Nico H. *The Emotions*. Cambridge, Eng.: Cambridge UP, 1986.

Frijda, Nico H., Antony S. R. Manstead, and Sacha Bem, eds. *Emotions and Beliefs: How Feelings Influence Thoughts*. Cambridge, Eng.: Cambridge UP, 2000.

Ghazinhour, Mehdi, and Jörg Richter. "Anger Related to Psychopathology, Temperament, and Character in Healthy Individuals—An Explorative Study." *Social Behavior and Personality* 37.9 (2009): 1197–1212.

Gibb, Jane, and Roger Sabin. "Who Loves Ya, David Simon? Notes Toward Placing *The Wire*'s Depiction of African-Americans in the Context of American TV Crime Drama." *The Wire Files*, special issue of *darkmatter* 4 (May 2009): 9–18.

Gikandi, Simon. "The Epistemology of Translation: Ngugi, Matigari, and the Politics of Language." *Research in African Literatures* 22:4 (Winter 1991): 162–167.

———. *Ngugi wa Thiong'o*. Cambridge, Eng.: Cambridge UP, 2000.

Glaister, Dan. "*Crash* Plus Cash Equals Oscar." *The Guardian*, 7 March 2006. Web. 1 October 2009.

Goldberg, David Theo. *The Threat of Race: Reflections on Racial Neoliberalism*. Malden: Blackwell, 2009.

Gonzalez, Juan. "Stéphane Hessel on Occupy Wall Street." Interview. *Democracy Now*. 10 Oct. 2011. Web. 24 Oct. 2011.

Goodwin, Jeff, James M. Jasper, and Francesca Polletta, eds. *Passionate Politics: Emotions and Social Movements*. Chicago: U of Chicago P, 2001.

Gopal, Priyamvada. "Protest and the Faculty of Outrage." *The Guardian*, 31 July 2011. Web. 8 August 2011.

Graham, Sandra, and Cynthia Hudley. "Attributions of Aggressive and Nonaggressive African-American Male Early Adolescents: A Study of Construct Accessibility." *Development Psychology* 30.3 (1994): 365–373.

Gregg, Melissa, and Gregory J. Seigworth, eds. *The Affect Theory Reader*. Durham: Duke UP, 2010.

Hall, Diane M., Elaine F. Cassidy, and Howard C. Stevenson. "Acting 'Tough' in a 'Tough' World: An Examination of Fear Among Urban African American Adolescents." *Journal of Black Psychology* 34.2 (August 2008): 381–398.

Hall, Judith A., and David Matsumoto. "Gender Differences in Judgments of Multiple Emotions from Facial Expressions." *Emotion* 4.2 (2004): 201–206.

Haney López, Ian F. "The Social Construction of Race: Some Observations on Illusion, Fabrication, and Choice." *Harvard Civil Rights—Civil Liberties Law Review* 29 (1993). Web. 1 June 2012.

Hart, F. Elizabeth. "The View of Where We've Been and Where We'd Like to Go." Review article. *College Literature* 33.1 (Winter 2006): 225–237.

Harvey, David. *The New Imperialism*. New ed. Oxford: Oxford UP, 2005.

Heinrich, Joseph, Steven J. Heine, and Ara Norenzayan. "The Weirdest People in the World." *Behavioral and Brain Sciences* 33 (2010): 1–75.

Helal, Kathleen M. "Anger, Anxiety, Abstraction: Virginia Woolf's 'Submerged Truth." *South Central Review* 22.2 (Summer 2005): 78–94.

Herman, David. "Narrative Theory After the Second Cognitive Revolution." *Introduction to Cognitive Cultural Studies*. Ed. Lisa Zunshine. Baltimore: Johns Hopkins UP, 2010. 155–175.

———. "Parables of Narrative Imagining." Rev. of Mark Turner's *The Literary Mind*. *Diacritics* 29.1 (1999): 20–36.

———. *Story Logic: Problems and Possibilities of Narrative*. Lincoln: U of Nebraska P, 2002.

———. "Storytelling and the Sciences of the Mind: Cognitive Narratology, Discursive Psychology, and Narratives in Face-to-Face Interaction." *Narrative* 15.3 (Oct. 2007): 306–334.

Herman, David, ed. *Narrative Theory and the Cognitive Sciences*. Stanford: CSLI Publications, 2003.

Hess, Ursula, Reginald B. Adams, and Robert E. Kleck. "Facial Appearance, Gender, and Emotion Expression." *Emotion* 4.4 (Dec. 2004): 378–388.

Hessel, Stéphane. *Time for Outrage (Indignez-vous!)*. Trans. Marion Duvert. New York: Twelve, 2010.

Hogan, Patrick Colm. *Cognitive Science, Literature and the Arts: A Guide for Humanists*. New York: Routledge, 2003.

———. *The Mind and Its Stories: Narrative Universals and Human Emotion*. Cambridge, Eng.: Cambridge UP, 2003.

Hoggett, Paul, and Simon Thompson, eds. *Politics and the Emotions: The Affective Turn in Contemporary Political Studies*. New York: Continuum, 2012.

hooks, bell. *Killing Rage: Ending Racism*. New York: H. Holt and Co., 1995.

Hopkins, Jim. "Conscience and Conflict: Darwin, Freud, and the Origins of Human Aggression." *Emotions, Evolution, and Rationality*. Ed. Dylan Evans and Pierre Cruse. Oxford: Oxford UP, 2004. 225–248.

Howard, Philip S. S., and George J. Sefa Dei, eds. *Crash Politics and Antiracism: Interrogations of Liberal Race Discourse*. New York: Peter Lang, 2008.

Hsieh, Lili. "The Other Side of the Picture: The Politics of Affect in Virginia Woolf's *Three Guineas*." *JNT: Journal of Narrative Theory* 36.1 (Winter 2006): 20–52.

Hsu, Hsuan L. "Racial Privacy, the L.A. Ensemble Film, and Paul Haggis's *Crash*." *Film Criticism* 31.1–2 (2006): 132–156.

"Inner Workings of the Magnanimous Mind: Why It Feels Good to Be Altruistic." *Science Daily*. N.p., 28 May 2007. Web. 5 November 2009.

Izard, Carroll E. "Emotion Theory and Research: Highlights, Unanswered Questions, and Emerging Issues." *The Annual Review of Psychology* 60.1 (2009): 1–25.

———. "Four Systems for Emotion Activation: Cognitive and Noncognitive Processes." *Psychological Review* 100.1 (1993): 68–90.

Jackson, Tony. "Questioning Interdisciplinarity: Cognitive Science, Evolutionary Psychology, and Literary Criticism." *Poetics Today* 21.2 (Summer 2000): 319–347.

Jaggar, Alison. "Love and Knowledge: Emotions in Feminist Epistemology." *Gender/Body/Knowledge: Feminist Reconstructions of Being and Knowing.* Eds. Alison Jaggar and Susan Bordo. New Brunswick: Rutgers UP, 1989. 145–171.

Johnson-Laird, P. N., and Keith Oatley. "The Language of Emotions: An Analysis of a Semantic Field." *Cognition and Emotion* 3.2 (1989): 81–123.

Keen, Suzanne. *Empathy and the Novel.* New York: Oxford UP, 2007.

Keltner, Dacher, and Jennifer S. Lerner. "Emotion." *Handbook of Social Psychology.* Eds. Susan T. Fiske, Daniel T. Gilbert, and Gardner Lindzey. Hoboken: Wiley and Sons, 2009. 317–352.

Kim, Sangwon, et al. "A Multiple Risk Factors Model of the Development of Aggression Among Early Adolescents From Urban Disadvantaged Neighborhoods." *School Psychology Quarterly* 26.3 (2011): 215–230.

Kim, Sue J. *Critiquing Postmodernism in Contemporary Discourses of Race.* New York: Palgrave Macmillan, 2009.

Kinder, Marsha. "Re-Wiring Baltimore: The Emotive Power of Systemics, Seriality, and the City." *Film Quarterly* 62.2 (2008): 50–57.

Kingston, Maxine Hong. "Cultural Mis-readings by American Reviewers." *Asian and Western Writers in Dialogue: New Cultural Identities.* Ed. Guy Amirthanayagam. London: Macmillan, 1982. 55–65.

———. *The Woman Warrior: Memoirs of a Girlhood Among Ghosts.* New York: Vintage, 1975.

Kitayama, Shinobu, and Hazel Markus. *Emotion and Culture: Empirical Studies of Mutual Influence.* Washington, DC: American Psychological Association, 1994.

Kochhar, Rakesh, Richard Fry, and Paul Taylor. "Wealth Gaps Rise to Records Highs between Whites, Blacks, Hispanics." *Pew Social and Demographic Trends.* Pew Research Center. 26 July 2011. Web. 6 Nov 2011.

Lakoff, George, and Mark Johnson. *Philosophy in the Flesh: The Embodied Mind and Its Challenge to Western Thought.* New York: Basic Books, 1999.

Lane, Richard D., and Lynn Nadel, eds. *Cognitive Neuroscience of Emotion.* New York: Oxford UP, 1999.

Langhaug, Lisa F., et al. "High Prevalence of Affective Disorders Among Adolescents Living in Rural Zimbabwe." *Journal of Community Health* 35 (2010): 355–364.

Lazarus, Richard S. "Cognition and Motivation in Emotion." *American Psychologist* 46.4 (1991): 352–367.

———. "The Cognition-Emotion Debate: A Bit of History." *The Handbook of Cognition and Emotion.* Eds. Tim Dagleish and Mick Power. West Sussex, Eng.: John Wiley & Sons, 2000. 3–19.

———. "On the Primacy of Cognition." *American Psychologist* 39.2 (1984): 124–129.

Lee, Sue-Im. "Suspicious Characters: Realism, Asian American Identity, and Theresa Hak Kyung Cha's *Dictee*." *JNT: Journal of Narrative Theory* 32.2 (Summer 2002): 227–258.

Leonard, Andrew. "The Bungled Politics of Bank Bashing." *Slate.com.* Slate Magazine, 6 Sept. 2011. Web. 21 Sept. 2011.

Li, David Leiwei. *Imagining the Nation: Asian American Literature and Cultural Studies*. Stanford: Stanford UP, 1998.

Lim, Shirley Geok-lin. "The Tradition of Chinese American Women's Life Stories: Thematics of Race and Gender in Jade Snow Wong's *Fifth Chinese Daughter* and Maxine Hong Kingston's *The Woman Warrior*." *American Women's Autobiography: Fea(s)ts of Memory*. Ed. Margo Culley. Madison: U of Wisconsin P, 1992. 252–267.

———, ed. *Approaches to Teaching Kingston's* The Woman Warrior. New York: Modern Language Association, 1991.

Lindfors, Bernth, and Bala Kothandaraman, eds. *The Writer as Activist: South Asian Perspectives on Ngugi Wa Thiong'o*. Trenton: Africa World, 2001.

Ling, Jinqi. *Narrating Nationalisms: Ideology and Form in Asian American Literature*. New York: Oxford UP, 1998.

Lorde, Audre. *Sister/Outsider: Essays and Speeches*. Trumansburg: Cross Press, 1984.

Lovesey, Oliver. *Ngugi wa Thiong'o*. New York: Twayne Publishers, 2000.

Lowe, Lisa. *Immigrant Acts: On Asian American Cultural Politics*. Durham: Duke UP, 1996.

Lubrano, Alfred. "In Hard Times, Americans Blame the Poor." *The Philadelphia Inquirer*, 15 Feb. 2010. Web. 4 Nov. 2011.

Lundegaard, Erik. "Oscar Misfire: 'Crash' and Burn." *MSNBC.com*. NBC, 6 March 2006. Web. 5 Aug. 2011.

Lutz, Catherine A., and Lila Abu-Lughod, eds. *Language and the Politics of Emotion*. Cambridge, Eng.: Cambridge UP, 1990.

Lyman, Peter. "The Domestication of Anger: The Use and Abuse of Anger in Politics." *European Journal of Society Theory* 7.2 (May 2004): 133–47.

Lyons, William. "The Philosophy of Cognition and Emotion." *Handbook of Cognition and Emotion*. Eds. Tim Dagleish and Mick Power. West Sussex, Eng.: John Wiley & Sons, 1999. 21–44.

Marcus, Jane. *Art and Anger: Reading Like a Woman*. Columbus: Ohio State UP, 1988.

Marx, Karl. "From *The Eighteenth Brumaire of Louis Bonaparte*." *Marxism and Art*. Ed. Maynard Solomon. Detroit: Wayne State UP, 1974.

Massumi, Brian. *Parables for the Virtual: Movement, Affect, Sensation*. Durham: Duke UP, 2002.

Matsumoto, David, Seung Hee Yoo, and Joanne Chung. "The Expression of Anger Across Cultures." *International Handbook of Anger*. Eds. Michael Potegal, Gerhard Stemmler, and Charles Spielberg. New York: Springer, 2010. 125–138.

Mauer, Marc. "Addressing Racial Disparities in Incarceration." *The Prison Journal*, supplement to 91.3 (2011): 87S–101S.

May, Stephen, and Christine E. Sleeter. *Critical Multiculturalism: Theory and Praxis*. New York: Routledge, 2010.

Mazrui, Alamin, and Lupenga Mphande. "Orality and the Literature of Combat: Ngugi and the Legacy of Fanon." *The World of Ngugi wa Thiong'o*. Ed. Charles Cantalupo. Trenton: Africa World Press, 1995. 159–183.

McMahon, Susan D., et al. "Community Violence Exposure and Aggression Among Urban Adolescents: Testing a Cognitive Mediator Model." *Journal of Community Psychology* 37.7 (2009): 895–910.

Mellard, James M. "'No Ideas But in Things': Fiction, Criticism, and the New Darwinism." *Style* 41.1 (Spring 2007): 1–29.

Miller, George A. "The Cognitive Revolution: A Historical Perspective." *Trends in Cognitive Sciences* 7.3 (March 2003): 141–144.

Minujin, Alberto, and Shailen Nandy. *Global Child Poverty and Well-Being: Measurement, Concepts, Policy, and Action.* Bristol: Policy Press, 2012.

Mittell, Jason. "All in the Game: *The Wire*, Serial Storytelling, and Procedural Logic." *Third Person: Authoring and Exploring Vast Narratives.* Ed. Pat Harrigan and Noah Wardrip-Fruin. Cambridge: MIT Press, 2009. 429–438.

———."Narrative Complexity in Contemporary American Television." *Velvet Light Trap* 58 (2006): 29–40.

Mohanty, Satya. *Literary Theory and the Claims of History: Postmodernism, Objectivity, Multicultural Politics.* Ithaca: Cornell UP, 1997.

Monga, Célestin. *The Anthropology of Anger: Civil Society and Democracy in Africa.* Boulder: Lynne Rienner, 1996.

Montado, Leo, and Angela Scheider. "Justice and Emotional Reactions in the Disadvantaged." *Social Justice Research* 3.4 (1989): 313–344.

Moretti, Franco. *The Way of the World: The Bildungsroman in European Culture.* London: Verso, 1987.

Moya, Paula M. L., and Michael R. Hames-Garcia, eds. *Reclaiming Identity: Realist Theory and the Predicament of Postmodernism.* Berkeley: U of California P, 2000.

Mukundi, Paul M. *Preventing Things from Falling Further Apart: The Preservation of Cultural Identities in Postcolonial African, Indian, and Caribbean Literatures.* London: Adonis & Abbey, 2010.

Muñoz, José Esteban. "Feeling Brown: Ethnicity and Affect in Ricardo Bracho's *The Sweetest Hangover (And Other STDs)*." *Theatre Journal* 52.1 (March 2000): 67–79.

———. "Feeling Brown, Feeling Down: Latina Affect, the Performativity of Race, and the Depressive Position." *Signs* 31.3 (Spring 2006): 675–688.

Mwangi, Evan. "Gender, Unreliable Oral Narration, and the Untranslated Preface in Ngugi wa Thiong'o's *Devil on the Cross*." *Research in African Literatures* 38.4 (2007): 28–46.

Myland, Sheryl. "The Mother as Other: Orientalism in Maxine Hong Kingston's *The Woman Warrior*." *Women of Color: Mother-Daughter Relationships in 20th-Century Literature.* Ed. Elizabeth Brown-Guillory. Austin: U of Texas P, 1996. 132–152.

Ngai, Sianne. *Ugly Feelings.* Cambridge: Harvard UP, 2004.

Ngugi wa Thiong'o. *Decolonising the Mind: The Politics of Language in African Literature.* Oxford, Eng.: Heinemann, 1986.

———. *Devil on the Cross.* Oxford, Eng.: Heinemann, 1982.

———. *Wizard of the Crow.* New York: Anchor, 2006.

Nguyen, Viet. "On the Uses of Rage and Anger." *Diacriticize.* Diacritics, 19 July 2012. Web. 23 July 2012.

Njogu, Kimani. "On the Polyphonic Nature of the Gicaandi Genre." *African Languages and Literatures* 10.1 (1997): 47–62.

Nussbaum, Martha. *Upheavals of Thought: The Intelligence of Emotions.* Cambridge, Eng.: Cambridge UP, 2001.

Oatley, Keith, and P. N. Johnson-Laird. "Basic Emotions, Rationality, and Folk Theory." *Cognition and Emotion* 6.3–4 (1992): 201–223.

Ogude, James. *Ngugi's Novels and African History: Narrating the Nation.* London: Pluto, 1999.

Okonkwo, Christopher. "Space Matters: Form and Narrative in Tsitsi Dangarembga's *Nervous Conditions.*" *Research in African Literatures* 34.2 (Summer 2003): 53–74.

Omi, Michael, and Howard Winant. *Racial Formation in the United States: From the 1960s to the 1990s.* 2nd ed. New York: Routledge, 1994.

O'Rourke, Meghan. "Behind *The Wire*: David Simon on Where the Show Goes Next." *Slate.com.* Slate Magazine, 1 Dec. 2006. Web. 15 Sept. 2011.

Ortony, Andrew, Gerald L. Clore, and Allan Collins. *The Cognitive Structure of Emotions.* Cambridge, Eng.: Cambridge UP, 1988.

O'Sullivan, Sean. "Broken on Purpose: Poetry, Serial Television, and the Season." *StoryWorlds* 2 (2010): 59–77.

———. "The Decalogue and the Remaking of American Television." *After Kiéslowski: The Legacy of Krzysztof Kiéslowski.* Ed. Steven Woodward. Detroit: Wayne State UP, 2009. 202–225.

———. "Old, New, Borrowed, Blue: Deadwood and Serial Fiction." *Reading Deadwood: A Western to Swear By.* Ed. David Lavery. London: I. B. Tauris, 2006. 115–129.

Palumbo-Liu, David. "Rationality and World-Systems Analysis: Fanon and the Impact of the Ethico-Historical." *Immanuel Wallerstein and the Problem of the World Scale.* Eds. David Palumbo-Liu et al. Durham: Duke UP, 2011. 202–222.

Palumbo-Liu, David, Bruce Robbins, and Nirvana Tanoukh, eds. *Immanuel Wallerstein and the Problem of the World: System, Scale, Culture.* Durham: Duke UP, 2011.

Parkinson, Brian, Alison Roper, and Gwenda Simons. "Appraisal Ratings in Diary Reports of Reasonable and Unreasonable Anger." *European Journal of Social Psychology* 39.1 (2009): 82–87.

Phelan, James. *Experiencing Fiction: Judgments, Progressions, and the Rhetorical Theory of Narrative.* Columbus: Ohio State UP, 2007.

———. *Living to Tell About It: A Rhetoric and Ethics of Character Narration.* Ithaca, NY: Cornell UP, 2005.

Phelan, James, and Peter J. Rabinowitz, eds. *A Companion to Narrative Theory.* Malden, MA: Blackwell, 2005.

Phelps, Elizabeth. "Emotion and Cognition: Insights from the Studies of the Human Amygdala." *Annual Review of Psychology* 57.1 (2006): 27–53.

Plantinga, Carl, and Greg M. Smith, eds. *Passionate Views: Film, Cognition, and Emotion.* Baltimore: Johns Hopkins UP, 1999.

Potegal, Michael, Gerhard Stemmler, and Charles Spielberger, eds. *International Handbook of Anger: Constituent and Concomitant Biological, Psychological, and Social Processes.* New York: Springer, 2010.

Povinelli, Elizabeth. *The Empire of Love: Toward a Theory of Intimacy, Genealogy, and Carnality.* Durham: Duke UP, 2006.

Power, Mick, and Tim Dagleish. *Cognition and Emotion: From Order to Disorder.* East Sussex, Eng.: Taylor & Francis, 1997.

Prinz, Jesse. "Which Emotions Are Basic?" *Emotion, Evolution, and Rationality*. Eds. Dylan Evans and Pierre Cruse. Oxford: Oxford UP, 2004. 69–80.

Probyn, Elspeth. *Blush: Faces of Shame*. Minneapolis: U of Minnesota P, 2005.

Rankin, Lindsay E., John T. Jost, and Cheryl Wakslak. "System Justification and the Meaning of Life: Are the Existential Benefits of Ideology Distributed Unequally Across Racial Groups?" *Social Justice Research* 22 (2009): 312–333.

Reddy, William M. *The Navigation of Feeling: A Framework for the History of Emotions*. Cambridge, Eng.: Cambridge UP, 2001.

Regan, Tom. "Is Being Good Based on Biology?" *NPR News Blog*. National Public Radio, 29 May 2007. Web. 20 November 2009.

Richards, Kimberly A. M., et al. "Counseling in Zimbabwe: History, Current Status, and Future Trends." *Journal of Counseling and Development* 90 (Jan. 2012): 102–106.

Richards, Kimberly A. M., Yegan Pillay, Oliver Mazodze, and Alexandra S. M. Govere. "The Impact of Colonial Culture in South Africa and Zimbabwe on Identity Development." *Journal of Psychology in Africa* 15.1 (Jan. 2005): 41–51.

Richardson, Alan. "Studies in Literature and Cognition: A Field Map." *The Work of Fiction: Cognition, Culture, and Complexity*. Ed. Alan Richardson and Ellen Spolsky. Aldershot: Ashgate, 2004. 1–30.

Richardson, Alan, and Ellen Spolsky, eds. *The Work of Fiction: Cognition, Culture, and Complexity*. Aldershot, Eng.: Ashgate, 2004.

Richardson, Alan, and Francis Steen, eds. *Literature and the Cognitive Revolution*. Special issue of *Poetics Today* 23.1 (Spring 2002).

Rodrigues, Angela Lamas. "Beyond Nativism: An Interview with Ngugi wa Thiong'o." *Research in African Literatures* 35.3 (Fall 2004): 161–167.

Rodriguez, Gregory. "Our Politics of Anger." *Los Angeles Times*, 1 Mar. 2010. Web. 10 July 2011.

Roseman, Ira J. "Appraisals, Rather Than Unpleasantness or Muscle Movements, Are the Primary Determinants of Specific Emotions." *Emotion* 4.2 (June 2004): 145–150.

Russell, James A., and Beverly Fehr. "Fuzzy Concepts in a Fuzzy Hierarchy: Varieties of Anger." *Journal of Personality and Social Psychology* 67.2 (Aug. 1994): 186–205.

Sadeh, Naomi, et al. "Gender Differences in Emotional Risk for Self- and Other-Directed Violence Among Externalizing Adults." *Journal of Consulting and Clinical Psychology* 79.1 (Feb. 2011): 106–117.

Safdar, Saba, et al. "Variations of Emotion Display Rules Within and Across Cultures: A Comparison Between Canada, USA, and Japan." *Canadian Journal of Behavioural Science* 41.1 (Jan. 2009): 1–10.

Saito, Leland. *Race and Politics: Asian Americans, Latinos, and Whites in a Los Angeles Suburb*. Champaign: U of Illinois P, 1998.

San Juan, E. *Racial Formations/Critical Transformations: Articulations of Power in Ethnic and Racial Studies in the United States*. Amherst, NY: Humanity Books, 1992.

———. *Racism and Cultural Studies: Critiques of Multiculturalist Ideology and the Politics of Difference*. Durham: Duke UP, 2002.

Savarese, Ralph. "Toward a Postcolonial Neurology: Autism, Tito Mukhopadhyay, and a New Geo-poetics of the Body." *Journal of Literary & Cultural Disability Studies* 4.3 (2010): 273–289.

Scheman, Naomi. "Anger and the Politics of Naming." *Engenderings: Constructions of Knowledge, Authority, and Privilege.* New York: Routledge, 1993. 22–35.

Schueller, Malini Johar. "Questioning Race and Gender Definitions: Dialogic Subversions in *The Woman Warrior.*" *Contemporary American Women Writers: Gender, Class, Ethnicity.* Ed. Lois Parkinson Zamora. New York: Longman, 1998. 51–66.

Sedgwick, Eve Kosofsky. *Touching Feeling: Affect, Pedagogy, Performativity.* Durham: Duke UP, 2003.

Seneca, Lucius Annaeus. *Anger, Mercy, Revenge: The Complete Works of Lucius Annaeus Seneca.* Trans. Robert A. Kaster and Martha Nussbaum. Chicago: U of Chicago P, 2010.

Shahinfar, Ariana, Janis B. Kupersmidt, and Louis S. Matza. "The Relation Between Exposure to Violence and Social Information Processing Among Incarcerated Adolescents." *Journal of Abnormal Psychology* 110.1 (2001): 136.

Shaw, Carolyn Martin. "You Had a Daughter, But I Am Becoming a Woman': Sexuality, Feminism and Postcoloniality in Tsitsi Dangarembga's *Nervous Conditions* and *She No Longer Weeps.*" *Research in African Literatures* 38.4 (Winter 2007): 10.

Shu, Yuan. "Cultural Politics and Chinese-American Female Subjectivity: Rethinking Kingston's *Woman Warrior.*" *MELUS* 26.2 (Summer 2001): 199–223.

Silver, Brenda. "The Authority of Anger: *Three Guineas* as Case Study." *Signs* 6.2 (1991): 340–370.

Simpson, Patricia, and Linda Stroh. "Gender Differences: Emotional Expression and Feelings of Personal Inauthenticity." *Journal of Applied Psychology* 89.4 (Aug. 2004): 715–721.

Sivanandan, A. *Communities of Resistance: Writings on Black Struggles for Socialism.* New York: Verso, 1990.

Smith, Craig A., and Leslie D. Kirby. "Appraisal as a Pervasive Determinant of Anger." *Emotion* 4.2 (June 2004): 133–138.

Smith, Greg M. *Film Structure and the Emotion System.* Cambridge, Eng.: Cambridge UP, 2003.

———. "Local Emotions, Global Moods, and Film Structure." *Passionate Views: Film, Cognition, and Emotion.* Ed. Carl Plantinga and Greg M. Smith. Baltimore: Johns Hopkins UP, 1999. 103–126.

Smith, James. "Race, Emotions, and Socialization." *Race, Gender & Class* 9.4 (Oct. 31, 2002): 94–110.

Smith, M. van Wyk. "The Emplotment of Ethnicity: Narrative Cognition and the Construction of 'Race.'" *The Journal of Narrative Technique* 27.3 (Fall 1997): 329–348.

Smith, Sidonie. "Maxine Hong Kingston's *The Woman Warrior*: Filiality and Woman's Autobiographical Storytelling." *A Poetics of Women's Autobiography.* Bloomington: Indiana UP, 1987. 150–173.

Smith, Sidonie, and Julia Watson. "The Trouble with Autobiography: Cautionary Notes for Narrative Theorists." *A Companion to Narrative Theory.* Eds. James Phelan and Peter J. Rabinowitz. Malden, MA: Blackwell, 2005. 356–371.

Smith, Sidonie, and Julia Watson, eds. *De/Colonizing the Subject: The Politics of Gender in Women's Autobiography.* Minneapolis: U of Minnesota P, 1992.

Spelman, Elizabeth V. "Anger and Insubordination." *Women, Knowledge, and Reality: Explorations in Feminist Philosophy.* Eds. Ann Garry and Marilyn Pearsall. New York: Unwin Hyman, 1989. 263–273.

Spolsky, Ellen. "Cognitive Literary Historicism: A Response to Adler and Gross." *Poetics Today* 24.2 (Summer 2003): 161–183.

Stevenson, Howard C. "'Missed, Dissed, and Pissed': Making Meaning of Neighborhood Risk, Fear and Anger Management in Urban Black Youth." *Cultural Diversity and Mental Health* 3.1 (1997): 16–52.

Stimmel, Dr. Theron, et al. "Anger and Shame as Predictors of Psychopathology." *Psychology Journal* 6.2 (2009): 78–86.

Swami, Viren, Rujeko Mada, and Martin J. Tovée. "Weight Discrepancy and Body Appreciation of Zimbabwean Women in Zimbabwe and Britain." *Body Image* (2012). 18 June 2012 (e-pub ahead of print). Web. 23 June 2012.

Symposium on Crash. Special issue of *College English* 69.4 (March 2007): 314–359.

Tan, Ed. S. *Emotions and the Structure of Narrative Film: Film as an Emotion Machine.* Trans. Barbara Fasting. Mahwah, NJ: L. Erlbaum Associates, 1996.

Tavris, Carol. *Anger: The Misunderstood Emotion.* Rev. ed. New York: Simon & Schuster, 1989.

Taylor, Astra. *Examined Life: Excursions with Contemporary Thinkers.* New York: The New Press, 2009.

Taylor, Charles. *Multiculturalism: Examining the Politics of Recognition.* Ed. Amy Gutman. Princeton, NJ: Princeton UP, 1994.

Thompson, Krissah. "Some Find Irony in Shirley Sherrod's USDA Incident." *The Washington Post,* 23 July 2010. Web. 20 May 2012.

Tobias, Steven. "The Poetics of Revolution: Ngugi wa Thiong'o's *Matigari.*" *Critique* 38.3 (Spring 1997): 163–176.

Treuer, David. *Native American Fiction: A User's Manual.* St. Paul: Graywolf, 2006.

Trotsky, Leon. "The ABC of Materialist Dialectics" (1939). *The Marxist Internet Archive.* N.p., 4 June 2007. Web. 20 May 2011.

Turner, Mark. *The Literary Mind.* New York: Oxford UP, 1996.

United States Dept. of Labor, Bureau of Statistics. *Usual Weekly Earnings of Wage and Salary Workers; Second Quarter 2012.* 18 July 2012. Web. 24 July 2012.

Vedantam, Shankar. "If It Feels Good to Be Good, It Might Only Be Natural." *The Washington Post,* 28 May 2007. Web. 20 June 2011.

Wakslak, Cheryl J., John T. Jost, Tom R. Tyler, and Emmeline S. Chen. "Moral Outrage Mediates the Dampening Effect of System Justification on Support for Redistributive Social Policies." *Psychological Science* 18.3 (2007): 267–274.

Warhol, Robyn. *Having a Good Cry.* Columbus: Ohio State UP, 2003.

West, Cornel. *Race Matters.* Boston: Beacon Press, 1993.

Whaley, Arthur L. "Cognitive-Cultural Model of Identity and Violence Prevention for African American Youth." *Genetic, Social & General Psychology Monographs* 129.2 (2003): 101–151.

Williams, Patrick. *Ngugi wa Thiong'o.* Manchester, Eng.: Manchester UP, 1999.

Williams, Raymond. *Marxism and Literature.* Oxford: Oxford UP, 1977.

The Wire: The Complete Series. Created by David Simon. Home Box Office, 2008. DVD.

Wise, Christopher. "Resurrecting the Devil: Notes on Ngugi's Theory of the Oral-Aural African Novel." *Research in African Literatures* 28.1 (Spring 1997): 134–140.

Wong, Sau-ling. "Necessity and Extravagance in Maxine Hong Kingston's *The Woman Warrior*: Art and the Ethnic Experience." *MELUS* 15.1 (Spring 1988): 3–26.

Wong, Shelley. "Unnaming the Same: Theresa Hak Kyung Cha's *Dictee*." *Writing Self, Writing Nation: Essays on Theresa Hak Kyung Cha's Dictee*. Eds. Elaine Kim and Norma Alarcón. Berkeley: Third Woman, 1994. 103–140.

Woodward, Kathleen. "Against Wisdom: The Social Politics of Anger and Aging." *Cultural Critique* 51 (Spring 2002): 186–218.

———. "Anger . . . and Anger: From Freud to Feminism." *Freud and the Passions*. Ed. John O'Neill. University Park: Pennsylvania State UP, 1996. 73–95.

———. *Statistical Panic: Cultural Politics and Poetics of Emotions*. Durham: Duke UP, 2009.

Yalom, Marilyn. "*The Woman Warrior* as Postmodern Autobiography." *Approaches to Teaching Kingston's* Woman Warrior. Ed. Shirley Geok-lin Lim. New York: MLA, 1991. 108–115.

Young, Kay. "Feeling Embodied: Consciousness, *Persuasion*, and Jane Austen." *Narrative* 11.1 (Jan. 2003): 78–92.

Young, Robert. "Postpositivist Realism and the Return of the Same: The Rational Subject and Post(post)postmodern Liberalism." *Cultural Logic* 5 (2002). Web. 20 May 2011.

Žižek, Slavoj. "Liberal Multiculturalism Masks an Old Barbarism with a Human Face." *The Guardian*, 3 Oct. 2007. Web. 10 May 2012.

Zunshine, Lisa. "Theory of Mind and Experimental Representations of Fictional Consciousness." *Narrative* 11.3 (Oct. 2003): 270–291.

———. *Why We Read Fiction: Theory of Mind and the Novel*. Columbus: Ohio State UP, 2006.

Zunshine, Lisa, ed. *Introduction to Cognitive Cultural Studies*. Baltimore: Johns Hopkins UP, 2010.

Achebe, Chinua, 131
ACORN (Association of Community Organizers for Reform Now), 156
Africa, 149, 177; languages of, 133–136; oral traditions of, 137–139. *See also* Kenya; South Africa; Zimbabwe
African Americans, 30, 82; anger/rage of, 49–53, 68, 184n9; in *Crash*, 72–76, 78, 79–82; poor urban, 155, 160–161, 164, 173
agency attribution (in appraisal theory), 18, 19–20, 41, 51, 154, 160, 173, 175
aggression, 1, 2, 13, 16, 23, 45, 93, 166, 168, 170; as distinguished from anger, 28, 181n7; and frustration, 20, 22, 24; in *The Woman Warrior*, 84–85, 88–93; in youth, 160–163, 192n7
Ahmed, Sara, 29, 52–53, 55
Aldama, Frederick, 4, 34, 86
American Indians. *See* Native Americans
anger: as affect, 56–60; appraisal theory of, 16–22, 38; and capitalism, 141–151; cognitive studies approach to, 3–4, 53, 177; as collective, 46–47, 54, 67–68, 96, 99; CNA model of, 23–25; cultural studies approach to, 3–4, 53–54; as dialectical, 6, 12, 63–64; as distinct from frustration, 16, 20, 175–176; as distinct from outrage, 12, 29–30, 99, 175–178; evolutionary view of, 2; feminist, 45–54; Freudian "hydraulic" model of, 2; as historical, 54–56, 68; individualized conception of, 5, 11, 67–68, 96, 99, 110, 123, 147; in Marxism, 45; in men, 1, 18, 46, 47, 49–50, 68, 140, 163, 183–184n5; neo-associationist model of, 22–25; physiological or neurochemical view of, 2; political, 44–54; pop psychological view of,

2; racial, 1, 5–6, 49–54, 68, 184n9; as related to systems, 68–69, 153–154; and social injustice, 29–30; in urban youth, 160–174; in women, 1, 45–46, 49–54, 68, 140, 144, 147, 150, 183–184n5. *See also* aggression; violence
apartheid, 102, 121, 190n7
Appadurai, Arjun, 45
appraisal theory of emotion, 11, 29, 37, 38, 41, 50, 53, 154, 165, 176, 181n10, 181–182n14; challenges to, 22–27; explained, 16–22
Arab Americans, 72, 78–79
Aristotle, 2, 46
Arnett, J., 31
Arnove, Anthony, 131
Asian Americans, 49, 72, 77–78, 82, 85, 89, 94–95, 96, 100, 188n13. *See also* Chinese Americans
Asian American studies, 92–93
associative processing, 18, 24
Atlas, John, 155–156
Autobiography of Malcolm X (Haley, 1987), 84
Averill, James, 180n4

Basu, Biman, 103, 113, 117, 189n3, 189–190n4
Beck, Glenn, 45
Berkowitz, Leonard, 2, 18, 20, 22–25, 27, 181–182n14
Berlant, Lauren, 54–55, 59, 66, 83
bildungsromans, 87–88, 95–96
black Africans, 119–122, 125–127, 147, 188–189n1, 190n7
blacks. *See* African Americans; black Africans
Blazhenkova, Olesya, 188–189n1
Book of Not, The (Tsitsi Dangarembga, 2006), 9, 12, 101–103, 116, 117–128
Bordwell, David, 34

Brecht, Bertolt, 60, 138–139. See also
  Verfremdung
Brennan, Teresa, 57, 67
Bridges, Chris "Ludacris," 77
Brooker, Peter, 190–191n3
Brown, Nicholas, 131
Bullock, Sandra, 80
Burke, Michael, 34
Burns, Ed, 154–155
Bush, George W., 83
Buss, Arnold, 24
Butler, Judith, 58, 98

capitalism, 31, 58, 79, 131, 137, 174; and
  control of affect, 139–151; Fordist
  model of, 160, 165; and language,
  136; and liberal multiculturalism,
  72; social changes wrought by, 159;
  system of, as a cause of injustice
  and racial anger, 5, 6, 10, 51, 61, 64,
  68, 97, 99, 110, 130, 154, 172, 175
Centerbar, David, 18–19, 25, 29
Chaddha, Anmol, 155–156
Cheadle, Don, 80, 186n5
Chen, Emmeline, 29
Cheng, Anne, 90, 179n3, 188nn9,10
Cheung, King-Kok, 90
China, 84, 96–100, 142
Chinese Americans, 89–92
Chow, Rey, 8
Christianity, 102, 107–108, 110, 111,
  113, 114
Clore, Gerald, 18–19, 25, 29
cognition, 68, 86, 95, 103, 127, 136, 164,
  175, 178; anger as, 13–42, 153, 156–
  157, 172–173; as learning, 152; physiological system distinct from, 44,
  56
cognitive narrative theory, 32–41
cognitive neo-associationistic (CNA)
  model of anger, 23–25
cognitive psychology, 6, 8, 154; on anger, 11, 13, 16, 17, 53, 60, 163, 176–
  178, 179n3; on emotions in general,
  3, 32, 34–35, 40–41, 181n10; research subjects for, 9
cognitive studies, 9, 53, 179–180n6,

180–181n5; and anger, 3, 6–7, 11,
  163; and cognitive narrative theory, 32–41; skepticism regarding, in
  cultural studies, 3–4; what it offers
  humanists, 7–8. See also cognitive
  psychology
Colbert, Stephen, 45
collectivity. See individuality vs.
  collectivity
Collins, Patricia Hill, 19
colonialism, 72, 82, 103, 107, 111, 113–
  116, 118, 120–122, 125, 134, 136; and
  language, 131–136; neo-, 5, 10, 102,
  130, 131, 136; and the new global
  marketplace, 124; as a system that
  oppresses and causes anger, 5, 110,
  111, 113; tied to cleanliness, 104,
  116; violating rules of, 108. See also
  postcolonial literature; postcolonial
  studies
Cook, David, 191n7
coping potential (in appraisal theory),
  18, 21, 41, 50, 53, 154, 158, 163, 173,
  175
Cose, Ellis, 49–50, 184n10
Cosmides, Leda, 15, 34
Cox, David, 17, 26, 181n7
Crash (Paul Haggis, 2005) 5, 9, 11, 70–
  83, 174
CSI, 157
cultural studies, 53–54, 179n1, 179–
  180n6; and anger, 3, 6–7, 11; importance of, to humanists, 7–8;
  skepticism in, regarding cognitive studies, 3–4; and understanding emotion, 26, 29. See also Asian
  American studies; ethnic studies; gender studies; Marxist studies; postcolonial studies; women's
  studies

Dagleish, Tim, 25, 28, 181nn6,10
Damasio, Antonio, 15
Dangarembga, Tsitsi, 9, 12, 101, 151,
  174, 188–189n1
Deater-Deckard et al., 161
de Beauvoir, Simone, 114

Decolonising the Mind: The Politics of Language in African Literature (Ngugi wa Thiong'o, 1986), 132–136
Deleuze, Gilles, 14
Derridean deconstruction, 44, 58
de Sousa, Ronald, 33, 48, 65, 87
Devil on the Cross (Ngugi wa Thiong'o, 1982), 12, 129–130, 136–145, 146, 150
Dickens, Charles, 185n18, 188n15; "Dickensian," 157
Dillon, Matt, 72
discrimination, racial, 186n9; reverse, 75, 80
Dollard, John, 20
Downey, Greg, 31
Dreier, Peter, 155–156

Ebert, Roger, 70
Eck, Lisa, 110–111
education. *See* schools
Ekman, Paul, 23, 28, 180n4
emotion, 4, 6, 11, 44, 58, 67, 68, 92, 138–139, 141, 153; appraisal theory of, 11, 16–22, 154; Aristotelian and psychoanalytic view of, 146; behaviorist view of, 14; as both individual and collective, 92, 93–95, 130; as bound up with prototypical narratives, 37–38; challenges to appraisal theory of, 22–27; control of, and capitalism, 144–150; in cultural contexts, 27–32; as distinct from affects, 56–60, 61; "epistemic potential" of, 48–49; genealogies of, 54–56, 61; information processing view of, 14; Marxist approaches to, 11, 60–65; narratological approaches to, 11, 65–67; as political, 45–54, 61; postcognitivist view of, 15; and reason, 130, 131, 136, 149; somatic view of, 13–14; and theory of mind, 35–36. *See also* anger
emotionologies, 40–41, 74, 188–189n1
English language, as language of colonizers, 131–136
Espiritu, Yen Le, 188n13

Esposito, Jennifer, 79
ethnic studies, 3, 7, 8, 49, 53, 54, 103
exemplum (in Hogan), 37, 38

Fanon, Frantz, 10, 121, 122, 130, 135, 188–189n1
Fauconnier, Gilles, 15
feminism, 53, 54, 65–66, 103, 136, 181–182n14; and anger, 45–54, 56; second-wave, 44, 94; in *The Woman Warrior*, 85
feminist studies. *See* gender studies; women's studies
fiction. *See* literature; narrative
film: anger in, 60; psychoanalytic theory of, 34; studying, as a source for understanding emotion, 5; as trigger for emotions, 27
Foley, Barbara, 184n7
Forgas, Joseph, 15
Forter, Greg, 92, 188n12
Foucault, Michel, 44, 54
Frank, Adam, 59–60
Fraser, Brendan, 80, 187n12
Freud, Sigmund: and model of emotions, 2, 46; and psychoanalysis, 8, 13
Friedman, Susan Stanford, 189n2
Frijda, Nico, 21, 181n13, 181–182n14
frustration, 5, 12, 22, 90–91, 98, 99, 175; as distinct from anger/outrage, 16, 20, 175–176; as a trigger for anger, 17, 19; and *The Wire*, 153–154, 158, 160, 165, 172, 173
frustration-aggression hypothesis, 20

Gaddafi, Muammar, 175
gender studies, 3, 4, 28. *See also* women's studies
Gikandi, Simon, 130, 136–138, 150
globalization, 10, 45, 102, 124, 126
goal blockage. *See* group norms (in appraisal theory)
Goldberg, David Theo, 10, 72, 83, 186n4
Gopal, Priyamvada, 178
Grant, Madison, 3

Grishakova, Marina, 34
group norms (in appraisal theory), 18–22, 41, 50, 53, 175

Haggis, Paul, 8, 11, 70, 187n13
Haley, Alex, 84
Harmon-Jones, Eddie, 18, 20, 23–25, 27, 181–182n14
Harrison, David, 17, 26, 181n7
Hau'ofa, Epeli, 10
Head, Bessie, 10
Heinrich, Joseph, 31
Helal, Kathleen, 54
Herman, David, 4, 15, 33–34, 39–41, 66, 74, 103, 183n23, 187n4, 188–189n1
Hessel, Stéphane, and *Indignez-Vous!*, 12, 176–178
Hispanics. *See* Latinos/as
Hogan, Patrick Colm, 4, 7, 19, 27, 31, 33, 34, 36–38, 44, 66, 182n21, 183n22
hooks, bell, 51–52, 173
Hsu, Hsuan, 70

imperialism, 31; anti-, 135; cultural, 110, 133; neo-, 10, 72, 82
individualism, 10–11, 57, 64, 72, 94, 137, 184n7
individuality vs. collectivity, 88, 92–94, 96, 113, 136, 142, 176–177
injustice. *See* social justice/injustice
International Handbook of Anger (2010), 17, 28

Jaggar, Alison, 45, 48, 67, 184n7
James, William, 13–14, 23
Johnson, Mark, 15
Johnson-Laird, P. N., 37, 183n23
Jost, John, 29, 30
justice. *See* social justice/injustice

Kamiriithu, 132
Keen, Suzanne, 4, 55, 65, 66
Keltner, Dacher, 17, 180–181n5
Kenya, 9, 132, 133, 136, 141, 145
Kim et al., 160–163, 192n7
Kinder, Marsha, 155

Kingston, Maxine Hong, 8–9, 12, 84, 151, 174, 184n8, 188n15
Kirby, Leslie, 18, 24
Kitayama, Shinobu, 28–29, 37
Kozhevnikov, Maria, 189n2

Lacanian psychoanalysis, 8, 44, 113
Lakoff, George, 15
Lange, Carl, 13–14, 23
Latinos/as, 58, 72, 78–82, 162
Law and Order, 157, 164
Lazarus, Richard, 18, 182n15
Lerner, Jennifer, 17, 180–181n5
liberal multiculturalism, 70–72, 74, 76, 78, 81, 82, 84, 94, 100, 174, 186n4, 187n13
literature, 7, 27, 95, 137; anger in, 60; and narrative theory, 65–67; and paradigm scenarios, 87–88; representation of collective experience in, 85–86; and structures of feeling, 63, 69; studying, as a source for understanding emotion, 5, 32–41
Lord, Audre, 49, 50, 52, 68
Lukács, György, 60, 139
Lundegaard, Erik, 70
Lyons, William, 14

magical realism, 136
Markus, Hazel, 28–29, 37
Marx, Karl, 10, 11, 184n11, 190–191n3
Marxism, 11, 45, 130, 131
Marxist studies, 7, 43, 179n1; and narratology, 60–67
Massumi, Brian, 56–57
Mazrui, Alamin, 130, 137, 190n2
McGee, Jack, 79
men, anger/aggression in, 1, 18, 46, 47, 49–50, 68, 140, 163, 183–184n5
mind reading. *See* theory of mind (ToM)
minorities, 49, 75, 78, 85. *See also* African Americans; Arab Americans, Asian Americans; Chinese Americans; Latinos/as; Native Americans; race; racism
Moretti, Franco, 87–88, 95

Morrison, Toni, 51–52
Moyo, Jason, 124
Mphande, Lupenga, 130, 137, 190n2
Mugabe, Robert, 122, 124
Muñoz, José, 58, 183n14
Mwangi, Evan, 138, 191n7

NAACP, 83
narrative, importance of, in understanding emotion, 32–41, 187n4. *See also* film; literature
narratology, 60–67
Native Americans, 72, 82
nativism, 130, 131, 133, 134, 136, 149, 150
neo-associationist model of anger, 22–25
neocolonialism. *See* colonialism
neoliberalism, 10, 71, 72, 144. *See also* liberal multiculturalism
Nervous Conditions (Tsitsi Dangarembga, 1988), 9, 12, 101–117, 118, 123, 127–128
Newton, Thandie, 73
Ngai, Sianne, 57–58, 61, 69, 185n16
Ngugi wa Thiong'o, 9, 12, 129–139, 174, 190nn1,2
Nguyen, Viet Thanh, 178
Nussbaum, Martha, 33, 48, 65, 95, 187n4

Oatley, Keith, 37
O'Brian, Patrick, 66
Occupy Wall Street, 175
Ogude, James, 131
Okenimpke, Michael, 191n7
Okonkwo, Christopher, 189n3
oral storytelling. *See* orature
orature, 136–139, 141
Ortony, Andrew, 19
O'Sullivan, Sean, 157
outrage (as distinct from anger), 12, 29–30, 99, 175–178

Paik, Greg Joung, 77
paradigm scenarios, 87–88
patriarchy, 51, 100, 102, 103, 110–114,

141, 144, 188n12; American, 97–98, 99; Chinese, 84, 85, 97–98, 99; Christian, 102, 107–108; and feelings, 139–140; gender roles of mainstream, 167–168; and male anger, 47; spaces of, 109; Western, 91
Pavlov, Ivan, 14
Pelecanos, George, 154–155
Peña, Michael, 80
Phelan, James, 66–67
Plantinga, Carl, 34
Plato, 2
postcolonial literature, 88, 103, 131, 190n5
postcolonial studies, 3, 7, 8, 49, 53, 54, 188n1
poststructuralism, 3, 8, 43, 52, 57, 59, 131
poverty, 29, 49, 98, 154, 156, 160, 167, 172, 177, 185n18
power: and coping potential, 18, 21; cultural studies concerned with, 3; economic, 142, 154; and emasculation, 51; and language, 133; lust for, 146; resisting and reinforcing, 91; structures/systems of, 50, 53, 78, 100, 103, 109, 110, 115, 117, 119, 120, 124, 127, 131, 134, 154, 156, 165; unequal relations of, 9, 75, 156; and vertical vs. horizontal relationships, 50, 68
Power, Mick, 25, 28, 181nn6,10
primal scream therapies, 2
Prinz, Jesse, 29
Probyn, Elspeth, 13–14, 55–56, 69
prototype (in Hogan), 37–38, 182n21

race, 9–10; and anger, 5–6; centrality of, to how we experience emotions, 30; correlated with innate cognitive ability, 3; in *Crash*, 70–83; as performance, 58; stereotypes about, 70–71, 79, 93
racism, 97–98, 99, 188n12; anger as reaction to, 49–53; covert vs. overt, 70; as reinforced in *Crash*, 11, 70–83, 186n6; reverse, 74, 75, 187n11;

racism (*continued*)
  in Rhodesia/Zimbabwe, 119–121,
  127, 189n1; structural, 49–50, 76–83,
  125, 187n11; in *The Wire*, 172
Rand, Ayn, 10
Rankin, Lindsay, 30
recession, economic, 175
Rhee, Alexis, 79
Rhodesia, 9–10, 102, 119–121, 188–
  189n1. *See also* Zimbabwe
Richards, Kimberly, 188–189n1
Richardson, Alan, 34
Rodrigues, Angela, 133
Rorty, Amélie, 33
Roseman, Ira, 24
Russell, James, 182n16
Russian formalism, 137

San Juan, E., 71–72, 82, 185–186n3,
  186n4
Sartre, Jean-Paul, 111
satire, 131, 136–139, 141–143, 146–147,
  149
Savarese, Ralph, 4
schema (in Hogan), 37, 182n21
Scheman, Naomi, 45
schools, 168–172
Sedgwick, Eve Kosofsky, 56, 58–59,
  184nn13,14
Seneca, 2
sexuality, 106–109
Shaw, Carolyn, 107
Sherrod, Shirley, 75, 186n9
Shona culture, 9, 102, 107–108, 111
Shu, Yuan, 91
Silver, Brenda, 45
Simon, David, 9, 154–155, 174
Skinner, B. F., 14
Smith, Craig A., 18, 24
Smith, Greg, 27, 34
Smith, James, 30
Smith, Sidonie, 88, 188n7
social justice/injustice, 12, 29–30, 49,
  52, 98–99, 101, 153
Soomekh, Bahar, 79
"source-tagging," 34–35
South Africa, 188–189n1

space/spaces, as important in production and perception of anger, 101–
  128, 189n2
Spelman, Elizabeth, 45, 46, 67
Spolsky, Ellen, 33
Steen, Francis, 34
Stewart, Jon, 45
Stoddard, Lothrop, 3
stories. *See* narrative
"storyworlds," 39, 40, 183n23
structural inequalities/racism. *See* racism: structural
"structure of feeling," 60–63, 69
structures of power. *See* power: struc-
  tures/systems of

Tan, E. S., 34
Tate, Larenz, 77
Tavris, Carol, 1, 2, 8, 10, 180–181n5,
  183–184n5, 188–189n1
Tea Party, 45, 48
temporality, 84–100
Terada, Rei, 58
theory of mind (ToM), 34–35
Third World, 149, 150, 177; anger of, 1–
  2; characterizations of people in, 49
time. *See* temporality
Tomkins, Silvan, 44, 56
Tooby, John, 15, 34
Toub, Shaun, 79
trauma studies, 188n12
Treuer, David, 86
Trollope, Anthony, 66
Trotsky, Leon, 179n5
Turner, Mark, 15, 33
Tyler, Tom, 29

United States: anger in, 1, 10; class exploitation, racism, and patriarchy
  in, 99; cultural differences between
  China and, 84; as source of most
  subjects in psychological studies, 31

Venkatesh, Sudhir, 155–156
Verfremdung, 131, 138–139, 190–191n2
violence, 153, 162; and anger/aggres-

sion, 1, 13, 45; and colonialism, 121,
122, 144; in *Devil on the Cross*,
143; domestic, by emasculated men
of color, 51; male, 47; in *Nervous
Conditions*, 106, 112; non-, 178;
structural, that produces racism,
55, 83; in *The Wire*, 164, 165; in *The
Woman Warrior*, 88–93, 188n9

Wakslak, Cheryl, 29, 30
Wallerstein, Immanuel, 185n19
Warhol, Robyn, 29, 65, 71
"warrior gene," 13
Watson, J. B., 14
Watson, Julia, 88, 188n7
Weep Not, Child (Ngugi wa Thiong'o,
1964), 136
Wendt, Albert, 10
West: notions of femininity and patriarchy in, 91, 93; as source of most
subjects in psychological studies,
31, 42
West, Cornel, 184n10
"Western Educated Industrialized
Rich Democratic" (W.E.I.R.D.), 31
whites/whiteness, 9, 96, 107, 155, 185–
186n3; in Africa, 102, 107, 114, 116,
118–122, 125–127, 142, 147, 150; and
anger, 1, 50, 51, 52; deemed "normal," 58, 72, 167; and liberal mul-
ticulturalism/liberal guilt, 71, 76,
78, 81, 82, 119; as nonrepresentative
sample of humanity, 9, 42; and reverse racism, 74

Williams, J. D., 164
Williams, Patricia, 49
Wilson, William Julius, 155–156
Winfrey, Oprah, 70
Wire, The, 6, 12, 152–174, 176
Wise, Christopher, 131–132, 133
Wizard of the Crow (Ngugi wa
Thiong'o, 2006), 5, 12, 131, 136, 139,
141, 144, 145–150
Woman Warrior, The (Maxine Hong
Kingston, 1975) 12, 67, 84–100, 121
women: anger in, 1, 45–46, 68, 140,
183–184n5; angry black, 52–53; con-
trol of bodies of, 106, 110, 126; dis-
enfranchisement and impover-
ishment of, 77; and emotion, 28;
sexual abuse of, 76
women's movement, 86, 97, 100. *See
also* feminism
women's studies, 3, 7, 8, 50, 92–93, 103
Wong, Sau-ling, 85
Woodward, Kathleen, 45, 46, 47–48, 55,
56, 67–68, 183n4
Woolf, Virginia, 35, 183n3

Yalom, Marilyn, 88
Young, Kay, 4, 34
Young, Robert, 184n7
youth, angry urban, 160–174

Zimbabwe, 10, 102, 119, 122, 124, 125,
127, 188–189n1, 190n7. *See also*
Rhodesia
Zunshine, Lisa, 4, 31, 34–36, 66, 95